Personnel Management: A Computer-Based System

Personnel Management

A Computer-Based System

SANG M. LEE
The University of Nebraska-Lincoln

CARY D. THORP, JR.
The University of Nebraska-Lincoln

PBI
a petrocelli
book
new york / princeton

To Laura and Peggy

Library of Congress Cataloging in Publication Data

Lee, Sang M   1939–
    Personnel management.

    Includes indexes.
    1. Personnel management—Data processing—Addresses,
essays, lectures.   2. Personnel management—Information
services—Addresses, essays, lectures.   3. Manpower
planning—Data processing—Addresses, essays, lectures.
I. Thorp, Cary D., joint author.   II. Title.
HF5549.L43   658.3'0028'54   78–25802
ISBN 0–89433–052–7
ISBN 0–89433–053–5 pbk.

Contents

Preface

Contents

Preface

While many changes have characterized organizational life in the 1960s and 1970s, two in particular have received central attention in most large, progressive organizations: the growth of electronic data processing that has made possible the development of sophisticated management information systems and the emergence of the function of personnel administration as one of the most influential areas affecting organizational success.

In view of the significance of these two activities, it is somewhat surprising that, until recent years, there had been very little indication of any major interrelation of the two. Bluntly speaking, personnel administration had lagged far behind the production, marketing, and financial functions in successfully applying data processing techniques to the resolution of problems. Early applications were limited primarily to payroll processing and basic record keeping of employee data. While the gap still exists, it is becoming increasingly evident that more and more organizations are now directing attention to the potential benefits of computer applications in personnel administration. This can partially be explained by the success of computerized information systems in other areas, partly by the growing awareness of the human resource as *the most* important resource of any organization, and partly by the expanded attention given the matter in professional journals—both in the field of management science and personnel administration.

This readings book attempts to provide a representative selection of some of the best articles appearing on a wide range of personnel subjects. In choosing the articles, three basic questions guided the editors' choice: (1) Was the article written on a plane that would shed light and comprehension to a student or practitioner who has little background or experience in information systems or management science techniques? Technical articles and articles directed primarily to an audience of management scientists and systems analysts were, with few exceptions, not chosen.

(2) Did the article provide an understanding both of the potential and the limitations of the application described? Articles which either "oversold" or denigrated computer-oriented problem-solving techniques in personnel were excluded. (3) Do the applications or techniques described have practical applications, or were they instead expressions of theoretical applications which some day in the future may find a place in the arsenal of management science tools?

While there are many excellent personnel textbooks available today, it is a fact that most give scant attention to the application of management science concepts and computer-based techniques. Hence, this book was designed to fill a void and to serve as a supplement to a basic personnel text in either upper-level undergraduate or graduate-level courses in personnel administration. The book could also be used effectively in courses designed to describe computer applications to management problems.

For the personnel practitioner, it is hoped that the articles selected will be thought-provokers and will lead to serious consideration of applying some of the methods described. Personnel, as a field, has gradually been shedding its reputation of being tradition-bound and shortsighted and has been taking on more and more of the trappings of a profession. Personnel administrators today often perform in the role of change-agents and instigators of innovations. For such persons, the offerings in this book should provide food for thought—to be shared with the resident pros in data processing, the systems analysts.

The book is organized into five sections:

Part I provides an introduction and overview of the "state of the art" as it exists today with respect to computer applications in personnel administration.

Part II describes the nature of Personnel Information Systems (also known as Human Resource Information Systems) and of skills inventories.

Part III deals with manpower allocation issues. Articles on manpower planning and on work scheduling provide the subject matter for this section.

Part IV focuses upon personnel programs—more frequently referred to as personnel functions. Topics covered include selection, affirmative action, performance appraisal, training, wage and salary administration, absentee control, and collective bargaining.

Part V explores three ticklish issues in the personnel-computer interface: conflict between managers and computer specialists, the role of time-sharing consulting services, and legal implications for information systems.

The editors are particularly indebted to the authors of the articles which give this book its heart and substance and to the publishers which granted permission to reprint these works. We are especially grateful to Mr. O.R. Petrocelli who encouraged us to initiate this project. Georgia Collins served as a research assistant on this project and we are grateful for her efforts in surveying the literature and gathering information. We would also like to thank those efficient ladies in our office who spent many hours for this book: Joyce Anderson, Sharon Blecha, and Diana Dittmer. Finally, we appreciate the work of Joan Shapiro who prepared the indexes.

S.M.L. and C.D.T.

Part I
Introduction and
Overview

Confusion still exists over the meaning of the term
"personnel administration." Some see no distinction
between this term and the more general concept,
"management." Others see it as synonymous with
"organizational behavior"—a subject area that focuses
primarily on such concepts as leadership, motivation, job
satisfaction, group dynamics, communication, managing
conflict, and managing change. Still others view it as that
set of activities carried out by a personnel department.

For purposes of this book, personnel administration
is defined as "those managerial activities dealing with
the procurement, development, maintenance, utilization,
and separation of a work force." As such it goes beyond
the activities of a personnel department and includes the
personnel responsibilities of line managers as well.
Specifically, some of the activities included within each
of the subfunctions are as follows:

Procurement— Manpower planning, affirmative action,
recruitment, and selection

Development—Orientation, training, management
development, career planning,
performance appraisal, and promotional
systems

Maintenance— Wage and salary administration, benefits
and services administration, safety,
health, disciplinary systems, grievance
systems, employee communications,
employee relations, and collective
bargaining

Utilization— Placement (job assignment), leadership,
motivation, job design, and work
scheduling

1

Separation— Pension administration, retirement counseling, layoff procedures, turnover analysis, and exit interviewing

Simply listing the activities hardly gives the full flavor of what is involved in personnel administration (or "human resource administration" as some modernists prefer to call it). Each of these functions requires varying degrees of *planning, implementation, and control*—activities that may be carried out at different levels of the organization by different people in different departments. Complicating the description still further, one should note that it is necessary to carry out the planning/control aspects of each function for both long-range and short-term horizons.

Given the broad encompassing nature of personnel administration and the growing awareness that it centers on the primary resource of the organization—the human resource—it is understandable that as an organizational function, personnel administration has been ascending in prestige and influence. It is also understandable that there is a great deal of literature in management journals aimed at upgrading personnel programs of various types. A significant number of these articles and books deal with computer applications for personnel problems—applications which to date have had limited acceptance in many organizations. This section provides an overview of the possibilities that exist for such applications.

In the lead article, the authors describe the emergence of personnel administration from its roots as a routine, service-oriented, lower-level administrative activity to its present place as a central, top-level management function. The authors also describe the lag in acceptance of computer-based personnel applications and then survey the wide range of potential applications. The challenges and problems of developing and effectively using a computerized personnel management information system are explored and the authors conclude that the personnel department with a computerized MIS is better equipped to play a greater and more important role in the organization.

This theme is continued in the second selection, Greenlaw's article on "Management Science and Personnel Management," where the point is made that personnel management is no longer to be looked on as a "weak sister," since, like other functions of management, it has moved ahead in the quantitative areas of management. Contrary to the widely held opinion that the "human resources management" area does not lend itself well to quantitative methods, the author shows that a number of management science techniques have been developed for personnel. Models have been designed for such personnel functions as recruiting, selection, manpower planning, safety, wage and salary administration, and collective bargaining. Among the methods that have been utilized for solving personnel problems are mathematical programming, Markov models, logarithmic learning curves, network techniques, and simulation techniques.

From this brief survey, it is evident that significant progress has been made toward wedding the techniques of management science to the resolution of personnel problems. Other articles in this collection indicate that further inroads have been made toward solidifying this marriage since original publication of Greenlaw's article.

1.
Personnel Management and Computer-Related Challenges

Sang M. Lee and Cary D. Thorp, Jr.

Personnel used to be a relatively simple administrative function. In the past a personnel manager had the basic responsibility of supplying needed manpower to functional areas of the organization such as the finance, sales, and manufacturing departments and of carrying out such routine services as maintaining employee records, administering benefit programs, and providing recreational activities. However, during the past several decades personnel has been transformed from a relatively obscure, low-level staff function to a central and top-level management function in the organization.

There are many socioeconomic factors that have affected the emergence of personnel as one of the most important management functions—unionization, professionalization, government legislation concerning labor and welfare pro-

Editors' Note: This article was written especially for this book.

grams, technological advances, and social recognition of human rights, etc. Perhaps the most important factor has been the general recognition of the "human resources" concept in organizations. Most, if not all, of today's managers believe that the primary resource of an organization is the human resource. All other resources, such as capital facilities, finance, and technology, should be supportive of the human resource.

The human resource model is a radical departure from the past concepts of personnel. The human resources model has undoubtedly received a great boost from many research findings of behavioral scientists. However, other important contributing factors have been the increasing complexity of organizational environment and rapid technological developments. A production manager, for instance, must rely on the personnel manager's judgment in order to formulate a comprehensive long-range production plan. The production manager must ask not only "can we get enough people to do such . . ." but also "what would be the manpower requirement in terms of technical and professional skills to implement the plan?"

Use of Computers in Personnel Systems

The increased scope and importance of personnel function have resulted in greater complexity to the field. In order to cope with the incredible volume of information and analysis the personnel department has to deal with, there is a need for computerized personnel systems. The computer is one of society's most important technological developments. In fact, Herbert Simon (1960) views the computer as the fourth greatest breakthrough in history to aid man in his thinking process and decision-making ability. (The first was the development of writing, the second was the emergence of the Arabic numerical system, and the third was the invention of analytical geometry and calculus.) While there are many problems in applying the computer, the fact remains that the computer has become an integral part of most organizations.

The use of computers for personnel functions has generally lagged behind computer applications in other functional areas. For example, many manufacturing firms began to use computers prior to 1960. Yet, the truly computerized personnel system is hard to find even today. The most widely computerized personnel functions are those which are routine, repetitive, or highly objective processes such as payroll, personnel statistics, employee benefits, personnel budgeting, etc. Many important personnel functions that require high-level decisions, long-range implications, or corporate policies are by and large uncomputerized. For example, there are not many computerized personnel systems that deal with collective bargaining, manpower planning, equal opportunity/affirmative action, or human relations.

Table 1: First Use of Computers

	Prior to 1960 (%)	1961 to 1965 (%)	After 1965 (%)	Computer Not Used (%)
A. Computer Department				
Federal	63	37	0	0
State	35	45	20	0
County	40	40	20	0
City	22	52	26	0
Private Sector	88	12	0	0
B. Personnel Department				
Federal	15	70	15	0
State	5	30	55	10
County	20	40	20	20
City	6	12	70	12
Private Sector	50	28	22	0

Source: Tomeski and Lazarus (1974), p. 169.

In a recent survey reported by Tomeski and Lazarus (1974), data on the use of computers were obtained from 87 large organizations in the United States. The organizations included in the survey were:

9 of 12 federal departments
22 of the 50 states
15 counties and 24 cities among the 50 largest populated areas
17 private firms among the Fortune 500

Table 1 clearly demonstrates that the first use of the computer to process personnel work lagged behind its use in other areas of organizations. Generally, federal agencies and private firms made earlier use of computers than did local governments. As a matter of fact, some local government units have yet to use the computer for personnel functions.

Table 2 presents the types of computerized personnel data obtained in the sample organizations. It is clearly shown that only routine and finance-related personnel functions are highly computerized. The uncomputerized functions include those which are more subjective, decision oriented, and not related to finance.

It can be concluded that computerization of the personnel function has not kept abreast with the development and application of computer technology in other functional areas. There is a general lack of computer application in important personnel functions such as decision making, manpower planning, and long-

Table 2: Computerized personnel data

	Federal (%)	State (%)	County (%)	City (%)	Private Sector (%)
Payroll records & reports	100	77	93	87	100
Employee benefit records & reports	78	59	66	66	76
Personnel statistics & reports	88	69	46	58	81
Position statistics & reports	66	73	73	46	77
Pay statistics & reports	99	73	87	62	91
Medical statistics & reports	22	27	13	29	29
Recruiting lists & analysis	11	24	0	12	10
Test scoring	22	18	20	16	10
Skills inventory	44	5	7	4	48
Performance evaluation	22	5	20	16	24
Work scheduling	44	9	0	4	29
Personnel budget & accounting	77	59	73	63	76
Collective bargaining reports	0	5	14	12	38
Manpower planning reports	44	10	7	8	39

Note: Percentages indicate the frequency with which respondents reported computerization of information.

Source: Tomeski and Lazarus (1974), p. 169.

range personnel planning for the organization. There is a need to develop a more comprehensive personnel management information system which can facilitate rational and effective utilization of human resources.

Development of Integrated Personnel MIS

In the past the approach frequently taken to computerize the personnel process was to computerize particular phases. This isolated or fragmented computerization was not very effective as it impeded coordination and necessitated duplication of work. A more widely accepted approach is to develop an overall personnel management information system. A broad perspective of an integrated personnel MIS is presented in Figure 1.

The personnel MIS is a systematic data handling process that organizes, maintains, and reports personnel information needs to top management, the personnel staff, employees, and governmental agencies. The system is intended to facilitate the performance of regular personnel activities and to provide management with information for decisions.

Figure 1: Broad perspective on personnel management information systems (Source: Burack and Smith, 1977, p. 430)

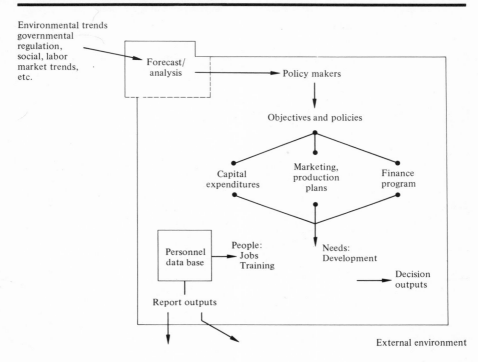

A typical personnel MIS is shown in Figure 2 and consists of five basic elements:

> Input—ability to receive information
> Storage—ability to retain information
> Operation—ability to manipulate information
> Logic—ability to control the process
> Output—ability to produce desired information

There are numerous advantages in an integrated personnel MIS. The following list presents a brief summary:

1. Stores and retrieves a vast amount of information about employees (this process may be impossible or too costly via manual means).
2. Expedites records and record preparation.
3. Improves quality and timeliness of information.
4. Provides the capability to manipulate information so that data can be classified, reclassified, or cross-classified.

Figure 2: Personnel integrated information system (Source: Tomeski and Lazarus, 1975, p. 188)

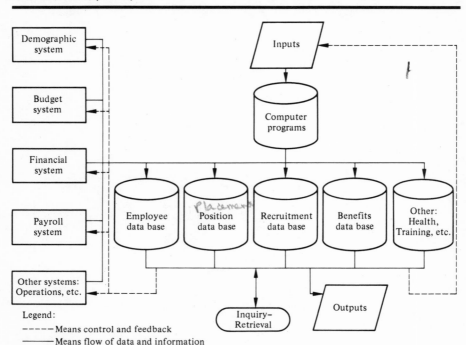

5. Eliminates duplicate records and functions.
6. Provides critical information for management decision making (i.e., analysis of personnel records may reveal prospective trouble spots and permit a timely action to alleviate labor/management difficulties).
7. Facilitates and improves corporate long-range planning, especially in the manpower planning area.

In order to develop an integrated personnel MIS, clearly stated objectives must be established. The scope, purpose, interrelations with other organizational systems, time and cost estimates, and possible benefits of the system must be carefully analyzed. Since the system design and implementation will involve and affect almost every function of the organization, a task force composed of representatives of various functions should be organized to undertake the task. The design and implementation phases should consider the personnel data needs for managerial decisions and for fulfilling legal and other report requirements. The typical data should include information about employees on skills, personal history, employment record, benefits, and the like. In addition, other internal and external data about employment trends, wage and salary information for various jobs, the personnel budget, and fore-casted manpower needs can be included.

Once the basic data needs are identified, the following should be determined for a successful personnel MIS:

What is the present system of personnel information?

How much and what kind of data should be collected, edited, manipulated, and stored?

How will the data be reported out of the system?

What should be the interrelationships among various files of the information?

Who will be responsible for the system?

How will the redundancy of handling, storage, and checking for accuracy and currency of data be taken care of?

How can the data retrieval system be designed that will allow the following types of reports?

Routine reports—to be produced at regular intervals

Special reports—to be produced on request

Demand information reports—to be produced to answer executives' questions.

How will employees be convinced that organizational policies are being applied consistently?

Once an organization's personnel MIS is completely computerized, it could even be interconnected with external systems such as an industrywide data bank, public and private employment offices, or government agencies. Such a comprehensive computer-based personnel system can provide opportunities for analysis of manpower data, timely wage and salary surveys, and a job-man matching system, etc.

Application Examples of the Computerized Personnel System

A carefully planned and implemented computerized personnel system can provide timely and accurate information for numerous personnel decisions. For example, a firm with an integrated (and computerized) personnel MIS can save thousands of dollars on recruiting specialists. As specific needs arise, the system can immediately identify existing personnel who have various skills that are required through computerized skills inventories. Also, the system can provide data for long-range personnel planning and development by analyzing the gap between the firm's long-term personnel needs and its present personnel strengths. Other specific applications are described below.

PERSONNEL RECORD KEEPING / Most computerized personnel systems begin here with savings in clerical time, increased speed and accuracy of report generation, and imposed standardization for routine and special reports. Some of the typical examples of the personnel record keeping applications are:

New hire report
Separations report
Personnel turnover criteria report
Personnel anniversaries listing
Employee status printout
Name, address, and telephone number list
Job history report
Wage and salary history report
Performance rating report
Vacation, sick leave, and absence
Employee earnings and benefits report
EEO/Affirmative Action report

EMPLOYMENT FUNCTIONS / There has been a great deal of interest in the use of computerized personnel systems for employment functions primarily because of the high cost associated with personnel recruiting and selection. The system allows a control of requisitions for open and projected jobs. Furthermore, it provides the personnel department speed in hiring decisions, coordinating internal routing of information and files concerning prospective employees. Some examples of the employment function applications of the personnel MIS would be:

Recruitment information system—applicants, job openings, and skill needs

Computerized man-job matching system

Analysis of sources of different types of job applicants

GRAD—information retrieval system linking employers with college placement offices

Computerized performance evaluation system of recruiters

Computer analysis of personality files

Computerized interpretation of psychological tests, biographical and job requirement data

WAGE AND SALARY ADMINISTRATION / A computerized personnel MIS allows timely and speedy analysis of effects of wage and salary changes; comparisons of wages and salaries by job class, department, and division; and preparation of data for external surveys. The following list presents some of the typical applications of the system for wage and salary administration:

12

Pay rate listing by employee

Pay rate listing by job classification

Pay rate analysis by several criteria—sex, education, age, geographical area, etc.

Analysis of compensation vs. experience

Salary increase analysis by group or companywide

Compensation trend and planning analysis

PERFORMANCE APPRAISAL / Although the application of the computerized MIS to performance appraisal has been relatively slow, there has been increasing efforts of application in this area. Some of the typical application examples are:

Annual merit rating reports

Comparison of employee performance with an ideal person on each of multiple performance criteria

Combination scheme between multiple criterion scores and overall merit figures

Analysis of performance over successive rating periods

Design and implementation of management science models to appraise or predict employee work performance

TRAINING AND DEVELOPMENT / There has been a trend of increasing applications of the computer to training and development, especially in the use of management games and simulation. Training and development via computerized games and management simulation (i.e., IBM Management Decision-Making Laboratory, UCLA Executive Games, Carnegie-Mellon Management Games, etc.) have proven to be effective for modifying organizational behavior under controlled conditions. Also, a computerized retrieval system for information and published documents enables one to keep current on a vast amount of new information on pertinent subjects.

SKILLS INVENTORY AND MANPOWER PLANNING / These are relatively new areas of computer application in personnel. Many firms now recognize that they must keep track of a multitude of employee skills to properly fulfill replacement or recruiting responsibilities. The computer-based personnel MIS provides management with up-to-date career-oriented information on both present and potential employees. Some examples of the skills inventory and manpower planning systems are:

Matching person and job

Manpower forecasting and planning

Future replacement candidates

Audit and update personnel data

Consistent personnel policy for replacement and promotion

Routine reports of corporate personnel strengths and weaknesses based on positions and salaries

Systematic employee searches

Tools for more efficient and rapid manpower planning and placement

COLLECTIVE BARGAINING / The computerized personnel MIS facilitates efficient and quick analysis, classification, and storage of information concerning union contract clauses. Furthermore, the system can be used for managerial analysis with respect to evaluation of actual or expected union demand alternatives through computerized simulation models. Some examples of the collective bargaining related applications of the system are as follows:

Local and/or industrywide union demands
Trend of wages and salaries
Fringe benefits and other costs
Forecast union and employee proposals
Potential strike issues
Limits to which union opposition is likely to concede
Composite historical records of grievance reports
Forecast probabilities of settling grievance
Systematic seniority update mechanism
Various safety related records

OVERALL PERSONNEL MANAGEMENT / In addition to the seven above mentioned areas of application, the computerized personnel MIS can assist the overall personnel management function. For example, management can easily obtain information concerning the manpower strengths and weaknesses of the firm with respect to any parameter (i.e., skills, equal opportunity and/or affirmative action categories, etc.). Several other reports that can be easily prepared by the system are:

Presentation of an organization chart on short notice

Information for budget planning and review

Trend data in personnel administration

Analysis of accession and separation rates

Analysis of longevity measurements

Analysis of manpower mobility

Analysis of personnel practices of other firms

Challenges and Problems of the Personnel MIS

Historically, personnel has been a process of *post audit*—determining the effectiveness of human resource related operations after the fact. However, with the computerized personnel MIS it is now possible to implement personnel functions as needs arise. The system can be used to determine whether or not human resource requirements of the entire firm are being satisfied effectively. Thus, the computer-based personnel system provides vital information for long-range management decision making as well as for routine operational effectiveness of the firm.

The computerized personnel system provides many new opportunities because of the capabilities of the computer, especially its speed and analytic power. For example, an organization can more easily decentralize its operations into individual profit centers so as to take its motivational effects as well as to promote an innovative and competitive spirit among centers. Also, the system may allow a firm to experiment with different types of organizational structures, i.e., a radial organization structure with the MIS at center and on-line use of the system for internal communication. The personnel MIS also provides a greater degree of individual freedom in the organization as the system provides clear organizational policies and rules so that each employee is more aware of the environment in which he works.

Another important development in the computerized personnel MIS is the time-sharing system. Time-sharing is based on the use of a remote terminal system which is hooked up with the computer of a service organization (or another firm). The system is usually based on "interactive processing" which enables a quick and economical means to process information. The interactive system adds a new dimension to the personnel MIS as it allows easy editing and filing of existing and new data. The time-sharing system is especially important for relatively small firms that can hardly have their own computers and analysts.

Implementation of the computerized personnel MIS has also resulted in a number of serious questions. The computer-based system brings changes to a firm's work procedures and organizational structure. Thus, the utilization process of human resources may be significantly modified. However, most systems analysts are often ill-equipped or not very sensitive to behavioral implications of these changes. Thus, very careful coordination and close communication between personnel and systems analysts from the beginning of the personnel MIS development are required. This preliminary step is also the key in preventing resistance to computerization by many employees. It is ironic in a way to see that organizations install multimillion dollar computer-based information systems and yet pay only minimal attention to the behavioral impact of such systems to interpersonal communications, job content of various positions, formal and informal organizational structures, and motivation of employees.

The complexity of the personnel MIS is vulnerable to computer-related embezzlement by employees who are knowledgeable about computer systems.

For example, an employee in the payroll system is said to have stolen millions of dollars by processing fictitious employee work cards and cashing the automatically printed checks. The roles and responsibilities of a personnel department for these types of white-collar crimes are indeed hard to determine.

The increasing rate of technological developments in computers and information sciences has reached the stage where large and complex data banks can now be economically established. This development allows rapid, accurate, and timely processing of tremendous amounts of information that are useful for effective management of various organizations. However, the availability of a vast amount of personnel information has raised the concern over potential invasion of privacy as well as other potential misuse of such confidential data. The Federal Privacy Act of 1974 is a direct response to such a danger. The act applies to federal agencies and private firms that supply goods or services to them. Since 1975 a number of states and foreign countries have enacted similar laws. In general, most privacy laws are concerned with three categories: operating procedures, access rights to information, and control of use procedures. In order for an organization to comply with privacy law, utilization of the computerized personnel MIS should implement several controls. For example, a log should be maintained for the use of personnel records by various authorized individuals, a procedure established for the disclosure of information to individuals inquiring about their records, and a process set up to correct any inaccurate personal information. It should be clearly evident that employees who handle sensitive personal data should be well trained concerning privacy laws, company policies, and work procedures in handling such information.

Summary

Automation and computerization have resulted in many profound changes for managers and the rank and file employees in most organizations. It has been argued that computers and other technological advances tend to dehumanize the management process. However, there have been numerous examples where responsible applications of contemporary technological advances greatly improved the welfare of employees by helping to humanize the workplace. Creative personnel managers can take advantage of modern technology to better utilize human resources in their organization.

The personnel department with a computerized MIS is better equipped to play a greater and more important role in the organization. It can obtain and process accurate, objective, timely, relevant, and analytical information about people. Thus, personnel managers can play important roles in setting long-range corporate objectives and planning as well as in helping employees to plan their careers. Personnel managers would be in a better position to develop effective recruiting programs, relevant training programs, and fair performance evaluation system. The computerized personnel MIS should create free time for personnel managers to expand their functions into a viable top-level decision-making area.

The computerized MIS can of course be abused and misused. In order to avoid this problem, a carefully designed and planned system of control is needed for any personnel data base. The data base contains private and confidential personal information and its utilization requires a clearly defined set of security rules. It should be recognized that computers are here to stay. The primary mission of personnel is to utilize modern technology to serve people in the most effective way.

REFERENCES

Burack, E.H. and R.D. Smith. *Personnel Management: A Human Resource Systems Approach.* New York: West Publishing Co., 1977.

Chruden, H.J. and A.W. Sherman. *Personnel Management,* 5th ed. Cincinnati: South-Western Publishing Co., 1976.

Greenlaw, P.S. and R.D. Smith. *Personnel Management: A Management Science Approach.* Scranton, Pennsylvania: International Textbook Co., 1970.

Miner, J.B. and M.G. Miner. *Personnel and Industrial Relations,* 2nd ed. New York: Macmillan, 1973.

Roter, B. "An Integrated Framework for Personnel Utilization and Management." *Personnel Journal* (December 1973).

Simon, H.A. *The New Science of Management Decision.* New York: Harper & Row, 1960.

Tomeski, E.A. and H. Lazarus. "Computerized Information Systems in Personnel—A Comparative Analysis of the State of the Art in Government and Business." *Academy of Management Journal* (March 1974).

————. *People-Oriented Computer Systems.* New York: Van Nostrand Reinhold Co., 1975.

Tomeski, E.A., B.M. Yoon and G. Stephenson. "Computer-Related Challenges for Personnel Administrators." *Personnel Journal* (June 1976).

2.
Management Science and Personnel Management

Paul S. Greenlaw

Personnel management as defined here refers to the functions of selection, training, wage and salary administration, etc. The focus of this article will be in these areas rather than in the area of human relations, i.e., leadership styles, discipline and the like. The purpose is to demonstrate that personnel management is no longer to be looked on as a "weak sister," since, like other functions of management, it has moved ahead in the quantitative areas of management. Specifically, it will be shown that mathematical programming, Markov models, logarithmic learning curves, network techniques, and two different classes of simulation have been designed for solving personnel problems.

Editors' Note: Reprinted with permission from *Personnel Journal,* Copyright November 1973.

Mathematical Programming

The classical article applying linear programming to personnel was done by Rehmus and Wagner [17] in the area of wage and salary administration. They developed a program for both executives and administrative-clerical personnel, whose objective function, which included numerous constraints,[1] was to develop via simplex both factor and degree values for jobs so that the differences between these values and actual existing job salaries would be minimized. One obvious criticism of this research is that existing salaries may be out of line and, therefore, will not provide a good basis of comparison.[2] On the other hand, a look at the authors' data indicates that their use of the simplex algorithm has met quite well their objective of minimizing differences between the computer generated weights and actual salaries.

Following Rehmus and Wagner's notion that simplex could be applied in the wage and salary area, there have been at least three other efforts in this field. Bruno [2] has developed a simplex model for salary evaluation in collective bargaining negotiations with teacher unions. Bruno's research is different from Rehmus and Wagner's in the following ways. First, the program provides for a dollar objective function so as to ensure that the linear program can meet the wage and salary budget available. Second, Bruno overcomes the objection of the Rehmus and Wagner research by *not* using existing salary data as a base. Rather, what he does is engage in an *a priori* subjective weighting of the degrees for each factor. Like Rehmus and Wagner, Bruno has a number of constraints in the model so as to ensure that a particular factor will not be weighted too lightly or too heavily. However, unlike the Rehmus and Wagner model, there are other types of constraints—e.g., establishing a constraint maintaining a minimum dollar spread between the highest and lowest positions in each job classification.

Two other papers have appeared in which simplex has been applied to wage and salary administration. Both of these are by Rodgers [18][19] and are unpublished. The first describes a wage and salary simplex program which was actually used in dealing in a $12,000,000 budget situation in the Youngstown, Ohio school system. Since "beginning teachers were seen as the least expensive over-all unit cost to the program and most critical to the curriculum" [19, p. 7], it was decided for the simplex program to maximize their salaries as the objective function within the limitations of the budget. This, of course, did not mean that superintendents, principals, other teachers, etc., were excluded from consideration, and their positions were included in the program. Thus, like Bruno, but unlike Rehmus and Wagner, we have a dollar-constrained budget. Further, more comparable to Bruno than to Rehmus and Wagner, a number of dollar constraints have been

[1]For example, placing constraints so that one job with a higher (or lower) degree than another, be given a sufficiently great (or lesser) weighting.

[2]The authors argue here that their use of existing salaries "is based on the premise that they may well give the best indication of the relative value of jobs to an organization . . ." (17, pp. 97–8).

built into the model—e.g., factor 5 must be no less than $50 and no more than $500.

Rodgers' second paper also had to do with the problems faced by a school district in Northeast Ohio [18]. Pointing out that there is an increasing tendency to pay school personnel extra for extra work, Rodgers has developed a simplex model for this type of allocation problem. He points out that the traditional method of paying school personnel for extra work as a percentage of their base salaries creates many inequities, which can be overcome with the simplex approach. Although not as large in scope as his other paper, the allocation of $40,000 over 80 positions and a little over 100 personnel were involved.

At least two pieces of research have been conducted utilizing simplex in personnel outside the area of wage and salary administration. The first of these, by Chisman [3], is a linear program which substitutes for traditional time study[3] in a work situation where all jobs contain the same discrete work elements, but these elemental *times* vary from task to task. Chisman's program in some ways parallels that of Rehmus and Wagner in that he attempts to minimize differences. A series of jobs are examined to determine how much/or how many of each element is present; and the simplex algorithm arrives at a time for each work element which minimizes "the sum, over-all jobs, of the absolute deviation between the actual total time for a job and the total time that would be calculated by summing the determined work-element times for that job" [3, p. 190]. Chisman's model was carried out in an electric utility (with work elements such as put up poles, number of crossarms, number of guy-wires, etc.), and the author admits that for different conditions (e.g., good versus poor weather), different work standards would have to be used, each calling for a different linear program. That this may be cost prohibitive is obvious. Chisman's basic technique, however, may be useful where jobs have the characteristics of variable element times, but where external conditions are more constant—e.g., possibly in a maintenance crew operation in a plant. Finally, it should be pointed out that when actual figures are placed in Chisman's simplex solution, they *do* come up to a high degree with his minimization of differences objective function.

Finally, Teach and Thompson [24] have developed a linear programming solution for a decentralized college recruitment planning in the IBM Corporation. IBM, to solve certain of its problems, had decentralized its college recruiting, had created four decentralized National Recruiting Organization (NRO) offices, and was searching for a means which would handle this type of operation efficiently. The Teach and Thompson linear program had to deal with a variety of problems —e.g., that there must be separate solutions for three classes of college personnel (engineering, other technical, and technical), and that costs were associated with

[3]Work measurement is treated here even though it more often falls within the domain of industrial engineering because it does have relevance to personnel. It is, by the way, treated in certain standard personnel textbooks, e.g., George Strauss and Leonard Sayles, *Personnel: The Human Problems of Management,* 2nd ed. (Englewood Cliffs, N.J.: Prentice-Hall, Inc.) 1967.

a visit or more of each individual recruit. In attempting to minimize costs as much as feasible, no attempt was made to gather actual individual costs, but rather, borrowing the "Center of Gravity" concept from physics, a "Center of Supply" and "Center of Demand" were calculated for each NRO area, and an appropriate equation was set up to estimate "the total average visit and move expense for a college hire from any NRO area to any location" [24, p. 289].

In summary, a majority of linear programming applications in personnel have been in the area of wage and salary administration. Also three out of four of these wage and salary studies have been connected with teachers organizations rather than with the business firm. Whether this teacher orientation will continue, or more firms will use simplex in the future is open to speculation.

Markovian Models

In a classic paper, John Merck at Lackland Air Force Base showed the possibilities of utilizing a Markovian model for projecting the movements of personnel through the air force system [13]. The paper is mathematically written, but the mathematics (e.g., state, transition probability, matrix of transition probabilities) is explained clearly and with the use of simple examples. Merck shows both how the organization may project the number of its personnel in various states in the future and how proposed policy decisions (e.g., accelerated promotions) can be entered into the model to test their effects. The one major limiting problem with Merck's model (and that of other regular Markov models) is that it assumes constant transition probabilities from period to period. (The writer has been informed, in fact, that the Merck model is no longer in use in the Air Force primarily because of this particular problem.)

Merck's work was followed up by Vroom and MacCrimmon [26], who examined 1964 and 1965 data in a business organization, derived transition probabilities from these data and, making certain assumptions about the firm's future manpower needs, used the transition matrix to project manpower needs in 13 categories (or states) up through 1969. Two comments are in order concerning this research. First, if the projections are to be accurate, Vroom and Mac-Crimmon must face up to the same problem as did Merck—the transition probabilities must be constant (or relatively constant). Second, although one might not put data for two succeeding years together in a matrix for non-Markovian analysis, simply looking at Vroom and MacCrimmon's 1964–65 matrix data does pinpoint certain problems of the organization—e.g., the percentage of promotions from one year to the next was lowest into the top level service positions (finance, public relations, legal, etc.) but highest in the firm from the lowest level to the middle level service positions. Thus, aside from being *prescriptive* as a Markov process, the data were usefully *descriptive* as to what actually did go on in the way of personnel movements during one year.

At least three other Markovian models have been developed relating to personnel management. First is an article by Rowland and Sovereign focusing attention on internal manpower supply and forecasting [20]. Although this article is interesting, it provides little new that Merck and Vroom and MacCrimmon do not cover, and will not be discussed here for this reason. A second article by Durbin [4] is interesting in that it attempts to apply Markovian analysis to two "hard core" youth training and employment projects in Los Angeles. By developing and comparing transition matrices among the two programs, Durbin identified differences in the two programs—e.g., the proportion of incoming population who move directly to employment varied considerably in the two programs. Here, again, as in the Vroom and MacCrimmon model, is the *descriptive-analytical* use of Markov models developed from raw data, as compared to the predictive use by powering the matrix several times, and where the constant transition probability problem comes in. Durbin goes on into the predictive aspects of his Markov chains, admitting this problem. He points out that the "question of stationarity and comparability of transition rates . . . cannot be definitely answered in advance, but fluctuations (nonstationarity) are probably predictable," [4, p. 13] and that "Likelihood Ratio tests for stationarity of a Markov process" [4, p. 13] have been developed.

Finally, Eaton has focused attention on studying mass layoffs through Markov chains [6]. Critical of previous research on mass layoffs, Eaton makes the point that the re-employment experience must be thought of as a process in time, with the basic measures being time rates of change. He then presents a *conceptual* Markovian model describing the re-employment process as a time-process phenomenon. He presents no numerical data to show that his model has been utilized, and this is one of the basic weaknesses of this research.

In summary, all of the Markov models discussed must face up to the problem of constant transition probabilities for predictive purposes. They all also have dealt with manpower movement in one way or another—movement within the firm, movement from training programs into a firm, and finally Eaton's movement of men from unemployed to employed (and sometimes again to unemployed) after mass layoffs.

Logarithmic Learning Curves

Several decades ago, T. P. Wright discovered in the aircraft industry that as the number of units produced doubled, the number of man hours to produce each unit decreased by a constant ratio [30]. Or, mathematically:

(1) $y = cx^k$
(2) $\log y = \log c + k \log x$

where y is the number of hours of direct labor to produce the xth unit; c, the number of hours of direct labor to produce the first unit; x, the unit number; and k, a constant parameter representing the rate of learning such that $k \leq 0$.

This logarithmic learning curve (often referred to as the manufacturing progress curve) has received considerable attention in the literature over the years. The learning curves have a number of uses, some of which deal directly with personnel. For example:

> More efficient production scheduling is possible when approximate improvement in worker performance is predictable . . . [and] . . . Hiring and termination of manpower over the life of a contract can be more efficiently controlled through use of learning curve data. [10, p. 130]

Those familiar with the logarithmic learning curve view the learning taking place as organizational learning, and would consider the learning curve as a predictive tool in the general area of manpower planning. In spite of its criticism (see [31]), the log-learning curve continues to be utilized, not only in the aircraft industry but in other industries as well (see, for example [1]).

Much less well known is the fact that the logarithmic learning curve model has been applied to the field of safety. In a study of the American petroleum industry, an accident-experience learning curve was developed by Greenberg [8]. This model corresponds closely to the logarithmic learning curve. To use Greenberg's words

> accident experience . . . is computed on a per-item-produced basis, and related to cumulative production to yield the model:
>
> $$Y = AX^b$$
>
> where Y is the accident experience for the Xth unit, A is the first unit accident experience, and b is the slope of the log-log-linear curve. [8, p. 43]

Greenberg reported that this model yielded results superior to the traditional Z16.1 safety rates. Whether Greenberg's results would be as good in other safety situations raises an important question. This is so because there is such a paucity of good safety measurement techniques that should his model be a general purpose one, it might be highly useful to personnel management in industry.

Network Techniques

For planning and controlling large scale projects, DuPont developed the critical path method (CPM), and for the Polaris Fleet Ballistic Missile Program, the Program Evaluation and Review Technique (PERT) was devised. Both of these are network techniques involving activities and events. Although technical differences exist between the two, as Moder and Phillips have pointed out, "the recent versions of the two original methods have become increasingly alike" [14, p. 337]. For this reason, we will generally use the one word PERT in the ensuing discussion.

In spite of the fact that PERT was developed for large scale projects (none of which are as large in the personnel department) it has been found that PERT can be a useful tool for certain types of personnel projects. First, PERT has been applied to the area of college recruiting. Schoderbek has pointed out how the Sandia Corporation in 1963 tailored the PERT technique's use to this area of endeavor [21]. He showed how the company broke down its recruiting process into 22 discrete functions, such as selecting schools and recruiters, training recruiters, etc. He also presented a case study of a large midwestern firm, using PERT for similar purposes, and encompassing 43 distinct activities. Both of these PERT applications, according to Schoderbek, involved the use of computers. It should be pointed out, however, that neither computers nor a mathematical orientation are necessary in order to use the technique.

These latter two points are confirmed by the other literature on PERT in personnel management. Steinmetz [23], who also deals with college recruiting, has indicated that PERT has not proved useful to the personnel manager when used in connection with three time estimates for each activity and computerization. Steinmetz does emphasize, however, the CPM methods mentioned earlier (which will be referred to as PERT) as being most amenable to simpler projects. Steinmetz illustrates one company's PERT program for college recruiting, showing such activities as "Analyze MS engineer hires," "Select schools for Ph.D. recruiting," and "Make required contacts with placement director."[4]

Two other applications of PERT in personnel deserve mention both utilizing noncomputer single-time estimates, as did Steinmetz. First, Foster has used a PERT program in the development of a programmed instruction program [7]. The particular PERT program developed included over 170 activities and, rather than dealing with policy decisions, was concerned with the actual writing and producing of the PI program. Foster's article illustrates to us another basic functional area of personnel to which PERT is amenable—the training function.

Finally, Varney and Carvalho have reported on the use of PERT in the installation of a new job evaluation program in their firm [25]. The company had: (1) spent four "frustrating" years attempting to install a job-evaluation program for 1100 salaried positions, (2) made some changes in their approach to installing the program to overcome prior weaknesses, and then, (3) with the utilization of the PERT program installed the program in 34 days. Why did the PERT program work so successfully? First, the success was partially due to the fact that some of the limitations in the company's prior methods of installation had already been overcome. Second, the use of a PERT program, according to Varney and Carvalho, appealed to the technically minded management. Third, the planning and involvement of managers with a visible indication of their own commitment (the PERT Chart) was a form of management by objectives. Thus, it appeared to be

---

[4]This may really be the Sandia PERT program mentioned by Schoderbek, since Steinmetz gives credit in his article to private correspondence with a Sandia executive when he presents his PERT chart.

not so much PERT per se, but PERT in a favorable environment which contributed to this company's success.

Simulation

For purposes of classification, simulation and personnel management will be broken down into two types: (1) ordinary and (2) cognitive process.[5]

By ordinary simulation we simply refer to the type of operations research technique which has grown so widely. It is often a technique utilized when no other cost-feasible or no other techniques at all will solve a problem. As Harvey Wagner points out in his work on operations research, simulation is a technique to be used "when all else fails" [27, p. 887].

There have been a few simulations developed in the personnel area. First, in the area of labor-management relations, Kaufman and Penchansky [11] have developed a simulation of union health and welfare trust fund management policies for unions in the construction industry. Various work rules determine when an individual becomes eligible for funds, and one of the basic problems of fund management is the control of dollars flowing into and out of the fund. Kaufman and Penchansky began the study with a suspicion that trust fund managers are drastically overconservative in their management of funds for fear of insolvency. The basic objectives of designing this simulation were (1) to build a "reasonable first-order" model of financial fund behavior to enable testing of different policies on the fund's financial behavior, and (2) to provide the trustees with a workable tool for measuring quantitatively the effects of policy changes. This model is based on historical data and, as such, must be tested further for validity. Nonetheless, the "tentative" results of the model do imply the authors' belief that fund managers are overconservative.

The writer has believed (without evidence) that simulation could provide a useful tool in collective bargaining—e.g., a firm could develop a model of its firm, "plug in" a union proposal, and get from the computer as output, the cost of the proposal. Although no article in an extensive literature search over a period of five years has described in detail any such simulation, in a survey by Pratt [15] of 460 companies, with 149 responses, a few companies were found that were using the computer in collective bargaining. Pratt discovered that the use of simulation was small in collective bargaining, but that it did exist. He found that *in preparation for* bargaining, 13 companies which had responded to the questionnaire had developed programs to analyze the costs of anticipated demands or offers, and that four firms had developed and were using mathematical or simulation models in preparing for bargaining. Fewer firms were found to be using such tools *during* bargaining, but here five companies were found to be using "simula-

[5]We will not treat educational simulation (or business gaming) in this article because it has been so widely treated in the literature. For a classic work on the subject, see (9).

25

tion or mathematical models of their contract to test and analyze the effects of alternative demand packages and company offers" [15, p. 61]. That this may be an area where simulation will grow in the future is indicated by Pratt's finding that previous surveys "found no evidence that any models were being utilized during the negotiation period. . . ." [15, pp. 61–62]

A quite different type of simulation has been developed by Wolf and Leo [29]. Their central concern is with wage and salary administration. They contend that it is extremely difficult, by normal means, to put an objective measure on an executive's *total compensation* package. They then describe analysis of an individual's pay package by a computer simulation they have developed, called "Compsim." They point out that the model can

> *determine the value of each item of compensation at the time it is actually received. Thus the model estimates the appreciation of stock, calculates pension fund growth and so on.* [29, p. 46]

The model also expresses each item in the package "in terms of equivalent salary dollars, thus discounting it back from time of receipt" [29, p. 46]. Finally the model is designed to generate, for each item of compensation, an efficiency index which relates the economic benefit (compensation) to the dollars paid for it. This type model seems most appropriate since it does consider factors not always covered by wage and people—that the cost of a wage item to a company before taxes can be quite different than dollars received by individuals after taxes, especially when the whole problem of time discounting of money is incorporated into the problem.

Cognitive Process Simulation

Some work of interest to personnel managers has been in the way of simulation of cognitive processes. As far back as 1962, it was reported by the Mayo Clinic [16], that the Minnesota Multiphasic Personality Inventory (MMPI) had been "automated"—i.e., a computer program had been written to in effect incorporate the thought processes of a qualified individual as he would interpret the test. These automated tests interpretations then served as data for psychiatrists at the clinic. Somewhat later, Kleinmuntz [12] obtained a computerized interpretation of the MMPI by a different manner—he actually simulated the thought processes of a psychologist, using the protocol method (the psychologist verbalized his decision-making process, which was tape-recorded, subsequently analyzed, and finally programmed on a computer). Kleinmuntz was interested in adjusted and maladjusted students in college, rather than providing data to psychiatrists as had been the case at Mayo. His program had a fairly high "hit" rate, i.e., if students (e.g., as rated by their peers or counselors) were adjusted, there was a fairly high probability that the computer would categorize the student's MMPI score as adjusted; and vice versa.

In a later piece of research, Smith and Greenlaw [22] extended Kleinmuntz's approach to personnel *selection* using the same protocol method. They simulated the psychological decision process of a psychologist working in a well known consulting firm. The subjects were a group of women applying for clerical and administrative clerical positions; and as inputs into the computerized model there were personal information about the applicant, 19 test scores, and job requirements. The program was so written that it printed out a *written evaluation* on each candidate as well as one of four possible hiring recommendations: (1) hire, (2) hire as fair risk, (3) check background further, and (4) reject. The authors ran eight new cases through the model (in addition to the 16 it had been built on), and the computer agreed with the psychologist in seven cases. It is unfortunate that it was not possible for the authors to carry out more validity testing on this model, for it extends considerably the work of Kleinmuntz (with his one test) and appears to have perhaps widespread application in industry.

In summary, this article has demonstrated that several endeavors in management science have been applied to personnel management. Three studies used automated programs or cognitive process simulation in personality assessment and/or personnel selection. Linear programming and PERT have been applied to college recruiting. Five Markovian models, and the logarithmic learning curve model have dealt with the area of manpower planning. The logarithmic model has been applied to safety, simplex to work measurement, and PERT to training (Programmed Instruction). In wage and salary administration, we find one application of PERT, one simulation model, and four linear programming models. Finally, with respect to unions we have the Kaufman and Penchansky simulation study as well as Pratt's survey reports on simulation in collective bargaining. Although one could wish for more, comparing this literature with that of a decade ago indicates that considerable progress has been made in the area of management science and personnel management.[6]

REFERENCES

1. Billon, S.A., "Industrial Learning Curves and Forecasting," *Management International Review,* Vol. 6, No. 6, 1966, pp. 65–79.
2. Bruno, James, "Using Linear Programming Salary Evaluation Models in Collective Bargaining Negotiations with Teacher Unions," *Socio-Economic Planning Sciences,* Vol. 3, No. 2, August 1969, pp. 103–117.
3. Chisman, James A., "Using Linear Programming to Determine Time Standards," *The Journal of Industrial Engineering,* Vol. 17, No. 4, April 1966, pp. 189–191.

[6]It should also be noted that the *only* models considered in this article are those which fall into some well defined operations research category. (e.g., simplex). There are also in existence several unique operations research models in the field of personnel. For example, Easton (5) has developed an n-dimensional Pythagorean model in the field of performance appraisal, and Whybark (28) has developed a manpower forecasting model for determining manpower needs until 1980 in civil aviation.

4. Durbin, E.P., "Manpower Programs as Markov Chains," Memorandum RM-5741-OEO, the Rand Corporation, Santa Monica, California, October 1968.
5. Easton, Allen, "A Forward Step in Performance Evaluation," *Journal of Marketing,* Vol. 30, No. 3, July 1966, pp. 26–32.
6. Eaton, B. Curtis, "Studying Mass Layoff Through Markov Chains," *Industrial Relations,* Vol. 9, No. 4, October 1970, pp. 394–403.
7. Foster, Jerry F., "PERT for Programmed Instruction," *Administrative Management,* Vol. 26, No. 10, October 1965, pp. 42–43.
8. Greenberg, Leo, "Safety: Can It Be Measured?" *Industrial Engineering,* Vol. 2, No. 3, March 1970, pp. 41–45.
9. Greenlaw, Paul S., Lowell W. Herron, and Richard H. Rawdon, *Business Simulation,* Prentice-Hall, Inc., Englewood Cliffs, New Jersey, 1962.
10. Greenlaw, Paul S. and Robert D. Smith, "Learning Curve Analysis: Some General Historical and Theoretical Considerations," in Greenlaw, Paul S. and Robert D. Smith (eds.), *Personnel Management: A Management Science Approach,* The International Textbook Company, Scranton, Pennsylvania, 1970.
11. Kaufman, Gordon and Roy Penchansky, "Simulation Study of Union Health and Welfare Funds," *Industrial Management Review,* Vol. 10, No. 1, Fall 1968, pp. 41–60.
12. Kleinmuntz, Benjamin, "Personality Test Interpretation by Digital Computer," *Science,* Vol. 139, No. 3553, February 1963, pp. 416–418.
13. Merck, John W., "A Markovian Model for Projecting Movements of Personnel Through a System," PRL-TR-65-6, 6570th Personnel Research Laboratory, Aerospace Medical Division, Air Force Systems Command, Lackland Air Force Base, Texas, March 1965, 14pp.
14. Moder, Joseph J. and Cecil R. Phillips, *Project Management with CPM and PERT,* Van Nostrand Reinhold Co., New York, 1970.
15. Pratt, Robert N., "Computer Utilization in the Collective Bargaining Process," *Industrial Management Review,* Vol. 11, No. 3, Spring 1970, pp. 59–66.
16. *Proceedings of the Staff Meetings of the Mayo Clinic,* Vol. 37, No. 3, January 31, 1962, "Symposium on Automation Techniques in Personality Assessment," pp. 61–82.
17. Rehmus, Frederick P. and Harvey M. Wagner, "Applying Linear Programming to Your Pay Structure," *Business Horizons,* Vol. 6, No. 4, Winter 1963, pp. 89–98.
18. Rodgers, William A., "Applying Linear Programming to the Extra Pay for Extra Work Model," unpublished paper, Kent State University, August 4, 1971.
19. _____, "Negotiating a Salary Structure with Modeling, Simulation and Linear Programming," unpublished paper, Kent State University, August 4, 1971.
20. Rowland, Kendrith D. and Michael G. Sovereign, "Markov-Chain Analysis of Internal Manpower Supply," *Industrial Relations,* Vol. 9, No. 1, October 1969, pp. 88–99.
21. Schoderbek, Peter P., "PERT in College Recruiting," *Management of Personnel Quarterly,* Vol. 3, No. 4, Winter 1965, pp. 40–43.
22. Smith, Robert D. and Paul S. Greenlaw, "Simulation of a Psychological Decision Process in Personnel Selection," *Management Science,* Vol. 13, No. 8, April 1967, pp. B409–B419.
23. Steinmetz, Lawrence, "PERT Personnel Practices," *Personnel Journal,* Vol. 44, No. 9, September 1965, pp. 419–424.
24. Teach, Leon and John D. Thompson, "Simulation in Recruitment Planning," *Personnel Journal,* Vol. 48, No. 4, April 1969, pp. 286–292, 299.

25. Varney, Glenn H. and Carvalho, Gerard F., "PERT in the Personnel Department," *Personnel,* Vol. 45, No. 1, Jan.–Feb. 1968, pp. 48–53.
26. Vroom, Victor H. and Kenneth R. McCrimmon, "Toward a Stochastic Model of Managerial Careers," *Administrative Science Quarterly,* Vol. 13, No. 1, June 1968, pp. 26–46.
27. Wagner, Harvey M., *Principles of Operations Research,* Prentice-Hall, Inc., Englewood Cliffs, New Jersey, 1969.
28. Whybark, D. Clay, "Forecasting Requirements in Civil Aviation," *Personnel Administration,* Vol. 33, No. 2, March–April 1970, pp. 45–51.
29. Wolf, Gordon and Mario Leo, "A Systems Approach to Total Compensation," *Business Management/Executive Compensation Report,* Vol. 37, No. 5, February 1970, pp. 44, 46, 48.
30. Wright, T. P., "Factors Affecting the Cost of Airplanes," *Journal of the Aeronautical Sciences,* Vol. 3, No. 4, February 1936, pp. 34–40.
31. Young, Samuel L., "Misapplications of the Learning Curve Concept," *The Journal of Industrial Engineering,* Vol. 17, No. 8, August 1966, pp. 410–415.

Part II
Personnel
Information
Systems

The successful utilization of any management information system is highly dependent upon the nature and quality of information contained in the system. This is equally true of personnel information systems (also known as human resource information systems). Historically, the personnel area was slow to develop computerized information systems that could be used effectively in making major personnel decisions. The earliest applications were primarily for the purposes of keeping records and processing the payroll. Such systems could be used for rapid preparation of such employee lists as addresses, seniority, retirement dates, eligibility for various benefits (life insurance, health insurance, vacations, pensions, etc.), departmental rosters, and pay lists by compensation levels. As more sophisticated "skills inventories" were developed to help locate talent within the organization, the personnel information system was able to yield valuable information to aid the decision maker in such areas as career planning, management development, promotions, and transfers. At this stage of development, many organizations began to make use of their information systems for manpower planning purposes—specifically focusing on manpower forecasts and assessment of the internal supply of manpower.

Further refinements have led to the potential application of the computer to a wide range of problems in nearly every facet of personnel administration. However, computerized personnel data systems are not necessarily cost effective for every organization. This section deals with such issues as the nature of personnel information systems, the situational factors most appropriate to the development of skills inventories, the expansion of systems to include behavioral information, and costs/benefits analysis of such systems.

The word "potential" should be emphasized in the study of personnel information systems. The fact that the potential exists does not necessarily mean that every organization should develop an automated personnel MIS. In some instances it is neither practical nor economically feasible to adopt a comprehensive system. The selections in this section have been chosen with an eye toward answering the basic question, When should an organization develop a computer-based personnel information system?

The first article outlines some important considerations in developing a comprehensive human resource information system and presents some suggestions and a sample form for implementing such a system. According to Anthony the basic purpose of the system is to provide managers with the information they need to maximize human resource decisions. Human resource information systems are discussed within the context of the four basic types of decisions that managers have to make: acquiring, utilizing, maintaining, and accounting for the human resources of the organization. The author describes the concept of human resource asset accounting and briefly analyzes six considerations that must be resolved in order to implement a comprehensive HRIS.

In his article "Missing Ingredient in Skills Inventories," Azevedo describes the historical development and current usage of skills inventories. A dilemma that has arisen over inventories is that they have contained too much overall information but too little of what is important to be useful tools for personnel planning. Based on survey results of skills inventory usages, the author postulates that they are most likely to be effective in capital-intensive industries—and that the work assignments in such industries are likely to be markedly different from work assignments in labor-intensive industries. This suggests the development of a new type of skills inventory in which the basic structure of the inventory involves the detailing of job families or subfamilies held by individuals rather than listing their educational and employment histories.

The authors of the third article hope to correct a deficiency which they perceive in current management information systems—an overemphasis upon the "mechanical" or "technical" aspects of the firm and insufficient attention to the *human* element. Starke and Ferratt recommend complementing the existing "mechanical" MIS with a "behavioral" MIS to constitute a truly complete management information system. In effect, the authors are proposing a behavioral information system (BIS) that provides to the organization on a systematic and periodic basis the type of information contained in what has traditionally been called attitude or morale surveys. The BIS is designed to generate information about (1) employee perceptions, preferences, and attitudes on important job-related issues such as pay, promotion, supervision, job content, job satisfaction, etc., and (2) specific issues which management and/or employees feel are important for their particular organization.

The concluding article in this section focuses upon the factors affecting the costs and benefits of human resource information systems. Tetz contends that a computer-based system is essential today for most personnel operations, although size/complexity are major factors in the type of system applied to a particular situation. The most *immediate* benefit of such a system is the greater accuracy of data with savings in clerical effort while the most *significant* value is the availability of the data resource. Evaluation of costs must take into consideration both development costs and operation costs. However, the estimated costs of a human resource information system should be tempered by the realization that there are current information costs in the noncomputerized system which will be reduced or replaced.

3.
Get to Know Your Employees— The Human Resource Information System

William P. Anthony

The attempt to account for, understand and use human resource information is one of the more significant challenges faced today by managers. We see and hear references made to "skills inventories," "abilities listings," "career plans," "human asset accounting" and "human resource information systems." What goes into each of these systems varies greatly among organizations which have implemented them. This article outlines some important considerations in developing a comprehensive human resource information system and presents some suggestions and a sample form for implementing such a system.

Editors' Note: Reprinted with permission from *Personnel Journal,* Copyright April 1977.

What Is an Information System?

An information system is a logical, valid and reliable grouping of interpreted data which is useful for management decision making. The key concept is that it is information that is relevant to management decisions and that serves to improve decision making. For this reason the term "management information systems" has become popular.[1] The idea of thinking of information as a system developed from the systems approach to examine and manage organizations, which evolved from the computers, aerospace and defense industries. Basically, the characteristics of a management information system (MIS) are the following:[2]

1. A system of information is designed which effectively integrates component parts of information sub-systems. The organization has a total information system which consists of integrated reports, letters, memoranda and electronic data processing.
2. The system is linked to electronic data processing facilities for ease of access, update, and analysis.
3. The information is gathered, analyzed and presented in the form desired by decision makers in the organization.
4. As a corollary, the information is presented in the *user's* language—not the gatherer's.
5. The information is timely and cost-effective. This means that the information is presented at a time such that managers can still use it to effect a decision. It isn't outdated. It also means that the benefits derived from using the information (effectiveness) outweighs the costs of gathering, analyzing, and reporting the information.
6. The information is accurate; that is, it is reliable and valid.
7. Only those portions of information are presented to individual managers which are relevant to the scope of their job and the decision requirements of their job. "Information overload" is thus avoided.

Notice that these requirements present us with a different focus on what has traditionally been viewed as the communication process of the organization. No longer is the focus of communication primarily on inter-personal exchange. No longer are EDP reports, letters, memoranda, etc., viewed as separate means of communicating. The focus shifts now to a total, integrated system of information exchange within the organization that is designed for decision making.

What Is a Human Resource Information System?

A human resource information system is a management information system designed for one particular function of an organization's operations—its human resource management function. The basic purpose of such a system is to provide managers with the information they need to maximize human resource decisions. Like any resource, these decisions fall into the four categories of acquiring, utilizing, maintaining and accounting for the resources of the organization. Decisions made in these areas are made to maximize human resource performance, and, therefore, the human resource contribution to the achievement of organizational goals.

The responsibility for human resource functions prior to the thirties rested with line managers. However, as certain aspects of human resource management developed and became more complex, specialized staff expertise became needed to handle many of the human resource decisions. Thus, personnel departments were formed and grew in the thirties, forties and fifties to handle many of these decisions. Unfortunately, in too many organizations the personnel department soon came to be viewed as the only area in the organization concerned with human resource management. Line managers, relieved that someone could now handle sticky people functions that interfered with their jobs of production or marketing, were happy to let personnel increase the scope of their activities. The line manager thought that if he/she could "keep the people happy" and that if personnel did their job, human resource management problems would be solved.

This development, unfortunately, led to a system of personnel record keeping which was often more self-serving to the personnel department than to the line managers. Records were kept on personnel dealing with such things as previous employment experience, medical history, marital status, previous education, and other demographic data. The information was useful for initial selection and job placement decisions but, since it was not often updated with appropriate information, it had little use for managerial decisions five, ten and twenty years after the initial date of employment. That is, the information seldom provided the timely, reliable, valid information needed by managers to maximize human resource effectiveness in the organization.

That's beginning to change. With the developments in the field of human asset accounting[3] and manpower planning,[4] many managers now realize that a different information system is needed that more accurately reflects an organization's human resource capability. No longer can human resource information be simply the province of the records units of the personnel department. Such information must be fully integrated into the management decision structure of the organization.

Components of a Human Resource Information System

The components of the information system should be made up only of information units which enhance effective human resource decisions. In other words, interpreted data should be provided to managers on relevant decision variables which need to be considered in making a human resource decision. If such data do not contribute to helping the manager make a good decision, it should not be obtained or appear in any report.

What kinds of data maximize human resource decisions? Data that will predict future human resource performance is that kind of data. Unfortunately, most of us are not good prognosticators so we tend to rely on historical information to predict the future. But what we implicitly try to do is to identify key variables that we think will affect future performance and focus on these. We may err in several ways. We may have not identified certain key variables that will, indeed, affect future human resource performance. We may have the right variables, but have inaccurately measured them. Or we may not accurately report them in a timely fashion even though we have accurately measured them. These problems are especially critical at this time in human resource decisions because of the claims for equal employment opportunity and the bias which exists in various selection, placement and promotion criteria now being used.

For example, most organizations use past educational and job experience as a valid predictor of future performance. But, do we really know whether it does predict future performance in a particular job? The only way we can answer this is to observe the performance of those with the particular educational and job experience and those without it and determine if those with it do, indeed, perform at higher levels. Few firms have done this. It's difficult research since care must be made to have a matched control group of people without the characteristic so that a fair comparison can be made.

In the absence of such criterion validation research, many organizations today still operate on the basis of subjective judgment formed on the basis of experience. Of course, they may eliminate an obvious characteristic which has been found not to be valid (such as a culturally based selection test), but most other predictor criteria are formed on the basis of subjective judgment, rather than research.

Given this limitation, but keeping in mind that all predictor criteria should be validated, we can still suggest some components of an information system which is useful to managers in the four areas of human resource decisions.

SELECTION / What factors should an employer look for in an employee for the initial job selection? Hopefully he/she will identify factors which will screen employees who can perform the job from those that can't. But does he/she want superior or adequate performance? If it is superior, is he/she willing to pay for it? Has the employer determined the difference between superior and adequate performance for the job? Is the employer selecting an employee for the initial job or is he/she making a selection that implies the employee can handle future jobs to which he/she may be promoted? These are important questions that need carefully thought-out answers prior to the determination of selection criteria.

Typically, initial job selection decisions are based on such criteria as past educational achievement, past work experience, employer and academic references, tests, and performance during an interview. Other data which are usually obtained are age, sex, race, marital status and number of dependents. These have no predictor validity but are thought to be important demographic information on the candidate and may be required for organizations under certain equal employment opportunity compliance and reporting regulations.

Why is the employer interested in educational achievement, work experience, references, etc.? Usually because these are substitute measures for the criteria he/she is really interested in and because they are convenient screening techniques to reduce the number of candidates to a more manageable level. The employer is really interested in measuring the candidates dependability, reliability, maturity, poise, responsibility and motivation. The employer also wants to know whether the candidate has the basic language and mathematical skills (if any) required for the job. For skilled and professional jobs, such as accounting and engineering, educational achievement serves as a measure of the candidate's knowledge and skills in the job areas, as does any certification (e.g., Certified Public Accountant) which the candidate may hold.

The employment interview also attempts to directly assess many of the same characteristics for which education and experience stand. The interviewer subjectively determines the candidate's communication ability, job knowledge, motivation level, reliability and dependability, and ability to get along with others. Even though interviewers are usually highly skilled, they still make a subjective assessment which may be neither reliable nor valid. Worse yet, interviewers often allow such factors as a candidate's dress, appearance and mannerisms to represent more important characteristics. Common observations reflecting this are, "He must not be highly motivated because he sure dressed sloppy." Or, "She sure wears a lot of makeup and a very short skirt; she must just be interested in getting a husband." This is not to say that appearance is not important for a job. For example, in jobs which require customer contact (e.g., sales or customer service representatives) appearance often represents the quality image of the organization to the customer and thus is important. But to use appearance as a surrogate measure of other characteristics in the interview is not appropriate.

So where does this leave us? How can an employer improve the human resource information needed to make selection decisions? There are several steps he/she can take as follows:

1. The employer needs to identify those factors which characterize effective job performance in each job class, in as explicit terms as possible. These ought to be stated in output terms, perhaps along the lines suggested by a system of management by objectives.[5,6]
2. The employer needs to determine whether a job candidate can achieve these outputs by measuring, as directly as possible, whether the candidate has and is likely to exercise the kinds of skills and knowledge needed by the job.
3. The employer needs to examine each criterion in his present job selection process to determine if it is a valid predictor criterion for the job class and, if so, if it is being objectively measured.

39

This will result in a tailor-made set of selection criteria which are valid for each particular job class in the organization.

A SELECTION EXAMPLE / Suppose an auto dealer is interested in hiring automobile salesmen. What criteria would he/she be interested in? The first question to ask is what characteristics do the best salesmen have? The dealer may define the best salesmen as those who have the highest dollar sales, or highest volume sales, or, even better, those whose sales make the greatest contribution to overall profit. Suppose he/she defines the following characteristics for these salesmen:

1. Extensive and detailed product knowledge, including features, economy and performance characteristics of all models.
2. The ability to empathize or see things from the customer's view.
3. A thorough understanding of the selling process including the role that oral communication, persuasion, and reflection play in the process.
4. The ability to make simple mathematical calculations.
5. The ability to write simple, yet effective, letters, memoranda and reports.
6. Attention to detail including follow-up on customer orders and post-purchase satisfaction of customers.
7. The ability to make meaningful input to the dealer on changing customer tastes and preferences which can be used in planning inventory ordering and sales campaigns.
8. A high level of aspiration and goal-directed behavior.

To assess these in job applications the dealer can do the following:

1. Review the applicants' sales performance in jobs held previously.
2. Administer a test covering:
    a. Product knowledge
    b. Sales techniques
    c. Simple mathematical and writing skills
3. Observe the candidate in a sample sales situation and grade the performance.
4. Administer a personality test covering goal-directed behavior. (This may be a behavioral test, such as a role-playing situation, rather than a paper and pencil test.)
5. Have the candidate, both orally and in written form, detail his/her level of aspiration and career plan.

Notice that educational achievement as measured by years of schooling is inconsequential in and of itself. The dealer wants to know if the candidate can perform well on the above measures. Now the candidate may have learned about selling, writing, mathematics and product attributes through some formal system of schooling, but the actual completion of the schooling is not important; it's whether the candidate possesses the required job skills and knowledge.

UTILIZING / In this area of human resource decision making we are concerned with two related kinds of decisions: job placement[7] and rewarding performance. Each of these are utilization decisions. In job placement we want to be sure that the requirements of the job meet the qualifications of the employee. We do not want employees who are either overqualified or underqualified for the job. As we indicated earlier, most employers pay particular attention to this in the initial selection interview, but many do not give this area enough attention in promotion and transfer decisions. The key concept here is to be sure that the candidate has the skills, knowledge and interest in the new job for which he/she is being considered. The information gathered at the time of initial hiring may be inappropriate or incomplete for consideration here and should be supplemented with additional information.

For example, in our earlier auto salesman case, it would be inappropriate to make a decision to promote a salesman to sales manager based on the information gathered at the time of initial selection. A sales manager's job is different from a salesman's and thus requires different skills. A sales manager would be expected to plan, schedule, control, reward, and otherwise use the sales force. He/she may be asked to help set dealer goals, to participate in hiring and other personnel decisions, and may even be involved in financial decisions. Certainly, he/she will need a higher level of interpersonal skills to manage the work force.

The decision to promote a salesman to sales manager should be made not on the basis of how well the candidate has sold cars, but on the basis of how well the candidate is likely to effectively exercise managerial skills. This is not to say that a knowledge of the selling process and product attributes are not important. It is. But other skills and knowledge are as important, if not more so, for a sales manager.

How can an organization determine if an individual will be effective in a new job to which he/she is to be promoted or transferred? There are several ways this can be determined:

1. What does the individual want to do? This requires a determination of aspiration level and interests, perhaps, through a career planning process.
2. Does the individual presently have or, alternatively, can he/she learn the new job skills or knowledge? This may involve subject matter tests, assessment center techniques, role playing situations, gaming, determination of "trainability," and trial periods in the new position (perhaps as an "assistant to").
3. What has the candidate's past job performance been? This would include a comprehensive review of the individual's performance appraisals, including objective measures of output achieved, as well as interviews with previous superiors.
4. What additional training and development has the candidate received since joining the organization and which specific skills and knowledge have been increased? This entails maintaining an up-to-date development log, keyed by job skill, on each individual.

Again many organizations do not go through such a thorough analysis when making a promotion or transfer decision. Rather, they rely more on subjective judgments of managers which may be formed on biased, inaccurate or incomplete information.

Rewarding performance is the second type of utilization decision which requires accurate human resource information. Here we are concerned with whether the individual met or exceeded the job requirements. These requirements should be stated, in objectively measured output terms, to the greatest extent *possible*. For an organization on a management by objectives system, such a statement is easily developed for each individual. The reward for performance thus becomes integrated with the MBO system so that a performance-appraisal-by-results system is developed.

An organization not on a formal MBO system can still develop a performance-appraisal-by-results system for its employees by stating in output terms the results expected of each employee for the performance appraisal period. This may be stated in terms of units produced, customer complaints satisfactorily resolved, units sold, letters and reports typed, clients counseled and placed, or any other measure of direct output associated with a position. The actual rewards received, then, based upon these outputs, should also be summarized. These might include such factors as the amount of a salary increase received (such as a bonus), the addition of more challenging and responsible job assignments, the awarding of greater job autonomy, promotions or other rewards provided by the organization.

MAINTENANCE / The third major area of a human resource information system is concerned with various human resource maintenance decisions. This includes health and life insurance accruals, pension accruals, standard salary progressions (as opposed to incremental financial rewards provided for outstanding performance such as a bonus), absence rates, tardiness rates, grievance rates, disciplinary actions, and all other data that reflect the maintenance activities organizations exercise with regard to their human resources. Routine training to maintain present skills would also be included here, as opposed to the training to increase or provide new skills which is included in the utilization category. Changes in demographic information such as current address, marital status and number of dependents (for income tax purposes) might also be included here.

The purpose of these data is to provide the organization with the information that is needed to maintain its human resources. This differs from the information required to utilize its resources. Although some may consider this to be a rather arbitrary dichotomy, utilization decisions should be separated from maintenance decisions because maintenance decisions should reflect the routine personnel decisions made with respect to human resources. Utilization decisions are non-routine decisions which should really be decisions made by line managers and not the personnel department. Such a distinction more clearly separates the responsibility for human resource decision making between line managers and the personnel department.

HUMAN RESOURCE ACCOUNTING / The final type of information needed is that required to give a full and accurate accounting of the value of human resources for an organization. Likert[3,7] has been a pioneer in developing a system for accounting for the value of human resources in organizations. Such a system essentially tries to answer the question: How much are the human resources worth to the organization?

Generally, such computations attempt to total the dollars invested in training and development, salaries paid to employees, investments made in pension and insurance plans, hiring costs, and so on. Much of this information can be gathered from other parts of the human resource information system and analyzed and summarized for this section of the report.

Human resource asset accounting is still very much in developmental stages and is not widely used by organizations because particular methods of accounting for human resources are not yet generally accepted by accountants and managers. New methods are being developed, however, and one recently developed by Likert[8] holds some promise. He suggests that it is important to ascertain the productive capability of an organization's human resources. This is done by measuring " . . . the key dimensions of (the) human organization at each time period, say, at one year ago (T_1) and now (T_2)." A key dimension which is suggested is the increase in an organization's profit which can be directly attributable to human resource performance. Thus if profit increases from $1,000,000 to $1,100,000 in one year and if 50% of this improvement came about through more productivity of salesmen in making sales, then we can say that the salesmen human resource increased by $50,000 for the organization. Presumably, the same kind of analysis can be made for non-profit organizations by examining the reduction in costs associated with more productive human resource effort. Thus, if such costs as turnover, absenteeism, tardiness, waste, etc., fall by $50,000 in a given year we can say that the value of human resources increased by $50,000 in a year.

While this method gives us an estimate of incremental increases (or even decreases in the case of increased costs or reduced profits) for human resources, we are still faced with the problem of determining total human asset worth. Perhaps a summation of annual decreases and increases in the value of human resources could give us an estimate of total human resource worth. The key point here is to try to relate human resource performance to some measure of unit or overall organizational effectiveness, such as profit improvement, and then to allocate a portion of this effectiveness to the worth of human resources in dollar terms.

Another method to assess the value of human resources is to look at the market replacement value of the organization's human resources. This approach attempts to answer the question: Assuming all of our employees left the organization today, how much would it cost us to replace them? An attempt is then made to put a dollar figure value on such costs as:

1. Recruiting
2. Selection and placement
3. Training
4. Knowledge of operations
5. Morale
6. Trust and cooperative working relationships
7. Salaries needed to attract the employees

Of course, some of these costs are indeed difficult to measure, but this approach is akin to placing a value on a machine by determining what it costs to replace the machine, not on the basis of what the original machine cost.

How Can a Human Resource Information System Be Implemented?

To implement a comprehensive human resource information system, decisions have to be made on the following issues:

1. Who has the responsibility for gathering data?
2. Who has the responsibility for analyzing the data?
3. How should the system interface with the organization's management information system?
4. How should the system interface with the electronic data processing system?
5. Who should receive human resource information and when?
6. What are some forms which can be used for gathering and reporting data?

Each of these issues is briefly examined in the remainder of the paper.

GATHERING DATA / The responsibility of gathering data rests with three groups: the employee who has to provide data, the personnel department, and line management. The key concept is that each share in this responsibility. It's up to the personnel department to exercise initiative and provide the structure for the gathering of the information. This includes the forms to be used and the processes whereby the information will be analyzed and reported.

ANALYZING DATA / Again the personnel department plays a key role here by doing much of the legwork involved in compiling, synthesizing, and summarizing the data. Of course the analysis which results should be written in the user's language which is useful for decision making. While personnel may be the user of much of the information, line management, particularly in utilization decisions, will also be the user.

MIS INTERFACE / Explicit attention needs to be directed to this issue. An MIS is a system of subsystems and care must be taken to insure that the human resource information system does not duplicate other components of the MIS. For example, production reports may include information on tardiness and absenteeism. The question then becomes should such information be duplicated in another human resource report. Perhaps it should, but it will depend upon the reason for the report and how it will be used.

EDP INTERFACE / This can be a difficult interface. Often EDP is set up for accounting, billing, or research purposes and not for human resource information purposes. However, several authors do provide some suggestions here.[9,10]

1. Develop particular data items for identified purposes.
2. Utilize personnel people trained in computers or computer people trained in personnel.
3. Keep paper work to a minimum.
4. Use existing information which already may be gathered and stored on computer in such areas as employee files, position files, recruitment files, benefit files, or in the payroll systems.
5. Provide analyzed data to managers, not simply computer printouts.

Receivers of Human Resource Information

Receivers of human resource information include line managers, the personnel department, government agencies, other employers, and the employee. Personnel needs the information so that it can be analyzed and used to recommend action to line managers. Line managers need information to make utilization decisions. Government agencies may need some parts of the information for equal employment opportunity matters. The employee should have access to the "file" to ensure accuracy and to give him/her an opportunity to contest items in the file. Other employers may receive parts of the information if the employee authorizes it for an employment recommendation. The primary users of the information, however, will be line managers and the personnel department.

The one person in line management who most needs the information is the employee's immediate superior, who needs it in a timely fashion to make appropriate reward, promotion and evaluation decisions. This may be weekly, monthly, quarterly or annually. Often times an annual report is not frequent enough, even though this is probably the most common reporting period. The key is that line managers should be the ones who dictate how often the information is needed and not some other party.

REFERENCES

1. Voich, Dan, William Shorde, Homer J. Mottice. *Information Systems for Operations and Management.* Cincinnati: Southwestern Publishing Co., 1975.
2. *Ibid.*
3. Likert, Rensis. *The Human Organization: Its Management and Value.* New York: McGraw-Hill, 1967.
4. Patten, Thomas H., Jr. *Manpower Planning and the Development of Human Resources.* New York: Wiley Interscience, 1971.
5. Morrisey, George. *Management by Objectives and Results.* Reading, Mass.: Addison-Wesley, 1971.
6. Carroll, Stephen, Jr. and Henry Tosi, Jr. *Management by Objectives: Applications and Research.* New York: Macmillan Co., 1973.
7. Some people refer to this as manpower planning but we avoid the term here because it varies so much in meaning among employers. To some it is simply manpower forecasting. To others it is the complete process of planning the acquisition, utilization and maintenance of human resources.
8. Likert, Rensis. "Human Resource Accounting: Building and Assessing Productive Organizations." *Personnel,* May–June, 1973, pp. 8–24.
9. Check, Logan M. "Personnel Computer Systems: Solutions in Search of a Problem." *Business Horizons,* August 1971, pp. 67–76.
10. Tomeski, Edward A. and Harold Lazarus. "The Computer and the Personnel Department: Keys to Modernizing Human Resource Systems." *Business Horizons,* June 1973, pp. 61–66.

4.
Missing Ingredient in Skills Inventories

Ross E. Azevedo

For many years, skills inventories were advocated as the "in" method for organizations to use to structure and control their work forces. The argument ran that, if the organization can establish an efficient and effective skills inventory, it can significantly improve upon its ability to select and promote from within as well as possess a useful tool for efforts at designing and effectuating internal manpower programming efforts. Moreover, the skills inventory promised to assist organizations in affirmative action programs. Certainly the technology existed, in terms of the computer capability and the technical expertise to operate it, and the only real problem seemed to be to design the proper system, put it in operation, and reap the rewards. Unfortunately, things have not worked out quite as planned.

Editors' Note: Reprinted by permission of the Association for Systems Management from *Journal of Systems Management,* April 1977.

The bloom has long since fallen from skills inventory, with the experts now beginning to modify their positions substantially or even coming full circle to condemn the skills inventory as a waste of time . . . too expensive to design, install, operate, or maintain.[1] Managers have been equally disappointed by the problems associated with skills inventories. They have spent vast amounts of time, effort, and money supporting systems designed and built by the personnel and/or management information systems departments only to find out too often that their endeavors were to prove fruitless. Their efforts to make use of the inventories frequently fell flat because of system failures, inadequate or insufficient information, out-dated records, limited scope of operation, and many other factors.

Obviously, neither of these views provides the complete answer to the dilemma of skill inventories. What is needed is a more complete statement as to the role skills inventories can play and the role they cannot. To over-define the anticipated functional performance is to get our expectations out of line with reality and to under-define them is to fail to use the system to its fullest capabilities. This article neither condemns nor advocates the use of skills inventories but rather suggests a new criterion which should be evaluated in deciding whether to implement an automated skills inventory system.

Why Skills Inventories?

Skills inventories are generally reputed to have been first employed by the military in its attempt to handle vast manpower pools. It was a useful tool, allowing the armed services to record the training received and skills possessed by anyone from the private out of boot camp to the general in command. Their existence was supposed to allow the selection of the individuals or group of individuals most competent to meet every demand that might arise. It was this capability that provided the early appeal of skills inventories to the private sector.

The initial utilization of skills inventories in the private sector, however, had military overtones. Defense procurement procedures of the federal government, particularly in aerospace projects, often required that organizations responding to requests for proposals (RFP's) be able to demonstrate their ability to perform the specific operations detailed in the proposals submitted. The easiest way to do this was to develop a skills inventory. This would allow the company to perform a search of its records to obtain a composite picture of the qualifications of those employees "available." A particular company, by demonstrating that its skills mix was especially well qualified to complete the projects outlined in the RFP, could expect that its chances of a successful bid were enhanced.[2]

The idea of skills inventories spilled over into other segments of the private sector where the growth in their advocacy and use paralleled the growth in the use of automated information systems in expanding companies. Larger numbers of employees, in more divisions and departments, have necessitated better methods of recordkeeping. Government regulations, in the areas of Social Security, income tax, equal employment opportunity, and pension reform—to name but a few—have imposed a premium on being able to retrieve vast amounts of data in relatively short periods of time. However, recordkeeping uses only a portion of what has been implied as possible for skills inventories.

During the late 1950's and early 1960's, the rapidly improving technical capability provided the opportunity to use the more sophisticated programming and computational procedures of the computer to expand the informational gains possible from the inventories. The thinking about the uses to which the inventories could be put also underwent rapid change. The fact that skills inventories could be used to describe certain characteristics of the people in the organization led to consideration of using them to include records of previous work experience. This inclusion of information on the jobs performed by individual workers marks the transition to a true skills inventory.

This thinking soon expanded to include the possibility that the inventory could be used to develop an entire manpower planning capability.[3] The inventory systems were now considered to be capable of allowing the organization to develop a strategy and technique for rationalizing the "vacancy filling" process. They could be used to develop an internal manpower planning function that would allow for the structuring of the future employment paths of present and future employees associated with the organization.

This "planning" capability had a certain attractiveness to it because it allowed its advocates to argue it was the perfect way to "select and promote from within." The supporters carried their case to management, arguing that they had *the* manpower planning system. Their argument seemed reasonable for they demonstrated potential systems with substantial technical capacity that could elicit the names of from a few to several hundred likely candidates for any position. They could select within or across departments, within or across divisions, within particular plants or even across the entire corporation. The promise of a completely rational system of job ladders and promotions appeared to be at hand, neatly laid out for management use.

While skills inventories have long been a part of the personnel function, and strongly supported as an optimal method of dealing with internal manpower policy, their relative success and depth of penetration into public and private organizations has been generally limited. Although the hoopla which accompanied their growth and development has continued unabated in some circles, the disquieting rumblings have become too persistent to be ignored. Far too often, inventories have not lived up to the promises of their advocates and their utilization has suffered as a result. While the reasons for these failures are doubtless varied, this article reports on a key variable which most certainly had an influence in all of them.

Dilemma of Skills Inventories

The primary emphasis throughout the period of skills inventory growth and development has been a concentration on the accumulation of information. The development of newer and faster computers with ever-larger memories fostered this process. Personnel directors and systems persons developed continually expanding formats into which more and more data points on individual employees could be entered. From name, age, sex, degrees earned, and previous jobs held within the organization, the list grew to embrace foreign language capability, special licenses, school projects, and hobbies, whether or not they had a relationship to any position the organization was trying to fill or *ever* would need to fill.

The reasons for this growth of information "consciousness" resided both within and outside the organizations involved. There were the above-mentioned efforts on the part of personnel specialists and systems people to sell the inventories. Simultaneously, there was a growth in software suppliers who developed skills inventories on their own. These companies put together bits and pieces of existing systems, added innovations of their own, and brought forth "omnibus" skills inventories. These were packages which were described by their creators as being complete personnel systems which would provide the organization with full manpower planning capabilities. They were represented as operating inventories which would provide "scientific" answers to the bulk of the problems facing the typical personnel officer in large organizations.

There were also governmental pressures inducing large organizations to move into skills inventories. During the 1960's the civil rights movements and the drive for equality on a variety of employment fronts led many to believe that at least partial resolution of the situation could be obtained through the use of skills inventories. These systems, the arguments ran, would allow the organizations an opportunity to describe the sex, age, and race mix of its work force, thereby assuring it of the ability to meet equality guidelines as established by the Federal Government. The skills inventory was to provide the foundations for the structural aspects of the affirmative action program of the employer. The only task remaining was for the employer to use the inventory to first determine the location of deficiencies in the organization, and then employ it to identify those individuals from minority groups best suited to move into the areas of inadequacy. All the organizations had to do then was place the right people in the right jobs and its problems would be solved.

While the process of information gathering and inventory building has continued under the impetus of the advocates of skills inventories and the Federal Government, the real challenge to skills inventories came about when there were attempts to expand their utilization beyond the production of reports and tabulations. The expectations that the inventory would answer employment problems of particular organizations all too often failed to be realized. There proved to be a vast chasm between the promises of the advocates and the realities for the users, causing untold frustration on the part of many of the latter.

50

The dilemma which arose over inventories was that they have contained too much information but too little of what is important to be useful tools for personnel planning. The advocates of skills inventories have described their potential with infinite detail but have failed to understand the actual demands which would be made by the "future."[4] It is this lack of linkage between the information included in inventories and the true needs of a manpower planning system which has forced many personnel practitioners to feel they are boxed into a mechanical structure which is unable to mesh with the operational structure of the organization. It is valuable to consider why this situation developed.

Positions vs. Skills—Past vs. Future

To detail the shortcomings of skills inventories, which must be recognized whether one decides to use a system or not, involves consideration of a variety of factors. In a sense we must ask what is the connection between what an inventory measures and what is demanded by particular jobs within a given organization. The nature of this linkage might best be considered by examining the meaning of skills inventories and what they truly constitute for the user.[5]

One basic difficulty involves the general concept of an inventory and the manner in which it is used in this context. An inventory is usually thought of as a storeroom, filled with rows or stacks of items. Within each of these rows or stacks, there are groups of identical items, each designed to serve the same specific functions, to which an individual can go and select those required to fulfill particular needs. The inventory stock can normally be refilled as required, using items purchased at a given price from suppliers, making it *always* available for use. The contents of the inventory are specified with precision as are the tasks or uses to which they can be applied.

The same situation does not hold for the skills inventory, for it is an inventory of *only* those current employees. It records only the skills of the individual associated with the organization and does not consider whether they can be replaced by recruiting a new worker from outside. Certain skills may be irreplaceable, or replaceable only at a cost which the organization deems prohibitive. Unlike the typical inventory, the skills included in the inventory may belong to different people, meaning that often there is no way to select one person who meets the demands of a particular position.

Equally challenging is the question of what constitutes a skill. The inventory records exactly what the individual is and what he or she has done, from years of schooling completed to the specific title of the current position held. But Webster's defines a skill as "The ability to use one's knowledge effectively; technical proficiency." The mere recording of the experience an individual has had does not indicate his or her potential to use that past experience for a job in the future. Complicating the issue is the fact that the same job title may cover a multitude of specific job duties. Putting these relationships together, it is easy to foresee that there will be difficulties involved in using a computerized record to locate a particular individual to fit a particular job slot.

This situation is compounded by the fact that the records of most individuals tend to be autobiographical. They represent the perceptions held by the participant as to his or her education, training, and experience. There is rarely an employer's perception as to what job was performed or what level of responsibility was assumed. This lack of alternative information can bias the available data in either direction in those situations where the respondent builds up or undervalues the experience he or she has had.

There have been further difficulties because managers feel they can make promotions and transfer selections just as well if not better on their own.[6] When promotions or other job changes become possible, these supervisors use more traditional "informal" lines of communication to obtain people to fill vacancies. Only if all else fails will they refer to the Personnel Department and ask for the use of the skills inventory to select possible candidates for the available job slot.

Perhaps the most serious problem facing skills inventories has been an inability to integrate them into the personnel requisition system. This failure is the result both of the limitations described above and of the deficiencies in operating inventory systems. The conventional system employs a procedure whereby requisitions, normally the product of joint consultation between supervisor and employment representative, describing open positions in terms of the specific duties required are sent to the personnel unit. At this point, the skills inventory may be searched or the personnel unit may elect to use other methods to fill the vacancy. This is the juncture at which the system often fails.

The job requisition typically is expressed in terms of job tasks, but the skills inventory is recorded in job experience and job titles. There is no quick method of tying the request to the inventory system. The only way to match up the two is to convert the job request into pieces which are consistent with the experience records. This process is often foregone because of its complications and in the interest of expediency, short-changing the potential of the skills inventory and causing many of the individual systems to fail to live up to the expectations of both the organizations and the staff members involved.

Shortcomings Provide a Clue

To detail the problems associated with skills inventories is to provide a criterion determining the relative success a skills inventory might have in a particular organization. In a sense, the measure of success of a skills inventory system will be related to the extent to which the items recorded on the inventory correspond to the characteristics necessary for the vacant job which is being filled. The closer the correspondence, the more successful the inventory is likely to be . . . the greater the divergence the less useful the inventory will be at providing the link between opening and candidate.

A recent survey of skills inventories in the Los Angeles area provides substantial support to this analysis. Approximately 45 firms were surveyed to ascertain their experience with skills inventories. The survey, which was designed to ascertain the relative success these firms had with their inventories, provided considerable insight into the operation of these systems. Success rates varied and the reasons for these differences were diverse as might be expected.

The results of this important aspect of the survey are detailed in Table 1, which provides detail on effectiveness of skills inventories known to be operating in the Los Angeles area. The table indicates the percentage of firms in an industry using some form of skills inventory, which range from five percent in education to 95 percent in those firms involved in personnel search, as well as subjective estimates of the effectiveness of the inventories in helping these organizations place people in new positions through promotion or transfer. Obviously, there is a wide variation in success rates and they are all relatively low. Table 1 also suggests a clue as to why success rates have differed.

The rightmost column of Table 1 indicates the capital/labor ratios, expressed in dollars per worker, for the industries represented by organizations known to be operating inventories. It is evident that higher success levels are associated with those industries which have the higher capital/labor ratios—such as petroleum refining—while lower levels of success are associated with those industries which

Table 1: Effectiveness of Skills Inventories

Industry	Percent of Employment	Estimates of Effectiveness	Capital Labor Ratio
Petroleum refining	60%	40%	$135,476
Aerospace	70	20	9,009
Miscellaneous manufacturing	20	15	5,904
Utilities	40	20	N/A
Retail trade	5	10	N/A
Banking	30	10	13,030
Insurance	15	5	11,618
Large personnel search firms	95	70	N/A
Health care	15	10	18,176
Education	5	10	N/A
Local government	20	5	N/A

Notes: Based on skills inventories known to be operating in the Los Angeles area.

Effectiveness measured as proportion of openings filled using skills inventory and applies only to those with inventories.

Data for capital/labor ratios are expressed in original cost minus depreciation except for hospitals which are in terms of actual replacement costs.

have lower capital/labor ratios—banking, for example.[7] This relationship points to some important implications for the use of skills inventories and suggests one breakthrough for the design of skills inventories generally.

The relative capital intensity of an industry is a prime determinant of most of the jobs involved although some jobs transcend nearly all industries. The two industries noted—banking and refining—provide an excellent comparison. Refining is a highly automated industry, with much of the processing being directed by automated electronic and mechanical systems. A large proportion of the work in the industry involves adjusting machinery and equipment to maintain the appropriate levels of output and assure the correct product mix. Banking is at the other end of the spectrum, with the work involving people processing the paperwork necessary for the financial arrangements of the community. In the work process, individuals and groups of people make day-to-day decisions about the financial affairs of others. It should be clear that these are extremely different types of work assignments . . . and that difference suggests a key element in skills inventory design.

Petroleum refining is an industry which has had "relatively" more success with skills inventories because it has jobs which have high technical content. This means that the jobs are centered on the manner in which a sophisticated technical system converts crude petroleum into the variety of products which are demanded in the market. By comparison, jobs in the banking industry have a high people orientation. The tasks performed are of a much more personal nature, requiring substantially higher levels of interaction with people than is generally the case in refining.

The skills inventories in use in the petroleum industry are quite traditional, they detail training completed and jobs held. This information is relatively satisfactory in the industry because of the commonality among jobs. Similar skills and training can be used across a wide range of positions as an individual moves upward through promotions. Variations in the content of successive jobs is relatively small in most cases and even if the person chosen for a job proves to be unsatisfactory, the losses which might be incurred are likely to be small before the situation is corrected.

On the other hand, the type of loss incurred in banking can be substantial if the inventory leads to an improper choice. The problems of poor loans, inadequate securities management, and deficient investment supervision can cost the bank large sums of money as well as create a poor image in the community. These losses, which may be substantial, cannot be turned around quickly or easily in most cases.

This comparison between the banking and petroleum industries suggested the development of a new type of skills inventory. The basic structure of this inventory involves the detailing of job families or subfamilies held by individuals rather than listing their educational and employment histories. This development marks two major changes in the possible use and potential of skills inventories.

Improvements in the use of skills inventory in the job-filling process are the

54

first gains yielded by this change. Job requisitions are specified in terms of job families and can be easily fed into the search structure of the inventory system. There is no longer the problem of translation, changing job titles into the terms which can be interpreted by the inventory. Openings are compared with the records of those who have worked in the same job family (or families) and it is possible to isolate potential matches quickly. The interview and selection process can then take place without the delays imposed by other systems.

The second, and perhaps most important, benefit coming from this new form of skills inventory is its provision of the basis for the development of an inventory system based entirely on function. This is because the inventory details the specific tasks which each employee has performed regardless of job title. Individual workers, together with the supervisor, will work out detailed listings of the functions discharged on each job. Titles will become relatively irrelevant and attention is to be focused on job content.

As the system develops, every job within the organization is going to be broken down through functional analysis to specify the tasks which are required in its performance. In a similar fashion, every position on individual job ladders will be decomposed to provide measures of the relative proportion of work time spent on individual functions, thereby yielding the mix of abilities which the person filling each job must possess.[8]

By using functional job families and ultimately moving to individual job functions instead of work experience, this new approach to skills inventories promises to allow better alignment between people and jobs—particularly in those industries which have not experienced success with inventories in the past. The internal search for replacements will be performed on the basis of functional job families and job functions. The process, in its final form, will compare the mix of functions involved in a job with a composite picture of the employees' functional experience. Those employees who have performed the tasks required will be the ones selected for further consideration. They will be the people within the organization, regardless of education or position held, best qualified to fill the tasks necessary to the job which is available.

Summary

At one extreme, skills inventories have been advocated as highly sophisticated tools to aid in the vacancy filling process within organizations. Others have complained that the inventories are nothing more than expensive recordkeeping efforts with little or no payoff. Unfortunately, both of these views are right in many respects. The thrust of the arguments raised here is that there is a middle ground which might answer the complaints of some who have condemned skills inventories.

The results which indicate that success with skills inventories has largely been related to the capital intensity of an industry are crucial for they provide an important variable to be considered by those contemplating a system. If an organization is characterized as capital intensive, it might profit from the installation of an inventory; one with low capital intensity might be better off refraining from going to the expense of operationalizing a system.

On the other hand, the developing form of skills inventories involving functional job families and ultimately job functions may provide an answer for those organizations with relatively low capital intensity—and even for those with greater amounts of capital per employee who have had only limited success with inventories. This new "technology" should facilitate substantial expansion of skills inventories among organizations for which this method would be appropriate for promotion and transfer decisions. Obviously, the controlling variable appears to be the degree of personal interaction involved in the jobs in question although the inventory system using job families and job functions would appear to be applicable in other situations as well. It is evident this new method requires extra cost and effort but, as is true with any such development, these must be weighed against the benefits the system will yield.

The purpose of what is written here is not to stand as an advocacy for either an expansion in the number of or a change in characteristics of existing inventories. Rather, the intent here is to inform decision-makers as to the existence of another important variable which must be evaluated before a decision is made. In this case, the management decision must evaluate both the technical and human content of the jobs within the organization and investigate the possibility of separating jobs into job families and ultimately building the system around job functions.

Additionally, the adoption of a new approach to skills inventories does not ensure that it will be any easier to solve internal organizational problems associated with such systems. Managers and others will continue to resist this type of change unless it can be demonstrated that better results are possible with this new approach.[9] At the same time, any skills inventory can provide only a list of alternative individuals who must be considered in promotion and transfer decisions. It cannot keep people from wanting to promote their friends.

Moreover, all forms of skills inventory requires periodic update and maintenance. The installation of a system with the expectation that it will run itself dooms one to failure from the start. An inventory is only an aid to the personnel process. It goes hand in hand with proper interviewing, evaluating and selecting. The approach to skills inventories discussed here cannot replace good personnel practices. At its best it can only supplement them by providing a much more complete indication of the internal candidates available for particular positions in certain situations.

FOOTNOTES

1. Fahnline, Richard H., "The Skills Inventory Put On," *Journal of Systems Management,* May 1974.

2. This demand led people to claim that firms in the aerospace industry were guilty of "hoarding" labor. The argument ran that the government's requirements that contractors have a "demonstrated ability" to complete a proposed project meant that these firms held excessively large staffs—particularly of scientists and engineers—in order to be ready if the contract were awarded. Obviously, the hoarding of labor produced market inefficiencies and caused problems for other employers.

3. There has been an on-going confusion between the use of skills inventories and manpower planning. Those who sell the inventories have often touted them as manpower planning systems but the most that can be said is that inventories can be an important tool in manpower planning.

4. Fahnline, Richard H., "The Skills Inventory Put On," *Journal of Systems Management,* May 1974.

5. This portion of the discussion benefits from Fahnline, *Op. Cit.,* pp. 15–17. Ibid.

6. This is a basic concern with the skills inventory. One which is to be used for advancement and upgrading should be installed only if a convincing case can be made that it will provide a better promotion procedure than can be operated through traditional practices.

7. The employee search firms are excluded from this comparison because of obvious differences between them and the other firms. They use skills inventories as a primary tool in their operation; the inventories are not just a tool which is incidental to the production process as is true in the other industries. It might also be noted that the search firms are much more likely to spend the time and effort necessary to maintain their inventories than are other users. The cost of upkeep is very high for these systems and is much more likely to be paid by those firms which depend upon them to a considerable extent.

8. There is an additional advantage to this system. If a new job is being established, or the basic nature of an old job is changing, it is possible to characterize with respect to the new combination of functions.

9. Those familiar with skills inventories will recognize the importance of this point. Even if the functional job family system is employed, it does not guarantee that people from different job tracts with the appropriate talent will move up the ladder in question. The supervisor may feel that a better candidate can be found elsewhere in the organization because of knowledge gained independently. It should be obvious that the use of pure job functions should ease this deficiency in the system, although it does not promise to change human nature.

5.
Behavioral
Information Systems

Frederick A. Starke and Thomas W. Ferratt

The use of the computer and related management information systems (MIS) has allowed management to efficiently gather large amounts of data about corporate operations. Not surprisingly, these management information systems have had a great impact on the functional operating areas of manufacturing and service organizations. To date, the MIS has been primarily concerned with providing management with data on the "mechanical" or "technical" aspects of the firm, i.e., operating, sales, and cost data. While improvements in these areas of the firm's operations are necessary and beneficial, the value of the typical MIS has been considerably reduced by two problems: First, when designing the MIS, management often does not consider which information is most useful for its

Editors' Note: Reprinted by permission of the Association for Systems Management from *Journal of Systems Management,* March 1976.

purposes. As a result, a great deal of information may be available that is never used, or information that is necessary may not be generated at all. This problem has been studied extensively elsewhere, and is not discussed further here.[1]

Second, restricting the MIS to the reporting of data on the *mechanical* aspects of the firm means that management will have only a vague and fragmented idea of how the *human* element is reacting to its leadership. Increased organizational effectiveness is most likely to be achieved if management improves its knowledge about both the mechanical and human elements in the firm. This improvement can be achieved by complementing the existing "mechanical" MIS with a "behavioral" MIS, the two constituting a truly complete management information system.

The Behavioral Information System

A behavioral information system (BIS) is designed to generate information about (a) employee perceptions, preferences, and attitudes on important job-related issues such as pay, promotion, supervision, job content, job satisfaction, etc., and (b) specific issues which management and/or employees feel are important for their particular organization. Ideally, this information should be collected periodically (for example, once a year) so that management and employees can observe changes (either improvements or declines) in each of the categories for which data are being gathered. Analysis of observed changes will suggest areas that are satisfactory as well as those that need improvement.

The focus of data gathering and analysis may be on the individual employee, groups of employees, specific departments within the company, specific job titles, or any other grouping which will give insights into the state of the human element in a particular organization. Critical time periods for gathering information on individual employees are at the beginning of employment, during active employment, and at the termination of employment. Although many organizations collect information from individuals *before* they join or *after* they leave the company (entrance and exit interviews), they do not systematically collect information from employees *during* their employment. Even organizations which do collect this information often do not get full benefit from it since it is not systematically analyzed.

Information gathered during employment can be collected on the same periodic basis as other critical management control information (quarterly, semiannually, or annually). In addition, such information may be collected before, during, or after any major change programs that are conducted.

Many devices exist that can be used to gather data of the type proposed here, the most common of which are questionnaire surveys. Figure 1 indicates some of the questions that the employee might be asked relating to the organization in general and his job in particular. Employee responses to these questions form the core of the BIS.

Figure 1: Examples of Questions Used In Employee Surveys

---

1. Attitudes

a. I would not change my job for another job.

| Strongly disagree | Disagree | Neither agree nor disagree | Agree | Strongly agree |

b. People in this organization are given recognition for a job well done.

| Strongly disagree | Disagree | Neither agree nor disagree | Agree | Strongly agree |

c. Taking into consideration all the things about your job, how satisfied or dissatisfied are you with it?
(1) Very dissatisfied
(2) Dissatisified
(3) Neither satisfied nor dissatisfied
(4) Satisfied
(5) Very satisfied

2. Perceptions and Preferences

1. The authority connected with my position:
(1) How much is there now?   (minimum)   1 2 3 4 5 (maximum)
(2) How much should there be?   1 2 3 4 5
(3) How important is it to me?   1 2 3 4 5

b. My job provides me with the opportunity to be creative and innovative:
(1) To what extent is this true now?

| Never | Seldom | Occasionally | Frequently | Always |

(2) To what extent would you like this to be true?

| Never | Seldom | Occasionally | Frequently | Always |

The questions indicated are only suggestive of the type which may be asked. Each organization will want to develop its own questions so that issues which are particularly relevant for that organization can be examined. In this way, the most benefit will be obtained from employee responses.

If the organization does not wish to conduct general questionnaire surveys, a variety of other approaches can be used to generate the data necessary for the BIS. For example, supervisory ratings of subordinates, peer evaluations, subordinate ratings of superiors, and comments by trained observers are alternate methods of gathering data. In addition, employee responses made during in-depth interviewing programs, in-house seminars, MBO consultations, and company training programs are all valuable pieces of information that will benefit management in assessing the human component of the organization. Although many companies are currently conducting these types of programs, there is very little systematic incorporation of employee experiences in them into the total organizational information system.

Thus, the BIS concept stresses the importance of taking the large amount of behavioral data that many organizations routinely generate, supplementing this information with other data where necessary, and systematically incorporating it into the total management information system. When this is done, management will be able to develop a much more complete understanding of the technical and human elements comprising the firm as well as the interaction between the two.

The Value of a Behavioral Information System

The primary value of a BIS lies in its ability to make management aware of the state of employee perceptions, attitudes, and preferences and how these may change over time. In much the same way that preventive maintenance and monitoring the condition of mechanical operations can minimize unexpected breakdowns and their associated costs, monitoring the state of the human element can minimize unexpected costs of employee dissatisfaction. What are the specific costs associated with employee dissatisfaction? Three costs which are frequently cited are turnover, absenteeism, and counterproductive behavior.[2] The costs associated with these problems vary widely from company to company, but on an aggregate basis they are very high. For example, a recent estimate of the cost of turnover to U.S. industry is 11 billion dollars per year.[3]

A brief analysis of the turnover problem will indicate the value of a BIS. It is important to determine *why* turnover is occurring before any logical attempt can be made to reduce it. Although management often attempts to do this in exit interviews, the information generated is of questionable value since the exiting employee may be reluctant to give the real reason for quitting. A BIS resolves this problem by routinely gathering information on employee attitudes and preferences *before* turnover occurs. This information allows management to more effectively anticipate and/or cope with turnover problems. Similar comments apply with respect to the costs of absenteeism and counterproductive behavior.

The second value of a BIS is that it gives management the ability (based on the data generated by the system) to logically and systematically analyze problems and suggest appropriate solutions. This can be accomplished using the two-stage analysis system discussed below.

STAGE ONE / The first step toward better utilization of the human element is for management to understand how both mechanical and human factors can affect employee performance (Figure 2). Employee job attitudes are determined by (1) their individual preferences for certain types of jobs, and (2) the extent to which their perceptions of organizational and job characteristics are in agreement with their preferences. Generally, the greater the extent of agreement, the more positive the employee's attitude toward his job. The existence of positive attitudes does not, however, guarantee job performance; employee skills relevant to the job must also be present. In addition to these employee-related factors are the "mechanical" factors such as the extent of mechanization of the job, required company procedures, and other job-related features which inhibit or facilitate job performance.

STAGE TWO / The second stage of the process involves using these relationships to systematically analyze the data generated by the BIS (Figure 3). After the performance of individuals from a given department has been assessed, and they have been classified as either high performers or low performers, the attitudes of the two groups should be examined. If there are no differences in the attitudes of the two groups, the cause of low job performance may be in factors unrelated to attitudes (for example, employee skill levels or other mechanical causes). If attitudes are different, individual preferences and perceptions of organizational or job characteristics should be examined as potential explanations of the different performance levels. If, for example, differences in individual preferences show up in the BIS data, this could be the cause of the different attitudes observed. One group may prefer more opportunity for growth and learning in their job while another group may prefer more opportunity for social interaction. These differences in preferences may suggest alternative ways of coping with the group having the negative or low attitude. The organization may wish to hold training sessions to change preferences; it may wish to select new employees who have the same preferences as the group with positive attitudes; or it may attempt to accommodate different preferences by increasing job flexibility. All these actions may be taken so that negative attitudes can be improved and blocks to performance eliminated.

The same type of systematic analysis of problems and possible solutions can be done with respect to perceived organizational characteristics and employee skill levels. In this way, the difficult task of assessing the impact that human and mechanical factors have on performance can be more readily accomplished.

Figure 2: The relationship between employee attitudes and job performance

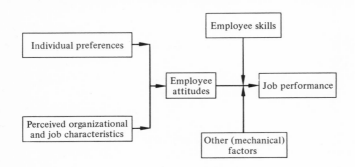

Figure 3: Analysis of BIS data

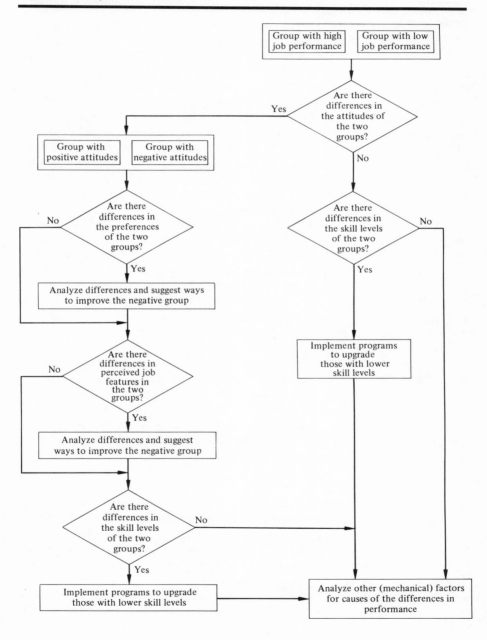

Implementing a Behavioral Information System

Recognition that a BIS has merit is simply the first step toward more complete information about the human element in the firm. Some practical steps must also be taken to ensure that the desired information is actually gathered. There are basically two approaches: Use an organization that is external to the company, or use a group within the firm.

THE OUTSIDE AGENCY / One of the crucial problems that has been encountered when organizations gather attitudinal data is the concern by employees that the information may be "used against them." To counter this legitimate concern (which often results in untruthful responses), it is important to ensure that employees see that confidentiality of responses is guaranteed. How can this be accomplished? The most straightforward method is to have the BIS administered by an agency which has competence in this area and is external to the firm (for example, a management consulting firm).

The typical procedure is to have a representative of the agency meet with management and employee representatives to determine the information desired and the frequency with which it will be generated. The actual gathering should be done by the outside agency to ensure that both management and employees see that impartiality is being maintained during the process. Once the data have been collected, the agency presents its findings to a joint meeting of management and employees. Discussion and analysis of problems (using the system proposed in Figure 3) can then take place in an atmosphere stressing problem-solving rather than confrontation.

What are the costs associated with this type of approach? Clearly, the direct dollar flows to the outside agency for operating the BIS are easy to calculate. However, these must be weighed against the benefits which accrue from operating the system. These include (1) the benefits of having the information about employees, and (2) the costs of not having the information. Given the high cost to industry of absenteeism, turnover, sabotage, and counterproductive behavior in general, it is likely that the benefits of having information on employee attitudes far exceed the costs of developing it.

THE INSIDE GROUP / In the event that management does not wish to utilize an outside agency because it has the competence within the firm to do the job (most likely in the personnel department), a degree of confidentiality can be maintained by having a competent individual or group administer the system. If an individual is used, it should be one mutually agreed to by both management and employees. If a group is used, representatives of both management and employees would constitute the group. Under this method, it is important that emphasis be placed on the gathering of data anonymously and the reporting of data in summary form.

In this way, the value of the information is not drastically reduced and employees are confident that individual responses cannot be traced.

These, then, are the two general approaches that can be used to implement a BIS. The method chosen depends on a variety of factors such as cost, availability of internal expertise, and the basic level of trust which exists between management and employees.

Summary

During the past few years, many firms have installed management information systems to monitor and report on important company activities. Unfortunately, they have not benefited as much as they might have from these systems because information typically is generated only for the technical aspects of the company's operations. In order to obtain full benefit from management information systems, it is suggested that existing technical information be complemented with behavioral information. When this is done, management will have data on both the human and non-human elements in the firm and will be able to make decisions that will most likely increase organizational effectiveness.

REFERENCES

1. Ackhoff, Russell L., "Management Misinformation Systems," *Management Science,* 14, December, 1967, 147–156.
2. Likert, Rensis, *New Patterns in Management.* New York: McGraw-Hill Book Company, 1961; see also Gibson, J., Ivancevich, J., and Donnelly, J., *Organizations.* Dallas: Business Publications, Inc., 1973, especially Chapter 5.
3. Augustine, Joseph, "Personnel Turnover." In Joseph Famularo (ed.), *Handbook of Modern Personnel Administration:* Chapter 62. New York: McGraw-Hill Book Company, 1972.

6.
Evaluating Computer-Based Human Resource Information Systems: Costs vs Benefits

Frank F. Tetz

As management struggles to increase profitability (or reduce costs) it is especially appropriate to look at the impact of a computerized human resource information system. How much does it cost? How much is it worth? These questions must be answered, not just at the time management is considering installation of a human resource information system, but through a constant evaluation process after it is operational. This evaluation requires assessment of the system with regard to:

> Effectiveness in meeting both immediate and projected needs of decision-making managers.

Editors' Note: Reprinted with permission from *Personnel Journal*, Copyright June 1973.

Costs and offsetting savings in time and money compared with former methods of meeting information requirements.

Information Systems in Human Resource Management

Before discussing specifically how to evaluate a human resource system for a particular situation, it is worthwhile to consider the overall place that management information systems have in Human Resource Management.

The human resource manager is uniquely fortunate to be dealing with the most vital, complex and expensive resource of the industrial equation—the human being—and there is a growing acceptance of the idea that a systematic approach to the management of people is one of the biggest, single challenges facing top management today.

Computerized management information systems are valuable and essential tools for meeting these challenges. They are not devices nor objectives which must be served in their own right. The system necessarily takes second place to the job to be done, although some degree of accommodation to an information system may be required to make it effective.

Factors Influencing Systems

In performing the job of managing our human resources, we cannot avoid having information systems of some type, whether or not they are computerized. These systems will grow "like Topsy" unless we plan them carefully. Overcoming the proliferation of special purpose systems—each operating independently of the others with little or no interchange—is one of the key factors influencing installation of a comprehensive human resource information system. Why have these special purpose systems been spawned with such frequency? Correspondingly, why are human resource information systems so necessary? Some reasons are:

The increasing difficulty including all useful information in decision making. Without a comprehensive human resource information system, decision-making is often necessarily based on limited information. The inclusion of all useful information which would contribute to a decision process is becoming more and more arduous. The natural result is to ignore some information and rationalize that we are being selective in what we consider.

A need to make more and quicker decisions. Our increasingly complex society requires that decisions with far-ranging consequences be made in a shorter time frame. The gestation period for change is shortening in business generally. More action is taken in a given period of time than was the case two, five, or ten years ago.

Organizational growth. Organizational growth has the obvious effect of requiring additional information and results in even greater impact on our decision-making.

Increasing costs for information maintenance and reporting. Clerical costs have increased as additional records and reports to support changing requirements are developed.

The Evaluation Process

Assessment of the effectiveness of a system should be made in the context of its objectives. These goals can be divided into "immediate" and "long-range" to achieve reasonable pay-back within an acceptable time frame/cost.

Typical goals provide immediate value through replacement of routine approaches for gathering, storing, and reporting information. Far more than just meeting today's requirements, however, a human resource information system provides a new capability for record maintenance and reports. Furthermore, it allows extension of human resource applications into new areas requiring complex analyses with numerous variables. The speed and depth of information availability in a sophisticated system will contribute substantially toward the quality of decision-making.

Typically, a human resource information system "signs up" an employee and initiates records for both personnel and payroll; triggers actions such as benefit plan membership, salary review, service awards; and satisfies special reporting requirements such as:

Meeting the growing requirements related to equal opportunity "Affirmative Action" programs.

Providing essential data for bargaining unit contract administration and negotiations.

Gathering human resource information for shareholders' meetings/annual reports.

Compensation studies/surveys.

Benefits planning.

System Benefits

Although few studies of tangible benefits from installation of a human resource information system have been undertaken, some personally documented findings of system impact include:

Improved accuracy resulted. Even facts as straightforward as population counts were found to be off by as much as 15% prior to system installation.

Clerical effort was reduced. There was no longer any need for manually posted employee record cards.

Labor negotiations, EEO, BLS, Pay Board reports, and other peak information requirements did not interrupt the regular work load.

Consistency was provided. It became possible for the first time to relate data between functional groups such as payroll, wage and salary, insurance, etc.

Savings came about, for example:

processing new employees—as much as ¼ less time

providing routine information—reported savings of 55%–90%

meeting increased EEO information needs—averaged 80% less effort

routine monthly reporting—60% less effort

handling seniority record keeping—up to 90% less effort

furnishing data to payroll—50% less

special reports (One plant reported $27,000 in savings per year using a computerized personnel system instead of EAM for *special reports alone*. In addition, there were documented clerical savings of over 600 hours per year in providing data to payroll, over 800 hours per year in weekly reporting, and almost 500 hours in preparing monthly, quarterly, and annual reports.)

In many situations, however, users report that they have not yet achieved all possible savings, even after several years of system operation. Why? There are many reasons, including neglect of these positive actions most often required for obtaining greater value from a human resource information system:

Overcoming resistance to change.

Increasing awareness of the system's capabilities.

Organizing in a way more suited to the system, such as utilization of a Human Resource Information Center concept (this does not mean that a system should dictate the Human Resource organization).

Demonstrating adequate support from both Human Resource and technical functions so that the system will perform as scheduled/required.

To achieve the foregoing benefits/savings through an operational computerized human resource information system, "one-time" costs will be incurred in the development of the system and in conversion to it. *Continuing* costs will result from operation and maintenance of the system. These costs must be compared with current costs which will be reduced or replaced to determine a true measure of the investment in the system.

Development Costs

"One-time" developmental costs include those for system design planning, detail design, software development, operation planning, documentation, management orientation, training, conversion, and parallel operation.

In an AMA study by R. T. Bueschel several years ago* six firms reported the average cost for in-house development of a personnel system, programming and conversion costs included, was about $15 per employee. In other instances, costs have been quoted as low as $6 per employee for systems installed with outside assistance, and as high as over $30 per employee for development and installation, because the scope of the systems, operating environments, and population sizes differ widely. However, experience can be a significant factor in reducing costs. For example, conversion costs alone were reduced more than threefold over a period of several years as a human resource information system was phased into the diverse operations of a major multi-location manufacturer. Development costs can likewise be reduced through application of experienced talent.

The wide range of costs serves only to reinforce the belief that it is useless to compare such figures.

Operation Costs

Consideration of operational costs is extremely important because of their recurring nature. These include costs related to human involvement, forms, data preparation, data control, system maintenance/documentation, and system reporting.

The AMA study showed nine firms reporting an average operating cost for a "system of comprehensive personnel records," including machine time and data preparation, of $5.50 per year for each employee. These costs are so dependent on variable factors that again, there is no general yardstick which can be applied with consistency and accuracy. Some of these factors are size of population, application of system options/capabilities, frequency of processing, volume of data, interfaces with other systems, organization and system administration/utilization, communications with remote locations, and internal billing practices.

Some original pre-installation estimates of $4–$5 per employee annually eventually ranged in actual practice from $2–$7. Why such a range? In some cases, higher costs reflected a correspondingly higher usage of the system. On the other hand, in too many situations the system cost resulted from inadequate controls, improper scheduling, and alarmingly high system operation set-up time in the computer room. The approach to the system operation can make a significant difference in its operational costs.

*AMA Management Bulletin #86—"EDP and Personnel."

Offsetting Costs

The estimated costs of a human resource information system should be tempered by the realization that there are current information costs which will be reduced or replaced. These offsetting costs include those for salaries, both for manual development of information and for its utilization by personnel, other staff activities, and operating management. They also include costs of mechanized systems with their associated data preparation, processing, and control.

Justification Based on Greater Capability

Computerized human resource information systems are not usually justified on the basis of savings and staffing reduction, even though they should result in directly attributable savings. What is more significant is that the Human Resource Management effort can be directed toward more meaningful and productive tasks in the time now spent on information development, maintenance, and reporting. More important, the additional capability for obtaining and manipulating information will allow the Human Resource function to provide substantially greater service to operating management than ever before. This service is all the more significant with the human resource becoming an increasingly critical—and expensive—factor in management.

Continuing Evaluation Necessary

The evaluation process should not end with the installation of the system. The effectiveness of operational systems can be measured on the basis of factors other than costs. When faced with an assignment to do just that in a short period of time with a system operating at two dozen locations with over 60,000 active employees, the approach used was a carefully structured "self-review" questionnaire with detailed assessments by Human Resource Management, Management Information Systems, and Auditing. With respect to each element in the system, in addition to costs, the evaluation considered:

Extent of use
Does it meet the location's needs completely?
Problems in meeting the organization's need—system, people, equipment
Most important benefits

Selected in-depth follow-up was undertaken after the survey was completed. This included structured interviews with all levels of personnel and operating management. Results were then analyzed and used as the basis for determining system improvements, the direction of further development efforts, and cost re-allocation.

Evaluation of a computerized human resource information system is an important process whether an organization is considering its installation or already has an operational system. Definite approaches have been developed for such evaluation to assure that essential factors are brought to the attention of management.

The writer's experience has indicated the following conclusions from such an evaluation:

1. The most *immediate* benefit is the greater accuracy of data with savings in clerical effort. The most *significant* value is the availability of the data resource with quick access by the Human Resource staff through a retrieval system designed for their use.

2. A computer-based system is essential today for most personnel operations, although size/complexity are major factors in the type of system applied to a particular situation.

3. Human Resource or Personnel operations with computer-based systems have made them a "way of life," and, therefore, have become *dependent* upon them. It would be costly and impractical to operate with former methods in these situations.

4. *Savings* over prior methods for collecting, maintaining, and reporting information have been substantial—and usually more than anticipated—even though such systems have not normally been "sold" on the basis of savings. Savings have been in terms of increased capability and cost avoidance, rather than staffing reduction—although there have been instances of such an effect on staff. Most important, computerization assists the company in using the talents of its people more fully.

5. *Resistance to change* continues as a factor which limits the system in making its maximum contribution toward most effective and economical operations.

6. A requirement for system success is a high level of Top Management, Human Resource Management, and Technical Systems interest and support. The Human Resource activity should provide the leadership in system design, installation, and operation, with the Systems activity assuring adequate computer scheduling, controls, and reliability.

Part III
Manpower Allocation:
Manpower Planning
and Scheduling

It has been said that the goal of personnel administration is to provide the right number of the right kind of people in the right place at the right time. To insure the efficient allocation of people, personnel has increasingly turned to formalized procedures designed to meet the demand/supply requirements of human resources in two time perspectives: the long range and the short term.

Manpower planning has evolved to provide guidance and direction in meeting the long-range manpower allocation problem. This personnel activity centers upon making forecasts of manpower needs (demand), assessing the likely availability and talents of current employees as projected into the future (supply), comparing any deficits between the two in terms of both quantity (how many) and quality (what qualifications), and developing programs to contend with those deficiencies (recruiting, management development, career planning, etc.).

The short-term manpower allocation problem is somewhat different in nature and calls for accommodating the peaks and valleys that occur in the demand for an organization's products or services—and hence the demand for employees by that organization. This is the area of scheduling. It has only been in recent years that organizations have begun to use sophisticated management science techniques to analyze and resolve the short-term scheduling problem.

The selections in this section describe some of the techniques that have been applied to manpower allocation problems.

Markov Analysis is a technique that has been widely used in manpower planning. It is particularly useful in examining the movement into, within, and out of the organization. In the first article in this section Heneman and Sandver review the applications and limitations of Markov Analysis for such purposes as describing the internal labor market, audit and control of human resources, career planning and development, personnel forecasting, and affirmative action programs. In general, Markov Analysis is said to be best suited to situations involving large numbers of individuals where substantial movement of individuals occurs on a stable basis among specific job states (e.g., promotion, transfer to another division, termination).

While the second article in this section, on work shift scheduling, may be too technical for some readers, it does provide insights into the potential application of computer-based heuristic techniques to accurately predict work load levels and to assign workers to shifts to meet the predicted demand. It describes an integrated work shift scheduling system developed and applied in the scheduling of 2,600 telephone operators in 43 locations of the General Telephone Company of California. With this scheduling system, the company realized a net annual savings in clerical and supervisory costs of over $170,000 in one year as well as achieving a 6 percent increase in work force productivity.

Another approach to handling work scheduling problems is offered in the article by Wallace and Spruill. The article focuses on the comparative merits of hiring temporary help when short-run demand exceeds staff capacity and the scheduling of overtime isn't feasible. The authors present a Peak Employee Demand Model (PEDM) in which the separate cost elements of each alternative are established and combined into a formula. The strength of PEDM is said to lie in its ability to show management how to minimize labor costs during peak cycles of labor demand by finding breakeven points within each cycle at which hiring becomes less costly than renting.

7.
Markov Analysis in Human Resource Administration: Applications and Limitations

Herbert G. Heneman III and Marcus G. Sandver

Virtually every aspect of human resource administration is affected by the movement of personnel into, within, and out of the organization. Effective management of such movement and its impacts first requires mechanisms for systematically identifying and analyzing it. One such mechanism is Markov Analysis (MA). This article describes MA and its applications in human resource administration, and then identifies and discusses its potential limitations. The latter is critical since most relevant MA literature tends to simply report examples of application and then either ignore or gloss over MA limitations.

Editors' Note: Reprinted by permission of the publisher from *The Academy of Management Review*, October 1977.

Markov Analysis: Description and Illustration

MA is potentially useful for studying and analyzing any time-series process. At the organization level it may be applied to personnel movement into, within, and out of the internal labor market between two time periods (t and $t + k$). A finite number of personnel moves may occur (remain on same job, promotion, transfer, demotion, exit) and MA may be used for investigating the rates and flows of such movement.

MA begins by translating the existing organization structure into a series of mutually exclusive and exhaustive "states" that individuals may occupy. States need not encompass the total organization; they may deal with organization segments such as product divisions. While states may be developed on the basis of any characteristic(s), they are most commonly based on function (marketing, services, general management, etc.) and hierarchical level within function. In addition, an exit state is created to reflect movement out of the organization. States are then arranged in a matrix, with the rows representing the states at t and the columns representing the states at $t + k$.

For the individuals in each state at t, the number and proportion occupying each state at $t + k$ is computed. For each row, the numbers of individuals in the cells represent the employment distribution of the individuals. This is simply the numbers of individuals who remained in the initial state or moved to another state. For each row, the number of individuals in each cell is then divided by the row total. The resultant proportions are defined as transition probabilities, the probabilities of remaining in the initial state or moving to another state.

The proportions form a transition probability matrix. The diagonal elements represent the proportions of individuals who did not move, and the off-diagonal elements represent the proportions of individuals who did move. In each row the sum of the proportions must equal 1.0, as the number of moves is finite and the states are mutually exclusive and exhaustive.

Underlying the application of MA are a number of important assumptions (13, 22). First, it is assumed that each individual makes only one move between t and $t + k$ (i.e., multiple moves are not detected). Second, probability of movement from t to $t + k$ is only conditional upon occupancy of the initial state (i.e., all individuals in a given state have the same probability of movement). Finally, if the results are to be used for making inferences about movement beyond $t + k$, the existing transition probabilities are assumed constant in the future time intervals. In turn, this requires the assumption of constancy of staffing policies and practices, and of the organization's environment (e.g., product demand, the unemployment rate).

Numerous results of MA as applied to personnel movement have been reported (2, 5, 12, 13, 14, 17, 18, 19, 21, 22). An illustrative example of a transition probability matrix, from the study by Vroom and MacCrimmon (22), is shown in Table 1. They investigated movement patterns of all college-trained personnel ($n = 2914$) in a large manufacturing organization between 1964 and 1965. There

Table 1: Transition Probability Matrix for Managers from 1964 to 1965 and Estimated Employment Distribution in 1969

Distribution of managers (1964)	1965													
	E_1	E_2	E_3	Mf_1	Mf_2	Mf_3	Mk_1	Mk_2	Mk_3	S_1	S_2	S_3	G	Exit
321 E_1	.79	.07	0	.01	0	0	.01	.01	0	.02	.01	0	0	.08
386 E_2	0	.84	.05	0	.01	0	0	.02	0	0	0*	0	0	.08
206 E_3	0	0	.90	0	0	0*	0	0	.02	0	0	.01	.01	.06
492 Mf_1	.01	.01	0	.86	.07	0*	0	0	0	0	0	0	0	.05
286 Mf_2	0	.03	0	.02	.83	.03	0	0	0	0	0*	0	0	.09
84 Mf_3	0	0	.02	0	.02	.86	0	0	.02	0	.01	0	0	.07
288 Mk_1	.02	.02	0	.01	0	0	.79	.06	0	0*	0	0	0	.10
293 Mk_2	0	.01	0	0	.01	0	0	.84	.06	0*	.01	.01	0	.06
160 Mk_3	0	0	.03	0	0	.01	0	.02	.86	0	0	.01	0	.07
136 S_1	.01	.01	0	0	0	0	.01	0	0	.81	.11	0	0	.05
149 S_2	0	.01	0	0	.01	0	0	.01	0	0	.84	.02	0	.11
101 S_3	0	0	.03	0	0	.01	0	0	.01	0	.02	.80	0	.13
12 G	0	0	0	0	0	0	0	0	.08	0	0	.08	.76	.08
Exit	0	0	0	0	0	0	0	0	0	0	0	0	0	1.00
Distribution of 1964 group in 1969	129	281	227	270	251	75	101	205	161	68	132	59	6	948

*There was a single individual in this cell, but the transition probability was zero when rounded to two significant digits.

SOURCE: Adapted from V.H. Vroom and K.R. MacCrimmon. "Toward a Stochastic Model of Managerial Careers," *Administrative Science Quarterly,* Vol. 13 (1968), 26–46.

were 13 states developed on the basis of five functions (E = engineering, Mf = manufacturing, Mk = marketing, S = services, G = general management) and three levels within each of the first four functions, plus an exit state.

The main diagonal indicates the probabilities of remaining in the same states; these ranged from .76 to .90. The data regarding promotion (higher level, same or different function) show that most occurred within function. The highest promotion rate was .11, for S_1 to S_2. Transfers (same level, different function) did not occur at high rates, although movement across function occurred for each function. For demotion (lower level, same or different function) the highest rate was .02, and with one exception (Mf_3 to S_2) demotion occurred within function. Exit rates varied from .03 to .13. The bottom row in Table 1 shows the number of 1964 individuals who are estimated to occupy each state in 1969 (procedures for this estimate are discussed later).

Administrative Applications

MA's original human resource application was in personnel forecasting by the armed services in the 1950s, but there are a number of other potential applications to human resource administration. This section reviews these applications, including forecasting, drawing upon examples from the literature.

DESCRIPTION OF THE INTERNAL LABOR MARKET / The results of MA provide a summary description of the operation of the organization's internal labor market; the data are perfectly descriptive of past events. It thus provides administrators with an overall "snapshot" of precisely what is occurring within the organization in terms of personnel movement. Moreover, the results are presented in a concise, readily interpretable form.

AUDIT AND CONTROL DEVICE / MA captures actual personnel movement, and thus functions as an audit of the "reality" of staffing practices and decisions within the organization. This "reality" may be compared to desired practices/ decisions in order to detect deviations. For example, the organization may have a policy that promotion can occur only within a functional area. Examination of a transition probability matrix would readily indicate any deviation (i.e., inter-function promotion) from this policy. In turn, this would lead to reconsideration of the policy or institution of control mechanisms to ensure compliance with the existing policy.

An illustration of this is provided by Mahoney and Milkovich (14), who studied personnel movement patterns in three organizations and compared them with stated organization policy. One organization was a steel firm whose nonexempt employees were covered by a labor contract. The contract specified new employees could be recruited only into the labor pool, which was one of the 25 MA-defined states. The results of MA indicated that new employees, on the average, were recruited into more than one-half of the job states, an obvious violation of the labor contract. These and other obtained deviations in the organizations led Mahoney and Milkovich to conclude that "manpower allocation processes within corporations cannot be inferred from personnel policies and union agreements" (p. 26). Without the descriptive evidence provided by MA, however, it is doubtful that this deviation from organization policy would have been so readily detected.

CAREER PLANNING AND DEVELOPMENT / For organizations concerned with long-range career planning and development, MA results can serve as an important input into program design and implementation (8, 15). Equally important, MA results may be useful and informative for individual employees in their own career planning. Through straightforward matrix algebra manipulations even more employee-centered information may be generated. Vroom and MacCrimmon (22) projected employees' expected number of years in each state and in the organization, and the probability of advancing from first-level to third-level positions in five and ten years. Other examples of such information "rearrangement", and attendant computational procedures, are provided by Turban and Meredith (19) and Uyar (21).

FORECASTING / MA results may be directly used for forecasting internal labor supply in future time periods. The internal supply estimates for each state may then be compared with demand estimates (independently derived) for each state to determine net personnel requirements. In turn, the projected shortages/surpluses may serve as a primary input into the overall personnel planning process (1).

One set of supply estimates concerns the likely distribution of only current personnel (i.e., personnel at t) among states in future time periods. To estimate the *proportions* of current personnel among states, the initial transition probability matrix is raised to the power of the number of time periods covered in the forecast. For example, if the time period is one year, proportion estimates for five years hence would require raising the original matrix to the fifth power. To translate the proportion estimates into *employment distribution* estimates, the original (at t) employment distribution is treated as a row vector and multiplied by the transition probability matrix (raised to the appropriate power). The bottom row in Table 1 shows the employment distribution estimates for the 1964 managers in 1969. They were obtained by multiplying the initial employment distribution by the matrix raised to the fifth power. Numerous other examples of such estimates have been reported (2, 5, 12, 13, 14, 18, 21, 22).

One disadvantage of the above estimation procedures is that they focus only on current personnel and thus ignore potential recruitment of personnel into the organization over the forecasting interval. With slight modification to the previously described estimation procedures, recruitment inputs may be incorporated into the internal labor supply estimates (14, 18, 22). Doing so requires assumptions about the total number recruited into the organization, and their proportionate distribution among states, in each time interval.

Affirmative Action Programs

All of the specific applications of MA noted above may be brought to bear upon affirmative action programs in organization. A fundamental requirement in such programs is that the organization must conduct detailed workforce studies (3, 20). Such "utilization analysis" is required to (a) determine present workforce composition and movement, (b) serve as a basis for affirmative action planning in the establishment of staffing goals and timetables for goal achievement, and (c) serve as an internal audit and reporting system to monitor affirmative action program effectiveness.

In essence, organizations are required to conduct the utilization analysis in a manner very similar to MA. Analysis is to be conducted by job classification (state), and separate subgroup analysis is to be conducted on the basis of sex and minority group status. The data must indicate numbers employed (employment distributions) and movement rates (transition probabilities) for each subgroup.

To date these requirements have been stated in somewhat loose and confusing terms. But clearly the thrust of the requirements is similar to conducting MA. Ledvinka (10) has translated these requirements into MA models and shown how the models may be used to assess organization compliance with the law and to establish goals and timetables for increasing the representativeness of the organization's workforce at all organization levels.

The results of utilization analysis, particularly movement rates (transition probabilities), are likely to lead to precise compliance standards for organizations. Differences in movement rates between subgroups (e.g., promotion rate of .50 for males and .30 for females) are considered evidence of adverse impact; but how much of a difference is "tolerable" or "acceptable" has never been precisely specified. Under the newly proposed *Uniform Guidelines on Employee Selection Procedures* (4), this would change.[1] It is proposed that "a selection rate for any racial, ethnic or sex group which is less than four-fifths (or 80 percent) of the rate for the group with the highest selection rate will generally be regarded as evidence of significant adverse impact . . ." (p. 4). Thus, if the highest rate for a group is .50, the rates for all other groups must be between .40 and .50. The term "selection" refers to *any* staffing decision (hire, promotion, etc.).

Potential Limitations

The strengths of MA are substantial and possible applications to human resource administration are numerous. But there are potential limitations, both practical and theoretical, on the appropriateness and usefulness of MA in these applications. These limitations, and in some instances possible solutions, need to be discussed.

CHOICE OF TIME INTERVAL / MA requires a decision about the time interval between t and $t + k$, and inherent conflicts underlie the choice. The time interval must be long enough for substantial movement to occur, and for minor cyclical/seasonal influences on personnel movement to cancel themselves out. Meeting these requirements is necessary for obtaining relatively stable transition probabilities. But the time interval must be short enough to minimize the occurrence of multiple moves during the interval (13). To the extent that multiple moves occur,

---

[1]A modified version of these guidelines was subsequently adopted by the Department of Labor, Department of Justice, and the Civil Service Commission and published ("Federal Executive Agency Guidelines on Employee Selection Procedures," *Federal Register,* Vol. 41, November 23, 1976, pp. 51734–51759). The "80 percent rule" is also contained in these new guidelines.

MA will understate the true amount of movement. Thus, MA is limited to those situations where the "long" and "short" time intervals are not substantially different.

SAMPLE SIZE / For a number of reasons, the usefulness of MA is directly related to the numbers of individuals occupying cells and states, and the total sample size. If the number of individuals in an initial state is small, the state transition probabilities will tend to be unstable. For example, in the initial G state in Table 1 there are only 12 individuals. The transition probability for G to Mk_3 is .08 (i.e., 1/12); inclusion of one more individual in the cell would increase the transition probability to .17, a rather substantial change.

More important, if the transition probabilities are treated or used as estimates of population parameters (as they are in forecasting), then the standard error of the estimate is influenced by the sample size. Specifically, for a given transition probability, the smaller the sample size (denominator of the proportion), the larger the standard error of estimate (16). And as the standard error increases, the confidence interval for the estimate increases, resulting in a decrease in the accuracy of the estimate.

Finally, use of small samples in MA tends to result in skewed probability distributions that do not approximate the normal curve (16). This inhibits hypothesis testing about transition probabilities, such as the significance of difference between two probabilities.

These considerations regarding transition probabilities are not unique to MA. Indeed, they are important whenever one is working with proportions. Unfortunately, these considerations are generally ignored in the MA literature, although they do establish some rather definite limits on MA applications. MA is simply most applicable in situations where there are relatively large numbers of individuals in cells and states.

Conditional Probabilities

As noted, MA assumes that all individuals in a state have the same probability of movement; movement is conditional only on occupancy of the state. This is tantamount to assuming perfect homogeneity among individuals within each state. Under most circumstances such homogeneity is unrealistic and it thus becomes necessary to investigate the consequences of nonhomogeneity.

An instructive example of a consequence of nonhomogeneity for forecasting accuracy is provided by Mahoney and Milkovich (12). They found that over five and ten year forecasting intervals the number of actual exits (turnover) was substantially overpredicted. Part of the reason for this was nonhomogeneity of length of service and age among individuals in the initial states, and the assumed constancy of these two variables over the course of the forecasting intervals.

Overcoming the nonhomogeneity limitations would require subgrouping individuals within states on the basis of personal characteristics assumed to influence probability of movement. The resultant subgroup transition probabilities could then be compared in terms of statistical and practical significance of difference. This is the approach underlying the subgrouping requirement in the proposed *Uniform Guidelines on Employee Selection Procedures* (4).

In a related manner, demographers are experimenting with the use of semi-MA to predict intergenerational mobility (6, 7). The semi-MA technique depicts the transition probability of movement between states in successive time periods as conditional upon both the state currently occupied and personal characteristics. It is a doubly stochastic model.

Unfortunately, application of subgrouping and semi-MA procedures is constrained by additional information requirements and sample size considerations. Subgrouping on the basis of job performance, for example, requires standardized measures of individuals' performance and enough individuals in each subgroup to make the performance distinctions statistically testable and practically meaningful. In the absence of large samples, MA will continue to be limited by the assumption of equal probabilities of movement.

CREATION OF STATES / States created for MA on the basis of organization characteristics (e.g., function and level) represent abstractions of the organization, or some segment of it, in varying degrees. Such states will be conceptually and administratively useful to the extent that they yield within-state differences among individuals that are less than between-state differences among individuals. This is simply an alternative way of dealing with the problem of homogeneity. Sample size problems thus may serve as a potential limitation in the development of states.

An example of possibilities, given a large sample, is provided by Merck (17). In this MA of Air Force recruits, Merck created 804 states on the basis of job and personal characteristics. This was made possible through a sample size in excess of 33,000.

Of course, this is an extreme case. The more usual case involves a substantially smaller sample size and number of states. Usually relatively general or abstract states are created, grouping relatively dissimilar jobs and thus individuals into each state. Perhaps this explains why, in the study by Vroom and MacCrimmon (22), the three "services" states included "finance, personnel, public relations, legal staff, etc." (p. 33). Vroom and MacCrimmon do not report why they created the "services" states in this manner. This is simply used to illustrate what could happen under sample size constraints. The point is that one can question the usefulness of such general states, regardless of why they were created.

One may similarly question why only a single exit state is typically created to reflect all movement out of the organization. The consequence is that one learns little, if anything, about the causes of turnover and thus its susceptibility to administrative control. Conceptually, it would be desirable to create multiple exit states in order to more precisely classify individuals according to reasons for leaving (e.g., voluntary-involuntary, avoidable-unavoidable). In practice, this may be difficult due to sample size constraints. In addition, there are substantial measurement problems associated with obtaining individuals' "true" reasons for leaving the organization (9, 11). The effect of these problems is that MA will probably continue to use only a single exit state with its attendant disadvantages.

FORECASTING ACCURACY / The question of forecasting accuracy is critical, particularly given the relative ease with which MA results may be used to generate internal labor supply forecasts. Accuracy is not only influenced by sample size; it is also dependent on the tenability of the assumptions underlying MA, particularly the assumed constancy of transition probabilities. Investigation of accuracy requires generation and comparison of predicted and actual employment distributions (or proportions) on a state-by-state basis. Both the statistical and practical significance of the differences are of interest.

Surprisingly few investigations of forecasting accuracy have been reported in the literature. Forbes (5) and Mahoney and Milkovich (12, 14) found considerable differences in accuracy among states over a given forecasting interval. Mahoney and Milkovich (12, 14) examined accuracy over successively longer forecasting intervals. As one would expect, they found that accuracy tended to decrease as the interval increased. It thus appears that there may be some definite limitations on MA for forecasting purposes.

Conclusions

The range of possible uses of MA suggests that it is often a necessary and/or desirable technique in human resource administration. It appears that the effect of current and proposed government regulations regarding equal employment opportunity will be to increase the use of MA, or something akin to it, in organizations.

At the same time, it is crucial to recognize the potential limitations on MA applications. In general, MA is best suited to situations involving large numbers of individuals, where substantial movement of individuals occurs on a stable basis among specific job states. The limitations regarding conditional probabilities and forecasting accuracy also involve essentially empirical questions, which have not been satisfactorily answered due to the paucity of research conducted on them. It is imperative that these areas receive considerably more research attention than they have so far.

REFERENCES

1. Albright, L. E. "Staffing Policies and Strategies," in D. Yoder and H. G. Heneman, Jr. (Eds.), *Staffing Policies and Strategies* (Washington, D.C.: BNA, 1974).

2. Bartholomew, D. J. *A Mathematical Analysis of Structural Control in a Graded Manpower System* (Berkeley, Calif.: University of California, Office of the Vice-President, 1969).
3. Equal Employment Opportunity Commission. *Affirmative Action and Equal Employment* (Washington, D.C.: Equal Employment Opportunity Commission, 1974).
4. Equal Employment Opportunity Coordinating Council. *Proposed Uniform Guidelines on Employee Selection Procedures* (Washington, D.C.: Department of Justice, 1975).
5. Forbes, A. F. "Markov Chain Models for Manpower Systems," in D. J. Bartholomew and A. R. Smith (eds.), *Manpower and Management Science* (London: D. C. Heath, 1971).
6. Ginzberg, R. "Critique of Probabilistic Models: Application of the Semi-Markov Model to Migration," *Journal of Applied Mathematical Sociology,* Vol. 2 (1972), 63–82.
7. Ginzberg, R. "Incorporating Causal Structure and Exogenous Information with Probabilistic Models: with Special Reference to Choice, Gravity, Migration, and Markov Chains," *Journal of Mathematical Sociology,* Vol. 2 (1972), 83–103.
8. Glueck, W. F. "Career Management of Managerial, Professional, and Technical Employees," in E. H. Burack and J. W. Walker (Eds.), *Manpower Planning and Programming* (Boston: Allyn and Bacon, 1972).
9. Hinrichs, J. R. "Measurement of Reasons for Resignation of Professionals: Questionnaire Versus Company and Consultant Exit Interviews," *Journal of Applied Psychology,* Vol. 60 (1975), 530–532.
10. Ledvinka, J. "Technical Implications of Equal Employment Law for Manpower Planning," *Personnel Psychology,* Vol. 28 (1975), 299–323.
11. Lefkowitz, J., and M. L. Katz. "Validity of Exit Interviews," *Personnel Psychology,* Vol. 22 (1969), 445–456.
12. Mahoney, T. A., and G. T. Milkovich. "The Internal Labor Market as a Stochastic Process," in D. J. Bartholomew and A. R. Smith (eds.), *Manpower and Management Science* (London: D. C. Heath, 1971).
13. Mahoney, T. A., and G. T. Milkovich. *Techniques for Application of Markov Analysis to Manpower Analysis* (Minneapolis: Industrial Relations Center, University of Minnesota, 1971).
14. Mahoney, T. A., and G. T. Milkovich. *Internal Labor Markets: An Empirical Investigation* (Minneapolis: Industrial Relations Center, University of Minnesota, 1972).
15. McNamar, R. T. "Identifying and Solving Corporate Manpower Needs," in E. H. Burack and J. W. Walker (eds.), *Manpower Planning and Programming* (Boston: Allyn and Bacon, 1972).
16. McNemar, Q. *Psychological Statistics,* 4th ed. (New York: Wiley, 1969).
17. Merck, J. W. "Retention of First Enlistment Airmen: Analysis of Results of a Mathematical Simulation," in P. S. Greenlaw and R. D. Smith (Eds.), *Personnel Management: A Management Science Approach* (Scranton, Pa.: International, 1970).
18. Rowland, K. M., and M. G. Sovereign. "Markov Chain Analysis of Internal Manpower Supply," *Industrial Relations,* Vol. 9, No. 1 (1969), 88–99.
19. Turban, E., and J. Meredith. "Absorbing States," in E. Turban and N. P. Loomba (Eds.), *Readings in Management Science* (Dallas: Business Publications, 1976).
20. U. S. Department of Labor. "Affirmative Action Programs (Revised Order No. 4)," *Federal Register,* Vol. 36 (1971), 23152–23157.

21. Uyar, K. M. "Markov Chain Forecasts of Employee Replacement Needs," *Industrial Relations,* Vol. 11 (1972), 96–106.
22. Vroom, V. H., and K. R. MacCrimmon. "Toward a Stochastic Model of Managerial Careers," *Administrative Science Quarterly,* Vol. 13 (1968), 26–46.

8.
An Integrated Work Shift Scheduling System

Elwood S. Buffa, Michael J. Cosgrove and
Bill J. Luce

One of the general problems which has emerged from the study of service and nonmanufacturing systems is work shift scheduling. The problem is essentially one of scheduling manpower to meet some variable demand pattern which is usually short-term, such as daily and/or weekly, but which also may be seasonal. The reason that the problem emerges in the context of service and nonmanufacturing systems is that they are characterized by variable short-term demand which cannot be backlogged and by an output which cannot be inventoried. This paper presents an integrated system of demand forecasting, conversion to operator requirements, shift scheduling, and operator assignment which is operating at the General Telephone Company of California.

The range of applications of work shift scheduling in the literature is an

Editors' Note: Reprinted by permission of the publisher from *Decision Sciences,* October 1976.

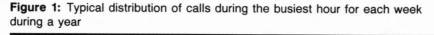

Figure 1: Typical distribution of calls during the busiest hour for each week during a year

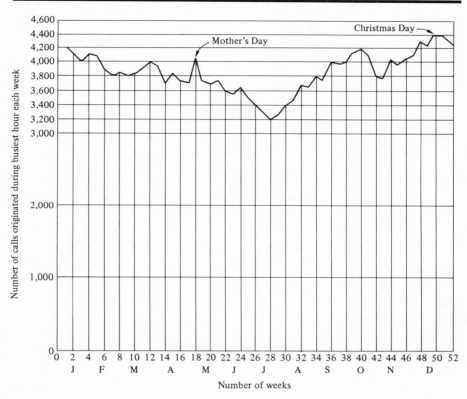

indicator of the importance of the problem. For applications to nurse scheduling see [1] [3] [21]. Other applications discussed in the literature are police protection, [7], airline reservation offices [16], supermarkets and retail stores [29], public transportation [5], bank tellers [20], the post office [25], and the telephone industry [8] [10] [11] [12] [17] [18] [19] [28]. A similar problem exists in scheduling manpower for continuous seven day manufacturing operations of employees who work only a forty hour week [4] [27] [29].

Demand for Service

The service offered is the telephone exchange by which operators are assigned to provide directory assistance, coin telephone customer dialing, and toll call assistance. The standard for service is supplied by the Public Utilities Commission in unusually specific terms: service must be provided at a resource level such that

Figure 2: Daily call load for Long Beach, January 1972

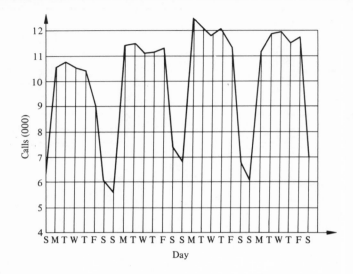

Figure 3: Typical half-hourly call distribution (Bundy D A)

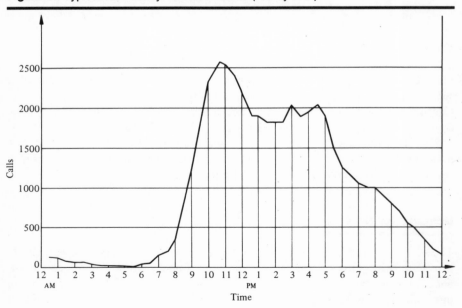

an incoming call can be answered within ten seconds, 89 percent of the time. The difficulty in implementing the response standard is in the severe demand variability of incoming calls.

Figures 1, 2, 3, and 4 show typical call variation during the year, the week, the day, and within a peak hour. Figure 1 shows the annual variation, highlighting the two sharp peaks which include Mother's Day and Christmas Day. The data indicate calls during the busiest hour in each of the 52 weeks. The minimum occurred in the 28th week (3200 calls) and the maximum during Christmas (4400 calls). The peak to valley ratio is 1.38. To accommodate seasonal variation, the company must provide about 38 percent more capacity at Christmas time than in the 28th week. Generally the summer months involve lighter loads than the rest of the year.

Figure 2 shows daily call load for January 1972. A pronounced weekly pattern emerges, showing the Saturday and Sunday call load to be only about 55 percent of the typical load for Monday through Friday. Although the telephone company offers lower weekend toll call rates to help smooth the load, the resultant weekly variation is still very large.

Figure 4: Typical intrahour distribution of calls, 10:00–11:00 A.M.

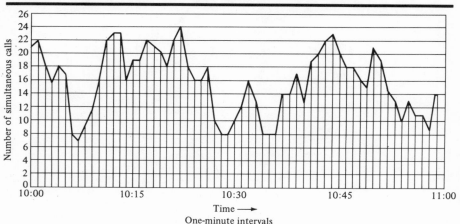

Figure 3 shows the half-hourly variation for a typical 24 hour period. Peak call volume is in the 10:30–11:00 A.M. period (2560 calls), and the minimum occurs at 5:30 A.M. (about 20 calls). The peak to valley variation for the typical half-hourly load is 128. The large variation in daily load levels apparent in Figure 3 suggests a daily problem of scheduling operator shifts.

Finally, Figure 4 shows the typical intra-hour variation in call load, indicating the number of simultaneous calls by one-minute intervals. This variation is random. In fact, continuous tracking of the mean and standard deviation of calls per minute indicates that the standard deviation is equal to the square root of the mean, a reasonable, practical test for randomness, and that the arrival rates are described by the Poisson distribution. For the sample of Figure 4, $X = 15.75$ calls per minute; $SD = 4.85$ calls per minute; and $\sqrt{15.75} = 3.99$. Therefore, the variation within the hour is taken as random. This variation cannot be accommodated by planning and scheduling, thus sufficient capacity must be provided to absorb the random variations.

The overall situation evidenced by the typical distributions of Figures 1, 2, 3, and 4 is that a forecastable pattern exists for seasonal, weekly, and daily variation. In addition, the call rate at any selected minute is adequately described by the Poisson distribution.

Figure 5: "Force management system"

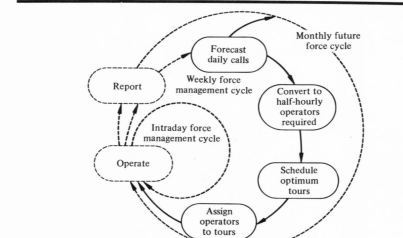

The Integrated System

Figure 5 indicates the system developed at General Telephone to accommodate demand for service. There are basically three cycles of planning and scheduling which involve information feedback of actual experience. The forecast of daily calls is the heart of the system. The forecast takes account of seasonal and weekly variation as well as trends. The forecast is converted to a distribution of operator requirements by half-hour increments. Based on the distribution of operator requirements, a schedule of tours or shifts is developed, and specific operators are assigned to tours. This sequence of modules is entirely computerized as indicated in Figure 5.

Besides the operator schedule, there are two additional cycles which operate on a normal basis. First, a schedule for "today" may be impacted by unintended events such as operator illness, an emergency increase in call load, and so on. Supervisors in local installations use the "Intraday Management Cycle" (Figure 5) to cope with such unintended events. In addition, there is the "Monthly Future Force Cycle" in which management can make higher level adjustments based on reports of actual operations or based on forecasts involving particular trend and seasonal factors. Hiring and training of operators is planned in the future cycle which projects up to 12 months forward [18].

Forecasting Demand

The demand forecasting system is based on a Box-Jenkins [6] model. The following major terms are used in forecasting the number of calls at a specific location for next Monday.

$$
\begin{aligned}
\text{Calls next Monday} = {} & \text{Calls last Monday} \\
& + \text{Weekly growth at this time last year (Monday}_{-52} - \\
& \quad \text{Monday}_{-53}) \\
& - \text{error last week} \times \theta \\
& - \text{error 52 weeks ago} \times \theta \\
& + \text{error 53 weeks ago} \times \theta \times \emptyset.
\end{aligned}
$$

θ is a non-seasonal moving average parameter, and $\emptyset$ is a seasonal moving average parameter.

In terms of actual operation, the computer inputs are last week's calls by day and type of service (toll, assistance, directory service), coefficients (work units per call) for the forecast week by day and type of service, and the board load (productivity) by day for the forecast week. The computer outputs are forecasts of daily calls up to five weeks in advance and a translation of the forecast into required operator hours by day up to five weeks in advance.

Figure 6 shows a typical record of comparison between forecast versus observed numbers of calls for Santa Monica. The uncanny forecast for day 151 is

Figure 6: Sample of forecast versus observed numbers of calls at Santa Monica

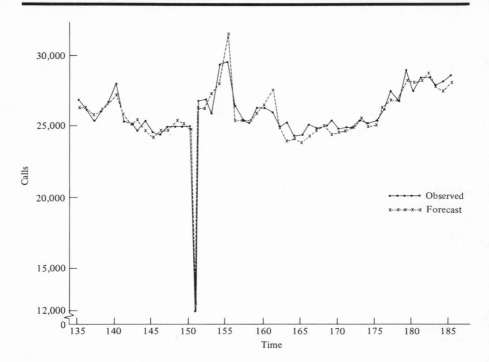

Thanksgiving when people are predictably more interested in dinner and family affairs than in communication. Average error for the forecasting system as a whole is 3.5 percent.

Conversion to Half-Hourly Operator Requirements

The total day operator hours must be distributed to the individual half hours of the work day to provide a required operators' profile for the shift scheduling stage. The daily distribution of operator requirements is developed by exponential smoothing of current and historical percent of total day requirements by half hours. These requirements are derived from actual counts of operators staffed each half hour and achieved speed of answer (response time). The M-M-C queueing model is used to adjust the actual operators staffed to reflect staffing required to meet the constraint of the response time standard.

The conversion process from estimate of calls to operators required is shown in Figure 7. The parameters which are required in the process are average call

Figure 7: Model for conversion of calls to half-hourly operator requirements (topline)

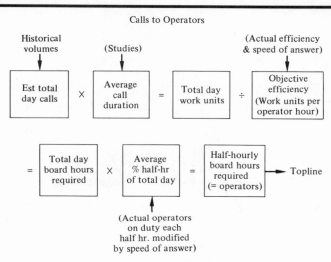

duration (coefficient) based on studies of actual times, operator efficiency (work units per hour), and the response time standard. The final product is a profile of operators required for each half hour of the day to process the call-load within the specified response time constraint.

Scheduling of Shifts

The graphical representation of an operator profile is shown in Figure 8. The problem in assigning tours or shifts is one of fitting in shifts so that they aggregate to the operator profile, as is also shown in Figure 8.

In order to be able to build up shifts so that they aggregate to the topline profile, flexibility is required in the types of shifts. Flexibility is provided by the shift length and the positioning of lunch hours and rest pauses. The set of shifts is constrained by state and federal laws, union agreements, company policy, and practical considerations. Shifts in the set are actually selected based on California State restrictions, company policy, and local management input concerning the desireability of working hours by their employees.

Each shift consists of two working sessions separated by a rest pause which may be the lunch period. Each working session requires a 15 minute rest pause near the middle of the session. The admissible shift set is limited by the following constraints:

Figure 8: Topline profile and concept for assigning tours to aggregate to the topline

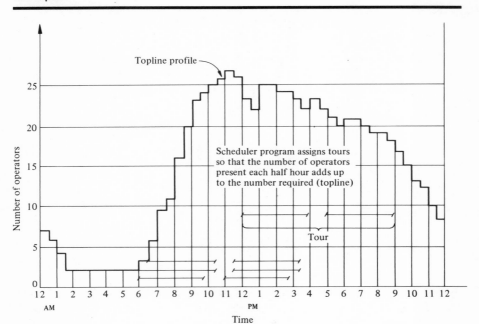

1. Shifts are 8, 7, or 6.5 hours.
2. Work sessions are in the range of 3 to 5 hours.
3. Lunch periods are either a half-hour or an hour.
4. Split work periods are in the range of 3.5 to 5 hours (split work periods are separated by substantial non-work periods).
5. Eight hour shifts end before 9 P.M.
6. Seven hour shifts end from 9:30 to 10:30 P.M.
7. Six and one-half hour shifts end at 11:00 P.M. or later.
8. Earliest lunch period is at 10:00 A.M.

Luce [17] developed a heuristic algorithm for choosing shifts from the approved set in such a way that the absolute differences between operators demanded by the topline profile in period i, D_i, and the operators provided, W_i is minimized when summed over all n periods of the day, that is

$$\text{Minimize } \sum_{i=1}^{n} |D_i - W_i| \tag{1}$$

The strategy is to build up the operator resources in the schedule, one shift at a time, drawing on the universal set of approved shifts. The criterion stated in (1)

94

is used to choose shifts at each step. Conceptually, as the schedule of W_i values is built up, the distance is minimized between the demand and operators supplied curves as illustrated by Figure 9.

At each stage in building up the schedule, there exists some remaining distance between D_i and W_i. The criterion for choice of the next shift is the following test on each alternate shift: add the contributions of the shift to W_i (1 for all working periods and 0 for idle periods such as lunch and rest pauses), and recalculate expression (1). Choose the shift which minimizes (1). In order to negate the preference of the preceding choice rule to favor shorter length shifts, the different shift lengths are weighted in the calculation. The longest shift is given a weight of 1.0, and shorter shifts are weighted by the ratio of the working times. Thus, if the longest shift is 8 hours, then, a 7 hour shift would be weighted $\frac{8}{7}$ = 1.14.

As the number of time intervals and shift types increase, the computing cost increases. Luce states that computing costs are moderate when the number of time intervals is less than 100 and the number of shifts is less than 500 [17].

As indicated in Figure 9, the final profiles for D_i and W_i do not coincide perfectly in any real case. Operators provided by the algorithm will be slightly greater or less than the demand, and the aggregate figures are a measure of the effectiveness of a given schedule. For example, in a typical output the aggregate

Figure 9: Concept of the schedule building process, using the criterion, minimize
$$\sum_{i+1}^{n} |D_i - W_i|$$

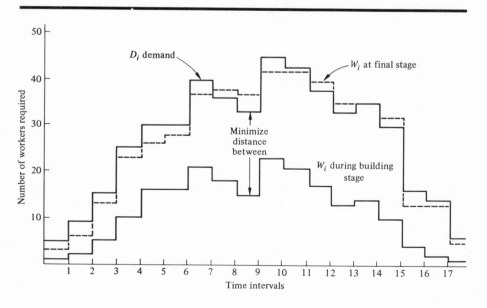

statistics were total hours required = 295 and total hours scheduled by half hours = 296.50.

For each ½ hour of the day, the computer output indicates the operators required and provided. The excess or shortage of operators provided is reported by half hours.

Also printed in the output is a list of shifts actually used. The shift length is shown, as well as the positioning of lunch and rest periods. The system also provides absentee relief (AR) allocations to be used as needed, based on experience factors.

Assigning Operators to Shifts

Given a set of shifts which meets the demand profile, the next step is to assign operators to shifts. There are many complications to this process which arise because of the 24 hour per day, 7 day per week operation. There are important questions of equity regarding the timing of days off and the assignment of overtime work which carries extra pay. There are also employee shift preferences and seniority status to be taken into account.

Luce [19] presents a computing algorithm which makes "days off" assignments:

1. At least one day off in a week;
2. Days off are one or two;
3. Maximize consecutive days off;
4. If days off cannot be consecutive, maximize the number of work days between days off;
5. Weekends are treated separately on a rotational basis in order to preserve equity because
   a. Overtime pay for weekend work and
   b. Weekends are the most desirable days off;
6. Requests for additional days off are honored on a first come first assigned basis.

The days off procedure must be carried out to assure that a final feasible schedule will result. Employee trading of days off is allowed. The actual assignment of operators to shifts takes into account employee shift preferences. Each operator makes up a list of shifts in ranked order. The list can have different preferences for each day of the week. Seniority is the basis for determining the order of satisfying preferences, and assignments are made to the highest ranked shift available for each operator.

The final employee schedule for each day is a computer output which specifies for each operator the beginning and end of two work periods (lunch between), and the time for each of two rest periods.

Concluding Remarks

The integrated work shift scheduling system described has been in operation at the General Telephone Company of California since 1973. The company routinely schedules approximately 2600 telephone operators in 43 locations using the system. The size of the work force at each location ranges from approximately 20 to 220 operators.

During 1974, the company realized a net annual savings in clerical and supervisory costs of over $170,000, as well as achieving a 6 percent increase in work force productivity, savings which were attributable to this scheduling system.

REFERENCES

1. Abernathy, W. J., N. Baloff, and J. C. Hershey. "The Nurse Staffing Problem: Issues and Prospects." *Sloan Management Review,* Vol. 13, No. 1 (Fall, 1971), pp. 87–109.
2. Abernathy, W. J., N. Baloff, J. C. Hershey, and S. Wandel. "A Three-Stage Manpower Planning and Scheduling Model—A Service-Sector Example." *Operations Research,* Vol. 21, No. 3 (May-June, 1973), pp. 693–711.
3. Ahuja, H. and R. Sheppard. "Computerized Nurse Scheduling." *Industrial Engineering,* Vol. 7, No. 10 (October, 1975), pp. 24–29.
4. Baker, K. R. "Scheduling a Full-Time Workforce to Meet Cyclic Staffing Requirements." *Management Science,* Vol. 20, No. 12 (August, 1974), pp. 1561–1568.
5. Bennett, B. T. and R. B. Potts. "Rotating Roster for a Transit System." *Transportation Science,* Vol. 2, No. 1 (February, 1968), pp. 25–34.
6. Box, G. E. P. and G. M. Jenkins. *Time Series Analysis, Forecasting, and Control.* San Francisco: Holden-Day, 1970.
7. Butterworth, R. W. and G. T. Howard. "A Method of Determining Highway Patrol Manning Schedules." ORSA, 44th National Meeting, November, 1973.
8. Church, J. G. "Sure Staff: A Computerized Staff Scheduling System for Telephone Business Offices." *Management Science,* Vol. 20, No. 4 (December, 1973), pp. 708–720.
9. Healy, W. E. "Shift Scheduling Made Easy." *Factory,* Vol. 117, No. 10 (October, 1969).
10. Harveston, M. F., B. J. Luce, and T. A. Smuczynski. "Telephone Operator Management System—TOMS." ORSA/TIMS/AIIE Joint National Meeting, November, 1972.
11. Henderson, W. B. and W. L. Berry. "Heuristic Methods for Telephone Operator Shift Scheduling: An Experimental Analysis." Working Paper No. 20, Center for Business and Economic Research, College of Business Administration, The University of Tennessee, February, 1975.
12. Henderson, W. B. and W. L. Berry. "Determining Optimal Shift Schedules for Telephone Traffic Exchange Operators." Paper No. 507, Institute for Research in the Behavioral, Economic, and Management Sciences, Krannert Graduate School of Industrial Administration, Purdue University, April, 1975.

13. Hill, A. V. and V. A. Mabert. "A Combined Projection—Causal Approach for Short Range Forecasts." Paper No. 527, Institute for Research in the Behavioral, Economic, and Management Sciences, Purdue University, September, 1975.
14. Jelinek, R. C. "Tell the Computer How Sick the Patients Are and It Will Tell How Many Nurses They Need." *Modern Hospital,* (December, 1973).
15. Larson, R. C. "Improving the Effectiveness of New York City's 911." In A. W. Drake, R. L. Keeney, and P. M. Morse, eds. *Analysis of Public Systems,* Chapter 9. Cambridge, Mass.: M.I.T. Press, 1972, pp. 151–180.
16. Linder, R. W. "The Development of Manpower and Facilities Planning Methods for Airline Telephone Reservations Offices." *Operational Research Quarterly,* Vol. 20, No. 1 (1969), pp. 3–21.
17. Luce, B. J. "A Shift Scheduling Algorithm." ORSA, 44th National Meeting, November, 1973.
18. Luce, B. J. "Dynamic Employment Planning Model." ORSA/TIMS, Joint National Meeting, April, 1974.
19. Luce, B. J. "Employee Assignment System." ORSA/TIMS, Joint National Meeting, April, 1974.
20. Mabert, V. A. and A. R. Raedels. "The Detail Scheduling of a Part-Time Work Force: A Case Study of Teller Staffing." Paper No. 531, *Institute for Research in the Behavioral, Economic, and Management Sciences,"* Purdue University, Sept. 1975.
21. Maier-Roth, C. and H. B. Wolfe. "Cyclical Scheduling and Allocation of Nursing Staff." *"Socio-Economic Planning Sciences,* Vol. 7, 1973, pp. 471–487.
22. Monroe, G. "Scheduling Manpower for Service Operations." *Industrial Engineering,* August 1970.
23. Murray, D. J. "Computer Makes the Schedules for Nurses." *Modern Hospital,* December 1971.
24. Paul, R. J. and R. E. Stevens. "Staffing Service Activities With Waiting Line Models." *Decision Sciences,* Vol. 2, No. 2, April 1971.
25. Ritzman, L. P., L. J. Krajewski, and M. J. Showalter. "The Disaggregation of Aggregate Manpower Plans." *Management Science,* Vol. 22, No. 11, pp. 1204–1214.
26. Rothstein, M. "Hospital Manpower Shift Scheduling by Mathematical Programming." *Health Services Research,* Spring 1973, pp. 60–66.
27. Rothstein, M. "Scheduling Manpower by Mathematical Programming." *Industrial Engineering,* April 1972, pp. 29–33.
28. Segal, M. "The Operator-Scheduling Problem: A Network-Flow Approach." *Operations Research,* Vol. 22, No. 4, July-August 1974, pp. 808–823.
29. Walsh, D. S. "Computerized Labor Scheduling: Supermarkets Jumping on the Bandwagon." 25th Annual Conference and Convention, *American Institute of Industrial Engineers,* May 1974.

9.
How to Minimize Labor Costs During Peak Demand Periods

Marc J. Wallace, Jr. and M. Lynn Spruill

Corporate manpower planners traditionally have utilized two prime options for staffing during short-run periods of peak labor demand—schedule overtime for current employees or hire new employees. With the growth of the temporary help industry, however, a third planning alternative has become increasingly available, and it is possible to "rent" labor in a growing variety of occupations for temporary demand periods. Occupational skills obtainable on a rental basis range from filing clerks through semi-skilled labor to highly skilled technicians, administrative secretaries, and even management-level executives.

The nagging question of relative costs has remained, however. A formula for determining the break-even point between paying overtime wages and hiring new

Editors' Note: Reprinted by permission of the publisher from *Personnel,* July-August 1975, © 1975 by AMACOM, a division of American Management Associations. All rights reserved.

workers has long been available (*Compensation Review,* Second Quarter 1969). But little has been done to provide managers with a systematic formula or model to determine when hiring new employees or utilizing the labor rental option is the least costly alternative for staffing during peak labor demand cycles.

Management can make this determination, however, by establishing the separate cost elements of each alternative and combining them into a formula—a Peak Employee Demand Model (PEDM)—which treats the combined labor cost associated with each option as a function of the time the additional labor will be needed. Designed as a research project, PEDM has been used in several typical peak demand situations to determine the break-even point at which the hire alternative becomes less costly than the alternative of bringing in temporary help on a labor rental basis.

Enumerating the Costs

The first step in designing and using PEDM is to identify each labor cost element associated with the hire and rent alternatives. To facilitate the hire-rent comparison, it is useful to reduce all cost elements to an hourly cost. While many labor costs such as the expense of recruiting an employee are considered to be fixed, they also can be treated as costs per hour by prorating them over the hours the additional labor is actually needed. For example, recruitment and selection costs are generally incurred just once, before the employee is hired. For each employee hired, however, the recruitment and selection cost can properly be apportioned over the number of additional hours labor is needed. If the peak demand period is short, prorated hourly recruitment and selection costs will be relatively high. As the peak demand period is extended, on the other hand, prorated hourly recruitment and selection costs will be relatively lower.

COST ELEMENTS OF THE HIRE ALTERNATIVE / The following cost elements were identified for the hire option:

1. Salary and fringe benefits.
2. Recruitment and selection costs.
3. Initial inefficiency costs attributable to the new employee's inexperience with the job and the employer.
4. Training costs.
5. The cost of supervising the employee. These cost elements were defined as follows:

S = The hourly wage plus fringe benefits paid to the hired employee. In addition to the hourly wage, the employer must pay the current social security tax rate imposed on employers, the unemployment insurance rate paid by the firm, the percentage of payroll paid for worker's compensation for the job classification, as well as paid vacation liability, the cost of paid holidays, the cost of sick leave, monthly health insurance premiums, payments to pension plan accounts, and any additional fringe benefit. For the sake of presentation, hourly fringe benefit costs were estimated to total 30 percent of the hourly wage.

R = Recruitment and selection costs associated with attracting a qualified applicant to the firm. These include the cost of newspaper and other media advertising and any fees paid to an employment agency. In addition, costs are associated with making selection decisions including the costs of receptionists, job interviewers' salaries, and the cost of testing.

E_H = The efficiency of an employee. PEDM assumes that most jobs require a period of experience with unique job demands before an employee reaches peak efficiency in carrying out his tasks. In other words, an inexperienced employee will take more time than an experienced employee in successfully completing a given task. The model defines the initial efficiency as the ratio of the time required by an experienced employee to complete job tasks to the time required by any other employee. The efficiency of an experienced employee is, therefore, defined as 1.00. The efficiency of an inexperienced employee (E_H) will take on values between 0 and 1 ($0 \leq E_H \leq 1.00$) depending upon the employee's experience with the job. For the sake of presentation and analysis, all new employees are assumed to reach peak efficiency after 120 hours of job experience. An employee's inefficiency is defined as $1 - E_H$.

M = The fixed cost of materials used in training the employee. These include books, manuals, machinery, tools, and space employed while formally training the new employee.

C = Supervision cost, defined as the supervisor's hourly wage rate times the fraction of each hour he must spend supervising the work of an employee. For the sake of analysis, this cost is defined as a constant cost per hour (C) during the period of employment.

H_S = The proportion of each hour the supervisor spends in directly training the new employee whose efficiency is zero. This is the time that would not have to be spent if the employee were perfectly equipped to perform the job. The amount of time spent will decrease as efficiency increases. The actual amount of time spent for an hour is $H_S (1 - E_H)$.

W_S = The hourly salary of the employee's supervisor.

t = Time, in hours, labor will be needed during the peak period.

Cost Elements in Peak Labor Options

Hourly Cost Components for Hiring	Hourly Cost Components for Renting
S	$S = 0$
C	$C = 0$
R/t	$R/t = 0$
$S (1 - E_H)$	$S (1 - E_H) = 0$
$H_S (1 - E_H) (W_S + S)$	$H_S (1 - E_H) (W_S + S) = 0$
M/t	$M/t = 0$
$P = 0$	P
$R = 0$	R
$P (1 - E_R) = 0$	$P (1 - E_R)$
$H_M (1 - E_R) (W_S + P) = 0$	$H_M (1 - E_R) (W_S + P)$

COST ELEMENTS OF THE RENT ALTERNATIVE / The following cost elements were identified for the rent option:

1. The hourly rental fees charged by the temporary help supplier.
2. Initial inefficiency costs attributable to the rental employee's inexperience.
3. The cost of introducing and orienting the rental employee to the job.
4. The cost of supervising the rental employee. Each component was defined as follows:

$P =$ The hourly fee charged by the rental agency.

$E_R =$ The initial efficiency of a rental employee. It is defined in exactly the same manner as the efficiency for a hired employee. For the sake of presentation and analysis, a rental employee is also assumed to reach peak efficiency within 120 hours of job experience.

$H_M =$ The proportion of each hour the supervisor spends in introducing and orienting the rental employee to the job. The amount of time spent will decrease as efficiency increases. The actual amount of time spent for an hour is $H_M (1 - E_R)$.

$W_S =$ The hourly salary of the supervisor.

$K =$ The constant supervision cost. This is defined similarly to C, the cost of supervising the hired employee.

The cost components for each alternative are summarized above. The components that are set equal to zero indicate that these elements do not influence the respective hire and rent decisions. The cost elements for both decisions can be combined algebraically to yield formulae for estimating the total cost for hiring and the total cost for renting as follows:

1. Total cost for hiring:

$$St + Ct + R + \sum_{i=1}^{t} S\,(1 - E_H) + \sum_{i=1}^{t} H_s\,(1 - E_H)\,(W_s + S) + M$$

2. Total cost for renting:

$$Pt + Kt + \sum_{i=1}^{t} P\,(1 - E_R) + \sum_{i=1}^{t} H_M\,(1 - E_R)\,(W_s + P)$$

The break-even point, where the cost of renting equals the cost of hiring, is determined by simplifying the two expressions and setting equation (1) equal to equation (2). The point at which equation (1) = equation (2) can be expressed as follows:

$$3.\ t = \frac{[P + H_M\,(W_s + P)] \sum_{i=1}^{t} (1 - E_R) - [S + H_s(W_s + S)] \sum_{i=1}^{t} (1 - E_H) - R - M}{(S + C) - (P + K)}$$

A SAMPLE SOLUTION / In cooperation with a major temporary help agency and a relatively large employer (6,000 employees) PEDM was used to determine the break-even point between hiring and renting for several peak demand conditions. In one case, costs were determined as follows: Recruitment (R), \$28.33; the supervisor's hourly salary (W_S), \$3.00; training materials (M), \$500; supervision for the hired employee (C), \$.36; supervision for the rented employee (K), \$.84; the hired employee's hourly wage rate (S), \$2.76; and the hourly rental fee (P), \$3.72. The proportion of a supervisor's hour spent in training a perfectly inefficient hired employee (H_S) and a perfectly inefficient rented employee (H_M) equaled 1.0, and the initial efficiencies of the hired (E_H) and the rented (E_R) employees were estimated to be equal to 0.6.

The only additional estimates required involve the learning curves for the new employee. In this case we estimated that employee efficiency increases by exactly the same amount in each hour until peak efficiency (1.00) is achieved. The time required to reach peak efficiency was estimated to be 120 hours. After 120 hours the expressions

$$\sum_{i=1}^{t} (1 - E_H) \text{ and } \sum_{i=1}^{t} (1 - E_R)$$

in equation (3) do not change because $(1 - E_H)$ and $(1 - E_R)$ equal zero beyond 120 hours. Beyond this point no costs of efficiency due to inexperience were incurred. Using the estimates in this case, the time lost because of inefficiency during the first 120 hours for both the rented and hired employee totaled 24.2 hours.

The cost estimates defined above were entered into equation (3) in order to determine the break-even point (t) beyond which hiring becomes the alternative

103

of least cost. The *t* value was 334 hours. In other words, the firm would minimize labor costs by renting if the duration of peak demand is estimated to be less than 334 hours. Beyond this point it would be less costly to hire.

Formula Adaptability

The major advantage of PEDM is that it provides a systematic method for determining whether hiring or renting will minimize labor costs during short-run periods of demand. In addition, the model can be adapted to many different firms by adding or dropping fixed and variable costs where appropriate. For example, if a firm using the model does not use training materials, this component can be dropped from the model. Similarly, in adding a cost component, the planner need only determine whether the cost is fixed or variable. If fixed, the cost need only be prorated by dividing the cost by the amount of time labor will be required. If variable, the planner need only specify the hourly amount of the cost component.

The most critical factor in PEDM is the information regarding cost components. The accuracy of the model will depend upon the quality of such information.

PEDM is relatively easy to set up and use because it requires only information regarding labor costs, rental fees, and employee efficiency. The latter component can be estimated by determining the typical time required to become proficient on a given job.

The model can rarely make a perfect prediction. But the planner can see what the limits for his costs might be for either alternative by varying the costs included in PEDM to show the costs associated with the worst possible outcome occurring once either alternative is chosen.

Little quantitative sophistication is needed to operate the model, although those with greater knowledge of math might want to use the tools of calculus to obtain a more elegant solution.

On the question of temporary demand peaks, PEDM is not designed to deal with cycles of labor demand and, therefore, does not assist manpower planners in scheduling production to avoid extra costs of hires and layoffs. There is no question that for a given annual level of output, cycles of labor demand peaks and troughs will be more costly than constant levels of demand throughout the year.

The strength of PEDM, however, lies in its ability to show management how to minimize labor costs during peak cycles of labor demand by finding break-even points within each cycle at which hiring becomes less costly than renting.

Part IV
Personnel Functions

When most people think of personnel administration, they think of such activities as recruiting, selection, orientation, training, management development, performance appraisal, wage and salary administration, benefits administration, health and safety, affirmative action programs, employee relations, etc. These are the so-called personnel functions that are common to all employing organizations, regardless of size, nature, location, or whether or not the organization has a personnel department. As organizations grow in size and complexity, it becomes necessary to formalize the policies, practices, and procedures associated with these activities. For many of these functions, responsibility for planning and execution is centralized in a personnel department. As the organization grows still further in size and complexity, and as the value of the human resource increases in significance, the feasibility of adopting computer-based techniques to solve problems in these functional areas becomes more and more realistic.

To describe all computer-based techniques that have been applied to the personnel function is beyond the scope of this book. Nor will any attempt be made to describe a technique for each personnel activity. Instead, articles have been chosen which describe possible applications in seven functional areas: recruitment/selection, affirmative action, performance appraisal, training, wage and salary administration, absentee control, and collective bargaining. The computer methods described *are* representative of the types of applications available, and the possibilities, pitfalls, and limitations of these techniques as described in the articles do alert the student or practitioner to the need for careful costs/benefits analysis of any proposed applications.

In the lead article in this section, Smith describes the traditional personnel selection process and gives consideration to computer models for improving the selection process. The role of the computer in this process is not to make the actual selection decisions, but to process information for candidates and employers to consider. The author reports on research that suggests the feasibility of utilizing computerized programs as prescriptive models for personnel selection in organizations. Interpretations for various lower-level positions can be made more quickly, objectively, and inexpensively by the computer.

Affirmative action programs have clearly become one of personnel administration's most important concerns. EEOC's increasing demand for facts, totals, and percentages can bog down personnel's clerical staff in endless details. A computer-based system may be the only way to achieve goals rather than just monitor an equal employment program. In Grauer's article on "An Automated Approach to Affirmative Action," practical tips are offered for establishing such a system.

Two articles in this section deal with performance appraisal programs. The first, "Rating the Boss Through a Computer," describes a method used by a German subsidiary of Exxon Corporation for providing subordinate evaluation of managers. The system makes use of a questionnaire distributed on a voluntary basis by managers with the results subjected to a computer analysis. Feedback to the managers, which is treated confidentially, provides them with an opportunity to assess their strengths and weaknesses and to improve their effectiveness as managers.

In many companies, performance review information has been collected and filed away with little effort made to develop those evaluated or to strengthen manpower resources. Polster and Rosen describe a Potential Evaluation Program that is intended to accurately measure what characteristics contribute to an individual's potential to advance within the organization. It is felt that a synopsis of organization trends and individual subordinates' growth can be charted with the result that the general overall ability of the organization to foster its own growth potential can be measured.

The potential application of the computer to training and learning problems appears to be virtually endless—though costs often prove to be a limiting factor in

Computer Assisted Instruction (CAI) and Programmed Instruction utilizing the computer for feedback. One technique that has been growing in use in both educational institutions and in corporations is that of computer simulation. This technique has the dual benefit of providing assistance in both training and planning phases of organization operations. Out of the many articles on computer simulation and business games, the article by Mahoney and Milkovich was chosen because of its unique appeal to the general readership of this book. The computer simulation for developing the skills of manpower managers was originally designed for research but was later discovered to have immediate application to the training of manpower planners. The two training objectives were to use the model in a manner which allowed managers to: (1) gain insight into the interrelationships among personnel decisions and the relationship of these decisions to organizational costs and profit, and (2) sharpen their decision-making skills and gain experience in the use of various manpower forecasting, analysis, planning, and modelling techniques.

The computer has long been used to assist in payroll administration, but it has only been in recent years that computer models have developed to aid the compensation manager in significant pay decisions. Steuer and Wallace have written a paper which makes an initial effort at systematizing a compensation planner's judgments in pricing a structure of jobs within an organization. The authors describe a set of OR/MS techniques for formalizing a planner's judgments and allowing him or her to systematically test and evaluate alternative policies for resolving conflicts between internal value judgments and external market forces. The interactive model also allows the planner to take explicit account of budgets and legal constraints on wage policies.

The control of absenteeism is a mandatory program in any business or industrial operation that seeks effective management of its workers. Where large numbers of employees are involved, a move to computerization from manual posting may be an effective and economical move. Scherba and Smith describe a computerized program which has two basic objectives: to accurately and efficiently record absence data and to establish a method of identifying problem absentees so that individual counseling or necessary disciplinary action can be taken as steps to reduce absenteeism and its accompanying costs.

One of the most significant personnel functions in many organizations—at least those which are unionized—is collective bargaining. Little is known, however, about the actual and potential uses of computers by management in the collective bargaining process. The selection by Caples represents one of the most comprehensive treatments of the subject to date. Caples reports on survey data of computer applications to bargaining as they existed in the late 1960s and offers several personal insights into the future of computer applications for collective bargaining from a management standpoint. He sees the rate of progress of information technology in this area as being dependent upon three factors: technological feasibility, economics, and the barrier of human acceptance and interpersonal relationships.

10.
Models for Personnel Selection Decisions

Robert D. Smith

In April of 1968, a team of eminent authorities in the fields of economics, politics, sociology, and industrial relations embarked on a study sponsored by the General Electric Company. Their assignment, and the focus of the research project, was to attempt to define the major environmental changes which would most likely confront managers in planning for the 1970's. Each of the predicted changes seems logical and not particularly novel when taken individually. When considered as an aggregate, however, they represent a challenge to the most imaginative and creative managers. This is especially true of personnel (manpower) management.

The General Electric study characterized social change over this decade as an interaction among eight significant variables: affluence, economic stabilization,

Editors' Note: Reprinted with permission from *Personnel Journal,* Copyright August 1973.

education, attitude toward work, growing institutional interdependence, emergence of the "post-industrial" society, individualism, and urban problems. The key features of this view of the future are:

1. A forty per cent increase in real per capita disposable income is predicted, bringing a dramatic change in American life style emphasizing leisure, travel, culture, and self-improvement activities.
2. The 1970's are expected to bring a declining birth rate, flattening of the business cycle, and lower frustration tolerance for hardships of all types. Between 1970 and 1975, 66 per cent of the net increase in the American work force will be in the 20–34 age group, which will contain proportionally more women and Negroes, and be more mobile and more professional.
3. Middle class America is expected to view money less and less as a motivator in and of itself and more as a means to such higher ends as status, belongingness, and self-actualization. Educational levels will continue to rise and approximate 14 years of free education by 1980. The process of learning and retraining undoubtedly will be continued throughout a person's working career. Since one's self-image is changed through education, there will be increasing desires for individualism and fewer organizational constraints. Individuals will have different and higher expectations of what they will put into a job and what they expect to get out of it. Work probably will be looked upon less as a duty and more as a right.
4. The information explosion will continue as instant feedback brings world problems to the forefront of human thought. Technology will bring computers which occupy only a cubic foot of space, respond in trillionths of a second, and cost only a fraction of typical third generation systems. Lasers, cryogenics, and electro-optics will become part of the high school vocabulary.

What this means is that effective manpower selection will, of necessity, require flexibility and the willingness to adjust to rapidly changing conditions. Yesterday's decision rules literally may be outdated by tomorrow. A critical problem in selection will be the diminishing marginal utility of income for job seekers and the need for first jobs which provide challenge, autonomy, and self-fulfillment.

Something else which the personnel manager probably will have to deal with is the desire for mobility dominant in youth. Restlessness, dissatisfaction, and a seemingly endless search for something "better" will dominate the early adult life patterns of many highly trained professionals. Thus, organizations will be in a state of flux and, potentially, in a state of turmoil unless more effective methods are developed to (a) select that type of manpower whose individual commitment would most probably fit with organizational goals, and (b) provide organizational design and development approaches which better accommodate "mobile" personnel.

It is to the former problem that this article is directed, namely, scientific, systematic, and flexible selection of effective human resources. The reader should note, however, that motivation, commitment, and performance are related to more than selection efforts. An effectively motivated and productive work force depends upon an integrated manpower system including acquisition, development, reward, appraisal, and feedback systems.

Classical Personnel Selection Methods

Traditionally, personnel selection processes have consisted of a series of obstacles which an applicant must hurdle in order to qualify for a particular position. The obstacles are comprised of initial application blank screening, personal interviews, reference checks, physical examinations, and often some form of psychological testing. While methods vary, the objective of the selection process is fairly consistent: to determine whether applicants who have been recruited meet the qualifications for a specific job, and to choose those applicants who are most likely to perform well in that job.

The development, refinement, and updating of decision rules to use during the selection process is a continuing problem for personnel management, a problem not immune to halo, bias, inconsistency, and other errors of commission and omission. The more scientific of the traditional selection procedures begin with the identification of statistical relationships between predictor and criterion measures for a sample of employees. Based upon the observed relationship, a decision rule is established and then cross validated for a second sample of workers. The predictor may be a single score or a combination of scores on a battery of psychological tests, while the criterion usually is some measure of job performance.

According to Mahoney (1965), such an approach errs in several ways. First, it fails to consider the actual probability of success or failure and implicitly assumes both probabilities equal to one-half. Neither does the traditional method provide for the cost consequences of selection decisions. For example, under tight labor market conditions, one may be willing to select an applicant whose probability of succeeding in a position is only 80 per cent, especially if the costs of recruiting a second candidate are high, say $2,000. This same applicant might be rejected if the cost of additional search and interview were only $500.

Computer Models for Improving the Selection Process

Miner (1969) points out that an organization should use appropriate models "to establish procedures that will in fact identify those individuals within an applicant group who are most likely to succeed." He further states that employees should be selected so as to maximize the probability of organizational goal attainment and that "there is little point in extensive recruiting if a company does not select from among those recruited, the specific individuals who will contribute most on an organizationally relevant basis."

Dill, Garver, and Weber (1966) state that the development of analytical models and more comprehensive techniques (e.g., Markov Chains, linear programming, network analysis) for personnel decision making has emphasized the importance of personnel records and other data as inputs to these decisions. This is specially true in large organizations where the mass of data makes computer storage an attractive alternative. Personnel information systems become a real possibility as management creates new applications for its human resource data. IBM Corporation, for example, has developed an integrated personnel data system (PDS). According to Pedicord (1966) the PDS is designed for both personnel planning and selection. In planning, the system provides an immediate picture of corporate manpower resources; in selection, the system permits operating management to consider all logical candidates within the corporation as the first step in filling a position. The same code numbers are used in accounting and personnel so each function can perform integrated analyses. The data base is used to maintain consistency of procedures by storing corporate policy documents on tape for retrieval by a key word index. A five year projection of corporate needs for personnel in the areas of engineering, mathematics, and physical sciences are made for various growth rates.

Personal history data has been found significantly valuable in predicting certain criteria of job success for clerical and sales positions. A number of studies have shown that such data can be weighted successfully for predictive use for one or a variety of jobs (Kirchner, 1957). Once the personnel data bank is computerized, application blank weights can be updated continuously to reflect changes in organizational goals, labor supply, supervision, product, and so forth. Such updating can be achieved with nominal costs since the data are available in the computer memory and the same program can be applied each time.

An example of a computer-assisted selection model may be found in Merck (1965) who developed a procedure for predicting the location (position, authority level) of an individual member of an organization at some future point in time. Using Markovian Analysis, Merck's approach enables an organization to estimate the number of (current) personnel who will be available to work on particular tasks in a future time period. Knowing this, current selection practices are modified (updated) to assure that sufficient personnel will be available for promotion as positions open at higher levels in the organization.

Using a computer-assisted selection procedure, it is possible to balance recruiting costs against misclassification costs.[1] The relative costs of the two types of selection errors can be allowed to vary with the situation. For example, if training costs were high in relation to recruiting costs, it would be wise to use

[1]Misclassification costs are those opportunity costs associated with the selection of a candidate who subsequently fails to perform on the job and rejecting a candidate who would, in fact, have succeeded in a particular position.

a selection decision rule which placed greater weight on the probability of rejecting a success candidate. The Expected Value criterion for decision making suggests this is an optimal approach to decision making over the long run. Prior to the availability of the computerized personnel data bank, these types of calculations were too costly and tedious to warrant the expense.

Kao (1959) emphasized the importance of considering, in an integrated fashion, the various cost factors involved in obtaining a given number of satisfactory employees. His model gives particular emphasis to the cost of hiring individuals who later prove to be unsatisfactory. Once the mathematical relationships between recruiting and selection costs, opportunity costs of hiring potential failures, and the probabilities of success for given criteria are established, it becomes feasible to simulate on a computer various selection decision rules to determine minimum cost strategies under varying labor market conditions. Thus, if an employer recognizes an increase in the availability of graduates (external labor market) with degrees in accounting, he may be well advised to alter his selection decision rules to achieve a decrease in recruiting costs which would be accompanied by an identifiable increase in selection standards.

Large-Scale Automation of Selection Decisions

A number of independent agencies recently have been established to aid employers in their recruiting and selection processes (Huber, 1969). The primary function of such agencies (e.g., Career-Ways System, Comp-U-Job, Graduate Resume Accumulation and Distribution) is to identify job applicant-employer pairs with high probabilities of entering into employment agreements.

Data on the qualifications of each candidate who volunteers to join the system are stored in computer accessible files. Also included in the data bank are employers' requirements, job characteristics, and candidates' job preferences. Upon request from either the candidate or employer, a computer search is made for all combinations which satisfy the minimum requirements of both parties. These matches are printed out and the employer and candidate are encouraged to establish a time for an interview. Some systems provide additional information upon request (e.g., GRAD) via real-time communications networks.

Sophistication has been added to this matching process in some systems, such as SEARCH (Arnstein, 1967), through computation of a relative ranking of potential candidate-employer pairs. The Labor Inventory Communication System (LINCS) of the California Department of Employment uses a "key word" approach which compares job requirements with candidate qualifications. A count is made of the number of key words which appear in both requirements and qualifications (hits) and pairings are printed out in rank order from highest to lowest number of hits.

The Federal Government has developed several computer-assisted personnel search systems. MOHR (Management of Human Resources) is used as a recruiting source by the Department of Agriculture at the upper spectrum of civil service grades (currently GS-15 and above). Approximately 2500 characters are stored for each employee. Some of the characters are used as selectors in the computer and others as narrative output to aid in the final selection decision. The MOHR system includes job preferences (both function and location), skills, educational experience, and other demographic data. Each time a job opening occurs, a search is made of all candidates within the system, with the best qualified being recommended to that executive having the job vacancy.

The Executive Assignment System developed by the United States Civil Service Commission in 1968 initially included 25,000 government executives at the level of GS-15 and above. Each executive fills in an extensive personal inventory which is then divided into two parts at Commission headquarters. The total form is put on microcards for a manual file, while certain information is keypunched and computer searchable. The total file consists of approximately 5,000 characters, of which 1,000 are searchable, and a complete printout is sent to each executive for verification once a year. Occupational officers working for the Commission, in conference with agency representatives, decide on search dimensions to be used when a job opening occurs. The search tape is used to screen for *mandatory* requirements, and a separate program search for *desirable* characteristics. Thus, it requires two passes (one hour per pass) to develop a set of "probables" and "possibles" for up to eight different positions. Next, the Occupational Officer goes to microfiles on probables in order to perform reference checks with immediate superiors. The list is then narrowed to a final referral printout which includes the total file and digest of reference checks of most promising candidates. This referral list is then delivered to the agency representative who is responsible for filling the vacancy. Admittedly, this system, at least in its initial stages of development, still requires a good deal of human search which could delay the selection process as much as several weeks. However, until such time as more executives become skilled in the use of computer systems, and until total files are accessible on a real-time basis, additional manmachine interface will be necessary.

According to Holt (1969), the role of the computer in the selection process is not to make the actual selection decisions, but to process large amounts of information and to present selected information and recommendations for the candidate and the employer to consider. Holt proposes a computer aided model which identifies those interviews which will tend to maximize expected gains in labor productivity and job satisfaction for all employers and job candidates participating in the labor market. The primary objective of introducing the computer to this particular selection model is to provide a better distribution of effort between man and machine, so that both the employer and the job candidate can concentrate time consuming interviews on a relatively small number of promising applicants and vacancies, respectively. Holt suggests that a computer-generated list, if it is better than a human-generated list, would result in better selections measured by increased productivity, job satisfaction, and job tenure. The Holt Model is based upon (1) the probability that an offer will be made, (2) the probability that it will be accepted, and (3) upon productivities and satisfactions which can be expected from a particular man-job match. A social utility function is generated which reflects the decision criteria of both the candidate and the prospective employer. The expected utility for a given man-job pairing is defined as: (Productivity + Satisfaction) times (probability of Offer) times (Probability of Acceptance) minus (Cost of Interview). Needless to say, measures of productivity and satisfaction present a complex and subjective problem which the authors attempt to deal with through multidimensional utility scaling, a topic which goes beyond the scope of this article. It is sufficient to understand that large-scale selection problems are being studied by scholars from various disciplines and that without the aid of the computer, little progress could be made in improving traditional methods.

The reader may question the reliability and validity of computerized approaches to employee selection. While it is true that personal contact between potential employer (supervisor) and applicant yields valuable information not contained in mechanized storage, there is much skepticism as to the actual value of this form of information in the selection process. Such factors as facial expressions, photographs, voice intonations, firmness of handshake, and width of tie do tell something about an applicant. They also tend to bias the interview, often overriding other qualifications of the job applicant.

The author is not suggesting that there be a complete replacement of human contact by machine in personnel selection, but that at least during the initial screening phases, the computer can be much less biased toward subjective characteristics and more likely to select on the basis of qualifications (objective criteria).[2] Given consistent inputs, the machine will be reliable, that is, the outputs will be consistent, which generally is not true for human decision processes. Research evidence (Mayfield, 1964) points to the lack of both reliability and validity in the personal interview process. Meehl (1954) found that in 19 of 20 studies, predictions based on statistical approaches were more effective than those based upon the personal judgment of experts.

Computer-Assisted Selection: a Research Study

In recent years, considerable attention has been given to cognitive simulations wherein the computer is used to replicate decisions normally made by human beings during the problem solving process. Such computer routines sometimes have been referred to as heuristic programs, and are based upon the following assumptions:

1. Humans, in making decisions, break down complex problems into numerous simpler but interrelated sub-problems.

[2]There are notable exceptions here involving, for example, professional-managerial classifications.

2. They develop decision rules to handle these sub-problems.
3. More complex thought processes can be represented by networks of relatively simple decision branches which reflect these decision rules.

In order to test the heuristic concept for personnel selection, the author undertook a study in a psychological consulting firm (Smith, 1967). A psychologist, who dealt with the selection of applicants for clerical-administrative positions, was asked to participate in the study. As inputs to his decision process, the psychologist used scores from a battery of psychological tests (Gordon Personal Profile and Inventory, Otis Mental Ability, Washburne Social Adjustment Inventory, and the Short Employment Tests). He also had information about the applicant's age and relevant job experience, as well as an indication of significant job requirements for the specific position for which the individual was being evaluated. In order to construct a model of the decision process used in evaluating these data, the protocol method was adopted. That is, the psychologist was asked to verbalize his thoughts as he analyzed a set of actual selection problems. These verbalizations were tape recorded, transcribed, and graphically synthesized by the researcher in the form of a decision flow-chart. In the completed form, the decision network contained approximately 600 simple branches together with 150 print statements. Computer output consisted of a short paragraph describing the individual's capabilities related to a particular clerical position (e.g., administrative assistant, billing clerk, statistical clerk, file clerk, etc.), as well as a decision whether to hire, reject, or further investigate the applicant.

In developing the computer model, relevancy of information became quite a critical matter. Using this clerical selection battery, twenty different test results are obtained, some of which range from a value of 1 to a value of 99 as with the Gordon tests. There are 1151 possible psychological test values in all, in addition to job and personal data which conceivably could be provided for in the model. It is clear that the number of combinations of variables quickly exceeds manageable proportions, even with the use of a computer. In fact, for this study, it would have required 10^{70} outcomes to provide a model encompassing all possible events. To avoid this situation, the researcher restricted the system's boundaries through the use of heuristics, narrowing relationships to those most relevant to solution of the decision problem.

Heuristics, derived from the Greek "heveiskein" (meaning to limit search), provide general decision rules which keep models of this type within the limit of man and machine capabilities. The heuristic problem solver turns his approach from a search for the optimum solution to one with a high probability of being suitable for his purposes. Ergo, a heuristic approach was adopted for this research study. Instead of providing for each possible value of a particular variable, relevant ranges for most variables were defined, while certain variables (e.g., Washburne series) were treated in their entirety. This type of model building involved heuristics actually used by the human analyst in his interpretations.

An example will help to clarify the procedure. The sociability score on the

Gordon Test could range between 1 and 99. The analyst, however, treated only particular ranges for certain job types. For the statistical clerk, a sociability score of 95 or greater, coupled with a low cautiousness score, led to a negative recommendation since the individual conceivably could become a "social butterfly" and be incapable of maintaining the prolonged concentration required for statistical work. Thus, the psychologist, in this and other restrictions, placed his initial and greatest emphasis on scores which appeared at the extremes of the rating scale. That is, he first recognized scores above 95 or below 25 on certain Gordon Tests which provided valuable "heuristics" for the researcher.

If certain combinations of variables were relevant but not provided for in the model, the computer was instructed to branch to the next applicant and leave the exception for human interpretation. In this manner, heuristics were effectively employed to reduce the number of combinations of variables within the system to those most relevant for solving the majority of cases.

To test the model, a set of cases not used in the original design was introduced and subjected to both human and computer analyses. Results of the automated interpretation regarding definitive statements about individuals compared favorably with acceptable psychological practice (as judged by an independent consultant) 94 per cent of the time. In seven of the eight test cases, the computer printed out the same final selection decision, while in the remaining case, the psychologist recommended hiring as a "risk" and the model recommended a further background check, both decisions expressed some reservation about the applicant.

This research suggests the feasibility of utilizing computerized programs as prescriptive models for personnel selection in organizations. Interpretations for various lower level positions can be made more quickly, objectively, and inexpensively by the computer. Such added speed would be of special value when large numbers of job applicants are screened during short time intervals. Computerized programs also provide better and more consistent decision making. In some large firms, for example, selection recommendations are made in geographically decentralized divisions by individuals with varying degrees of psychological expertise. In such cases, utilization of a common program derived from the mental processes of the "most expert" interpreter(s) should lead to both better and more consistent recommendations being made throughout the firm.

Another factor which must be considered is that the expert interpreter would not be required to spend as much time and skill on fairly routine types of decisions. Rather, he would be able to expend energies on interpreting information for higher level positions for which the selection decisions are far less structured, thus demanding more human judgment. Another reasonable outcome of this approach to selection is the eventual improvement of the selection decisions themselves. Nothing was said about the validity of the decisions in this study, since the objective was merely to stimulate the psychologists' thought processes. With an automated decision process, however, it becomes feasible to develop a data base wherein the effectiveness of the decisions could be measured through feedback on job performance. If the control loop were closed, the model would become adaptive and learn or "update" decision rules based upon subsequent performance results of applicants chosen for employment. Admittedly, adaptive computer programs for personnel selection are still fantasy, but only a decade ago such present-day technology as multi-programming, optical scanning, and laser implanted memory also was fantasy.

The concept of "economic man" in search of higher pay and job security has received considerable criticism during the past decade. Especially at managerial and professional levels, such variables as autonomy, esteem, challenge, and self-actualization become significant factors in the decision to accept or reject a new position. In view of this research study, it may be possible to bring the opportunity for similar behavioral considerations into lower level positions without adding significantly to the selection costs.

A well thought out program of personnel selection will yield a variety of benefits to the organization. In this era of prosperity, employees seek fulfillment of more higher level needs than those typically found twenty years ago. According to a recent edition of the College Placement Annual, the first job a man is assigned to in an organization is the most important job. Every effort should be made to select applicants with the type of background commensurate with the skill, challenge, and autonomy requirements of the open positions. It is this researcher's opinion that the extra cost of more scientific selection will, in the long run, increase overall profitability through a highly motivated work force which learns more quickly, produces better quality outputs, and stays on the job longer.

REFERENCES

Arnstein, G. E. *Design for an Academic Matching Service.* Washington, D. C.: National Educational Association, 1967.

Auerbach Corporation. *A Survey of Computer-Assisted Placement Systems.* Philadelphia: Auerbach Corporation, 1968.

Bureau of Executive Manpower. "Employment Under the Executive Assignment System," Chapter 35 of *Federal Personnel Manual,* 1967.

Burr, Allen. "The Mobile Young Manager: A Corporate Dilemma." *Management Personnel Quarterly* (Spring, 1969).

Chruden, H. J. and Sherman, A. W. *Personnel Management.* Cincinnati: Southwestern Publishing Company, 1968, pp. 135–166 on "Selection."

Dill, W. R., Garver, D. P., and Weber, W. L. "Models and Modelling for Manpower Planning" *Management Science,* XIII, No. 4 (December, 1966), B-144.

Ford, F. B. "A Technique for the Evaluation of Recruiting Strategy with Fluctuating Availability and Known Demand." *Technical Documentary Report PRL-TDR-62-22.* Lackland, Texas: Personnel Research Laboratory, 1962.

General Electric Company. "Developing Trends and Changing Institutions: Our Future Business Environment." Department of Personnel and Industrial Relations, April, 1968.

Greenlaw, P. S. and Smith, R. D. *Personnel Management: A Management Science Approach.* Scranton: International Textbook Company, 1970.

Holt, C. C. and Huber, G. P. "A Computer Aided Approach to Employment Service Placement and Counseling." *Management Science*, XV, No. 11 (July, 1969), 573–594.

Huber, G. P. and Falkner, C. H. "Computer-based Man-Job Matching: Summary of Current Practice." in *Proceedings of the Twelfth Annual Midwest Management Conference*. Des Moines, Iowa: Drake University, 1969.

Kao, R. C. and Rowan, T. C. "A Model for Personnel Recruiting and Selection." *Management Science*, V, No. 2 (January, 1959), 192–203.

Kellogg, F. "Computer Aids to the Placement Process for Internal and External Labor Markets." in *Proceedings of the Twentieth Winter Annual Meeting*. Washington, D. C.: Industrial Relations Research Association, 1967.

Kirchner, W. K. and Dunnette, M. D. "Applying the Weighted Application Blank Technique to a Variety of Office Jobs." *Journal of Applied Psychology*, XLI, No. 4 (1957), 206–208.

Leiman, J. M. "Man-Job Matching and Personnel Information Management." Paper presented at the NATO Conference on Operational and Personnel Research in the Management of Manpower Systems, Brussels, Belgium, August, 1965.

Mahoney, T. A. and England, G. W. "Efficiency and Accuracy of Employee Selection Decision Rules." *Personnel Psychology*, XVIII (Winter, 1965), 361–377.

Mayfield, E. C. "The Selection Interview—A Review of Research." *Personnel Psychology*, XVII (1964), 239–260.

Meehl, P. E. *Clinical Versus Statistical Prediction*. Minneapolis: University of Minnesota Press, 1954.

Merck, J. W. "A Markovian Model for Projecting Movements of Personnel Through a System." PRL-TR-65-6. Lackland Air Force Base, Texas: Personnel Research Laboratory, 1965.

Miner, J. B. *Personnel and Industrial Relations: A Managerial Approach*. London: The Macmillan Company, 1969, p. 539.

Pallett, J. E. and Hoyt, D. P. "An Empirical Approach to Criterion Specification in General Business." Journal of Applied Psychology, LI, No. 2 (1967).

Pedicord, W. J. "Advanced Data Systems for Personnel Planning and Placement." *Computers and Automation* (September, 1966), 20–22.

Smith, R. D. and Greenlaw, P. S. "Simulation of a Psychological Decision Process in Personnel Selection." *Management Science*, XIII, No. 8 (April, 1967), B-409.

11.
An Automated Approach to Affirmative Action

Robert T. Grauer

By taking an automated approach to affirmative action, organizations can best respond to external requests for updates and analyses of their programs. A computer-based system also helps firms achieve their equal employment opportunity (EEO) goals and related affirmative action objectives.

The system described below is used by several organizations. In addition to reducing clerical operations and providing a level of information retrieval not possible with conventional clerical methods, this data processing approach:

> Provides both standard reports and special requests more accurately and on a timely basis.

Editors' Note: Reprinted by permission of the publisher from *Personnel,* Sept.-Oct. 1976, © 1976 by AMACOM, a division of American Management Associations. All rights reserved.

Permits identification of problems and provides information for corrective action so that affirmative action can be achieved instead of merely monitored.

Collection of Data

Figure 1 shows the input form for an applications usage of the system plus a partial set of input codes. (Because the variety of possible EEO reports is so great, this discussion focuses only on handling data pertaining to job applicants.) Information is typically transcribed from the employment application to this form, although in some instances it may be entered directly. If, for example, John Smith applied in January 1976 and was referred by state employment services, then 0176 would be coded in columns 29–32 and 8 would be entered in column 33, indicating date and source, respectively. Other information is entered in similar fashion. The completed form is sent to key punch and subsequently entered into computer files.

Available Reports

An organization may be required to prepare equal employment or affirmative action reports for a number of federal, state, county, and city agencies. To compound the problem, each of these agencies is apt to ask for different information; even if they request the same information, they are likely to ask for different formats, different time spans, different sort sequences, and so forth. In order to accommodate these varied requirements, a series of 15 reports can be preprogrammed and offered as listed below:

1. Applicant Log
2. Applicant Analysis
3. Referral Log
4. Referral Analysis
5. Offer Log
6. Offer Analysis
7. Hire Log
8. Hire Analysis
9. Applicant/No Referral Log
10. Applicant/No Referral Analysis
11. Referral/No Offer Log
12. Referral/No Offer Analysis
13. Offer/No Hire Log
14. Offer/No Hire Analysis
15. Summary Analysis

Figure 1: Input Form for Applicant System

SOCIAL SECURITY										NAME																INITIALS	
1	2	3	4	5	6	7	8	9	10	11	12	13	14	15	16	17	18	19	20	21	22	23	24	25	26	27	28

DATE			SOU-RCE	AGENCY		REF	DEPARTMENT				TITLE				DISP	EDU	INT	FT/PT	E/S	RACE &SEX	CAT	HAN	VIET
MONTH	YEAR																						
29	30	31	32	33	34	35	36	37	38	39	40	41	42	43	44	45	46	47	48	49	50	51	52	53

33 – Source

1 – Advertisement
2 – Employee Referral
3 – External Referral
4 – Co-op High School
5 – Co-op College
6 – Resume
7 – College Recruiting

46 – Education

1 – Less than High School Graduate
2 – High School Graduate
3 – Vocational/Technical Training
4 – Some College/No Degree
5 – 2-Year Degree
6 – 4-Year Degree
7 – 4-Year Degree, no experience

50 – Race & Sex

1 – Male Nonminority
2 – Male Black
3 – Male Oriental
4 – Male Indian
5 – Male Spanish surname
6 – Female Black
7 – Female Oriental
8 – Female Indian
9 – Female Spanish surname
0 – Female Nonminority

122

8 – State Employment
9 – Walk-In
0 – Other, Unknown, Agency

45 – Disposition
1 – Not Interviewed
2 – No Position Available
3 – Does not meet requirements – Education
4 – Does not meet requirements – Skills
5 – Does not meet requirements – References
6 – Offer Declined
7 – Pending
8 – Offer Accepted
0 – Other, Unknown

8 – More than 4-Year Degree – no experience
9 – More than 4-Year Degree – experience
0 – Unknown, Other

48 – Full/time-Part/time
P – Part Time
F – Full Time
X – Unknown

49 – Exempt, Nonexempt
E – Exempt
N – Nonexempt
X – Unknown

51 – Category
1 – Official and Managers
2 – Professional
3 – Technician
4 – Sales Worker
5 – Office and Clerical
6 – Craftsman
7 – Operatives
8 – Laborers
9 – Service Workers

A log report, which lists the names of applicants, usually is required by government agencies for compliance reviews. An analysis report contains summary totals and percentages and may be used by management in assessing affirmative action. The two reports are a matched pair in that the analysis statistics in a given report are substantiated by the names in the corresponding log.

The applicant log and analysis reports contain information for all prospective employees. Referral reports contain only those applicants actually sent by personnel to a department for an interview; thus referrals are a subset of applicants. Similarly, offers are a subset of referrals, and hires are a subset of offers. Reports 9 through 14 provide similar data, but present it in different formats, enabling management and/or external agencies to review applicants who were not referred, referrals who did not receive offers, and so on.

Any of these canned reports is available for any time span. The user merely enters the starting and ending dates, and the system selects only those applicants who entered in the designated time frame. Each report may list applicants in any desired order—alphabetically, by date of application, by disposition. Thus the 15 basic reports translate into literally thousands of possible reports when date and sort sequences are varied. Naturally, no organization needs all or even a fraction of these, but the essential capability is there. External reporting requirements are in a constant state of flux, making the ability to respond quickly and accurately highly desirable.

Applicant Log and Applicant Analysis

These reports contain information on every applicant in the system. Assume, for example, that an applicant log and analysis have been requested for 1975 (Figures 2 and 3, respectively).

The sample log is an alphabetic listing of all applicants plus relevant data—name, date, sex, race, EEO category, and disposition. The analysis divides this information by sex and race. Thus, of 520 applicants during the year, 157 (30.2 percent) were male and 363 (69.8 percent) were female; 129 (24.8 percent) of the total applicants were caucasian males, 18 (3.5 percent) black males, 9 (1.7 percent) oriental males, and 1 (.2 percent) American Indian male. A similar breakdown is provided for females.

Applicants, Referrals, Offers, and Hired
(summary analysis)

Figure 4 illustrates how applicant statistics can be summarized. Of the 520 applicants, 199 (38.3 percent) were referred to individual departments, 139 (69.8 percent) of those referred received an offer, and 115 (82.7 percent) accepted.

The summary analysis also contains valuable information about the progress

Figure 2: Applicant Log

NAME		DATE	SEX	RACE	EEO LEVEL	DISPOSITION
ADAMS	T	1/75	F	CAUCASIAN	CLERICAL	NO POS AVAILABLE
BARGE	CP	8/75	F	CAUCASIAN	CLERICAL	NO POS AVAILABLE
BARNES	M	7/75	F	CAUCASIAN	CLERICAL	OTHER/UNKNOWN
BEASLEY	NJ	10/75	F	BLACK	PROFESSIONAL	OTHER/UNKNOWN
BILLS	S	1/75	M	CAUCASIAN	OPERATIVES	NO POS AVAILABLE
BLOOD	B	8/75	F	BLACK	OPERATIVES	NO POS AVAILABLE
.						
.						
WALASKI	NS	8/75	F	BLACK	CLERICAL	MORE QUAL CAND
WILKIE	KJ	9/75	M	ORIENTAL	PROFESSIONAL	NO POS AVAILABLE
WILLIAMS		7/75	M	CAUCASIAN	CLERICAL	OTHER/UNKNOWN
WILSON	BJ	7/75	F	CAUCASIAN	PROFESSIONAL	OTHER/UNKNOWN
WOODFORD	M	7/75	F	CAUCASIAN	CLERICAL	NO POS AVAILABLE
ZOSA	JM	7/75	F	ORIENTAL	PROFESSIONAL	OFFER ACCEPTED

TOTAL APPLICANTS IS 520

Figure 3: Applicant Analysis

ALL APPLICANTS

	TOTAL	MALE	FEM	M A L E					F E M A L E				
				C	B	O	AI	SSA	C	B	O	AI	SSA
APPLICANT	520	157	363	129	18	9	1	0	320	37	6	0	0
%	100.0	30.2	69.8	24.8	3.5	1.7	0.2	0.0	61.5	7.1	1.2	0.0	0.0

of the company's affirmative action program. Thus, while 38.3 percent of all applicants were referred, only 30.6 percent of the male applicants were referred compared with 41.6 percent of female applicants. Some 69.8 percent of the referrals received offers, but only 52.1 percent of males compared with 75.5 percent of females. Finally, 82.7 percent of all those receiving offers accepted, but only 76.0 percent of males accepted compared with 84.2 percent of females. Analogous breakdowns by race can also be extracted. Further, log reports for referrals, offers, and hires are available to supplement the summary statistics.

Applicants by
Exempt/Nonexempt Classification

Figure 5 illustrates how the applicant analysis can be further divided to provide data on job status. In this related series of examples, the 520 can be sorted to reveal that 300 of the job candidates applied for exempt jobs and 220 for nonexempt. Over all, 157 applicants were male, of whom 135 were considered for exempt and 22 for nonexempt jobs, but while 30.2 percent of the applicant total was male, only 10 percent of the nonexempts were male compared with 45 percent of the exempts. This difference may or may not be important to the organization or to external agencies. The significance of this example, however, is in the demonstration of the "sort" feature.

The system is capable of sorting on any input parameter for which data has been collected. Returning to the input document of Figure 1, one could sort by source, agency, disposition, and so on. One could not, however, sort by age because no information was collected on applicant birthdate.

Figure 4: Summary Analysis

ALL APPLICANTS				MALE					FEMALE				
	TOTAL	MALE	FEM	C	B	O	AI	SSA	C	B	O	AI	SSA
APPLICANT													
	520	157	363	129	18	9	1	0	320	37	6	0	0
%	100.0	30.2	69.8	24.8	3.5	1.7	0.2	0.0	61.5	7.1	1.2	0.0	0.0
REFERRAL													
	199	48	151	39	8	1	0	0	134	13	4	0	0
%	38.3	30.6	41.6	30.2	44.4	11.1	0.0	0.0	41.9	35.1	66.7	0.0	0.0
JOB OFFER													
	139	25	114	23	2	0	0	0	108	4	2	0	0
%	69.8	52.1	75.5	59.0	25.0	0.0	0.0	0.0	80.6	30.8	50.0	0.0	0.0
HIRE													
	115	19	96	19	0	0	0	0	90	4	2	0	0
%	82.7	76.0	84.2	82.6	0.0	0.0	0.0	0.0	83.3	100.0	100.0	0.0	0.0

EXPLANATION
APPLICANT LINE LISTS ALL APPLICANTS
REFERRAL PERCENTAGES RELATE TO ALL APPLICANTS
OFFER PERCENTAGES RELATE TO ALL REFERRALS
HIRE PERCENTAGES REFER TO ALL OFFERS

Unforeseen or Special Reports

Invariably management will require a special report—that is, one not previously defined. This calls for substantial clerical effort in most organizations with nonautomated systems. Indeed, even in organizations utilizing a computer, a one-time program must usually be written and debugged. Either way, response time is often unacceptably slow, and initial results tend to be inaccurate. The solution proposed here is a very general "report writer" computer program that is an integral part of the applicant EEO system.

A report writer program consists of a series of "English" commands that are prepared by the user and programmed into the computer. Among the more essential commands are: SORT to arrange the data, SELECT to choose only those applicants with specified characteristics, TOTAL to sum the number of selected applicants, and PRINT to display desired information about selected applicants.

Assume, for example, that we need a list, for the first quarter of 1975, of all minority applicants who have at least a four-year college degree. Further, the information is to be arranged by EEO category and alphabetically within each category. Before proceeding further, the reader must fully realize that:

1. This request cannot be satisfied by any one of the existing reports listed on page 121.
2. The input document of Figure 1 contains the necessary data to prepare this report. Note that the date is coded in columns 29–32, race in column 50, education in column 46, and EEO category in column 51.

The first command is to SORT. Since the report is to be arranged by EEO category, we use the command SORT CATEGORY. The system then rearranges

Figure 5: Applicant Analysis by Job Status

ALL APPLICANTS				MALE					FEMALE				
	TOTAL	MALE	FEM	C	B	O	AI	SSA	C	B	O	AI	SSA
APPLICANT													
	520	157	363	129	18	9	1	0	320	37	6	0	0
%	100.0	30.2	69.8	24.8	3.5	1.7	0.2	0.0	61.5	7.1	1.2	0.0	0.0
EXEMPT													
	300	135	165	115	13	6	1	0	130	30	5	0	0
%	100.0	45.0	55.0	38.3	4.3	2.0	.4	0.0	43.3	10.0	1.7	0.0	0.0
NONEXEMPT													
	220	22	198	14	5	3	0	0	190	7	1	0	0
%	100.0	10.0	90.0	6.3	2.3	1.4	0.0	0.0	86.4	3.2	.4	0.0	0.0

Figure 6: Minority Applicants with At Least a Four-Year Degree 1/75 to 3/75

NAME	DATE	EDUCATION	RACE	SEX	CATEGORY
JONES AJ	2/75	4-YEAR DEGREE	BLACK	F	OFF/MGR
WONG M	1/75	4-YEAR DEGREE	ORIENTAL	F	OFF/MGR
		TOTAL APPLICANTS FOR OFF/MGR IS 2			
LOPEZ	3/75	4-YEAR DEGREE	SSA	M	PROF
.					
.					
.					

TOTAL APPLICANTS FOR PROFESSIONAL IS 4

all records so that officials and managers (code 1) appear first, professionals (code 2) next, and so on.

Because the report calls for minority applicants only, we must eliminate male and female nonminorities; that is, those applicants who have either a 0 or 1 coded in column 50. In effect, we want only those applicants whose race is greater than 1. The appropriate command is SELECT RACE GREATER THAN 1.

We also require only those applicants with at least a four-year degree; that is, those with a 6, 7, 8, or 9 in column 46. Thus we use SELECT EDUCATION GREATER THAN 5.

In order to get only first-quarter applicants, we use two more SELECT commands SELECT DATE GREATER THAN 12/74 and SELECT DATE LESS THAN 4/75.

The number of applicants in each EEO category is accomplished by the TOTAL command TOTAL APPLICANTS BY CATEGORY.

Finally, certain information is to be printed for each selected applicant—name, date, education, race, sex, and category. The appropriate command is PRINT NAME DATE EDUCATION RACE SEX CATEGORY.

The above commands may be given in any order. Hypothetical results are shown in Figure 6. If the user has an interactive terminal available, response is almost immediate. If a "batch" system is in use, response is most likely overnight. Either way, it is timely and accurate, two essential characteristics not available with nonautomated systems.

12.
Rating the Boss
Through a Computer

Roy Hill

Have you ever wondered what your employees really think about you and your management style? Esso AG, the German subsidiary of Exxon Corp. of the US, has designed a system to tell its bosses just that.

Managers receive from the computer room a print-out giving the average response of their subordinates to each of 32 statements. These statements, reproduced on page 132, identify the strengths and weaknesses of the boss as a manager.

The qualities judged range from whether the boss is a rational manager to whether he fosters efficient teamwork to whether he stands up for his subordinates against third parties.

Because of the sensitive nature of such evaluations, Otto Daniel, the Hamburg-based company's employee relations manager, insists on keeping the exercise entirely voluntary and confidential.

Individual managers are under no obligation even to issue the questionnaire to their employees. If they do, they need not reveal the results to anyone, even their own boss or the personnel department.

"I don't want to know," insists Daniel. "The questionnaire is not a matter of control. It is nothing more than a tool which managers can use to improve their self-knowledge."

But Daniel is sure that the majority of managers have in fact distributed the questionnaire. He guesses that many will have been surprised to learn just how their employees view them. And he hopes that in some cases they will be better managers as a result.

It took three years to perfect the questionnaire and convince managers that it could be beneficial. "Especially when something is voluntary," Daniel says, "you want as many people as possible to take a positive attitude. So you must 'sell' your scheme carefully."

First, Daniel and his deputy devised a small "pilot" questionnaire with only ten questions. These included "Am I informed about the goals within my department?" and "Do I have the necessary authority to do my job or is somebody interfering too often?"

They gave the questionnaire to section heads for distribution to the staff within the personnel department. Then they invited the staff to have a beer, after normal hours, to discuss the results.

"The next step," Daniel says, "was to broach the idea to other department heads and the board of directors. We have a training system and within it we have a course for management in which a couple of hours are devoted to appraisal systems. That seemed the best place to make the idea more widely known."

About half of the managers presented with the idea reacted favorably. "A minority thought it was brilliant and another minority thought it was ridiculous," Daniel comments.

He distributed a short questionnaire, very much like the "pilot" effort, to all those department heads who were willing to try it. "The very strong people said 'that's fine' and took it. The very weak people didn't like it," Daniel says.

Reactions to the questionnaire were mixed. There were criticisms that it wasn't detailed enough and that some of the questions could be improved.

Daniel met with some of the department heads to agree in general terms on a better questionnaire. But before he attempted to design it in detail he wrote to Esso's 120 managerial employees, all over Germany, explaining the trials and asking them if they were interested in such a system.

Every manager responded, 118 of them saying that they thought it was a good idea.

Daniel grins as he recalls the replies of the two dissenters: "One of them wrote: 'I know exactly what my people think about me. They need not write it down.' The other said: 'I'm the boss, That's enough.'"

In the light of the discussion with department heads, Daniel's department then designed a better questionnaire which he despatched to the managerial employees for their comments. Nearly 40 responded with ideas on how to phrase questions, or with suggestions for new ones.

"Their chief concern," Daniel says, "was that they didn't like negative questions. They wanted to have everything with a positive aspect. They didn't want to ask, 'how bad is your superior?' but 'how good is he?' "

In the light of these suggestions 44 questions were condensed to 32 statements, most of them positive on management attitudes and qualities, which employees were asked to comment upon.

These were sent off to managers with a covering letter which re-emphasized that it was up to individuals whether or not they distributed the questionnaire to their subordinates. It was also stressed that they must not force any employee to participate against his will.

Daniel does not doubt that most of the employees are eager to co-operate. "After all," he points out, "if I am a subordinate I must sit down and listen to my boss when he is explaining to me why he appraised me this way or that way. Why shouldn't it be the other way round?"

If a department chief decides to subject himself to evaluation, he simply hands out the forms to the employees. They fill in the rating and hand their secret ballot to a fellow employee in charge of collecting them.

It is possible that an employee might feel that his superior delegated well to him but not to the other members of his group. He may therefore rate the boss objectively for the group, or subjectively for himself. No guidance is given on this point.

Once the survey is completed, all the responses are delivered to the computer room. The computer averages out the answers to each statement and expresses the average mathematically.

The results are delivered to the manager, who can sit back in his office and, with varying degrees of approval or dismay, digest his ratings. He may already have known he is bad at communicating, so his poor rating in that category comes as no surprise. Another rating may take him by surprise.

Then, Daniel hopes, he will call his people together and say: "Can you explain this to me? Why do you think I am no good at this?" Says Daniel: "We hope that this will lead to a constructive discussion and better understanding of mutual problems and attitudes."

He recommends that when a boss discusses the response with his employees it should be with one spokesman, rather than with them all. "Otherwise," he says, "it might become apparent to the boss which individuals thought that he was no good at such and such. Then, even if the boss did not hold it against them, they might not feel like taking part in future questionnaires."

Daniel also recommends that an appraisal should be administered to not less than five people and not more than about 15.

By early January this year, Daniel was certain that up to 80% of the com-

Boss Evaluation—80% of the company's managers distributed this questionnaire.

Employees rate their bosses on 32 statements related to various management attributes. The employee puts a cross against one of five possible responses to each statement: almost never, rarely, occasionally, frequently and almost always.

The statements on the form, loosely translated from the German, are as follows:

1. He (the superior) analyses and plans carefully.
2. He utilizes his employees and his means rationally.
3. Even under extreme conditions, he works safely and thoughtfully.
4. Employees have to do work which they think is unnecessary.
5. Employees have enough opportunity to use their capabilities.
6. He is always trying to develop efficient teamwork.
7. He gives enough scope to others in the team to express themselves.
8. He is prepared to listen to suggestions.
9. He likes to make decisions.
10. If employees, within their area of competence, make a decision, the superior feels he is not being consulted and does not like it.
11. He offers his employees the opportunity to make their own judgments, if that is in the interests of the work, and encourages them to co-operate in decisions.
12. He stands up for his employees against third parties.
13. He uses his employees as far as possible in accord with their abilities and will to work.
14. The employees have the impression that they have to work under unnecessary stress.
15. He gives his employees all available information which is necessary to fulfill their task.
16. He enables his employees to gather the necessary information for their work.
17. He has defined a clear line of responsibility.
18. He adheres to this.
19. The employees get enough feedback of information to judge the results of their work.
20. The employees have to fulfill tasks without the necessary guidelines.
21. He understands the need to activate his employees not by hectic behavior but by well-directed activity.
22. The employees feel that they and their work are fairly judged.
23. He promotes his employees and looks after their development.
24. If employees have a work problem they can ask him for support.
25. If an employee makes a mistake, he criticizes him on a factual and unbiased basis.
26. In his conversations with his employees, he creates an easy-going atmosphere.
27. When he points out mistakes and shortcomings he helps by suggesting corrections.
28. If an employee has done a very good job, he tells him so.
29. He puts forward propositions by other people as if they were his own.
30. He deals with his employees as equals without losing their respect.
31. If he has personal problems, or problems with management, he doesn't vent them against his employees.
32. If one of his employees has made a mistake he does not continually hold it against him.

pany's managers were, in fact using the questionnaire. "That is more than we expected."

He reached this conclusion not from receiving precise information but through informal feedback. "Department heads meet on the first Monday of every month," he says. "It is easy for me to ask them how the action is going."

He guesses that most managers will discuss the findings with their people. "Those who filled in the questionnaire will be interested in the result," he points out. "So the boss will be under great pressure to discuss it."

So far as he knows, Esso AG is the first Exxon subsidiary to try boss evaluation. "If it seems to be a complete success I will inform Esso Europe in London and Exxon in New York," Daniel says.

"But I will only do that when I have enough feedback. Not in results, but in satisfied people."

13.
Use of Statistical Analysis for Performance Review

Howard Polster and Harvey S. Rosen

The ability to draw sound conclusions from performance review data remains one of the most complex problems encountered in the personnel field. To deal with this challenge, four years ago the American Greetings Corporation* initiated a program to systematically evaluate and document, on a corporate-wide basis, an individual's ability to handle increased responsibilities. Although studies had shown that the company was doing a fair job of documenting a person's performance in his assignment, it had no way of determining who was one step away from "the Peter Principle."[1]

*When this article was written, Howard Polster was Management Development Administrator at the American Greetings Corporation in Cleveland.

[1]The Peter Principle, Dr. L. J. Peter and R. Hull, Wm. Morrow & Co., 1969.

Editors' Note: Reprinted with permission from *Personnel Journal,* Copyright July 1974.

The *Potential Evaluation Program* was set up to accurately measure what characteristics contribute to an individual's potential to advance within the organization. A second purpose was to make sure that the evaluation data provided a reliable basis on which to make judgments about people. The program is not as much a measure of performance in a present job as it is a measure of potential to handle increased responsibility, since it is realized that there is a close tie-in between the two. Although performance behavior characteristics have been used as a basis for some of the input, nevertheless the primary aim is to forecast potential. The performance evaluation received was of secondary importance although these ratings were subsequently incorporated into the long-established annual performance review report for each person.

The *Potential Evaluation Program* was divided into separate projects, the first of which was concerned with the gathering of objective information. To help guarantee that the input would be objective, the "coached-rating" method of gathering data was adopted.[2]

A trained personnel "coach," who is skilled in interviewing and counseling, sits down with each management person in the company who supervises non-hourly personnel. During this session, the manager or supervisor evaluates the subordinates under his jurisdiction on a series of seven performance behavior scales. The factors involved have previously been determined to be important indicators of future managerial success within the organization. The scales themselves are divided into five broad categories, with each category subdivided into three smaller segments. Administering this type of performance evaluation involves getting a rating for each subordinate on all seven scales. It was previously found that this method eliminates much of the "rating bias." The raters must justify their evaluation and reasons to the coach. The latter also acts as a sounding board for the rater and helps clarify any interpretation in the questionnaire.

The "pitfalls of rating" of particular concern are:

a. Judging on typical performance, NOT isolated incidents.
b. Recalling performance over the entire rating period, NOT recent events.
c. Comparing your employees to the objective of the job, not to yourself.
d. Using the extremes of the rating scale where it applies. Not always "playing it safe" in the middle category.
e. Basing the rating on job behavior or "how the person actually performs," NOT "how we think or want him to perform."
f. Basing the rating on "job behavior," NOT how the person acts away from the job.
g. Allowing overall performance to affect the ratings on the individual factors: "HALO."
h. The inability of a person, due to the nature of his position, to demonstrate his ability in the area(s) being measured: "Opportunity Bias."

[2]This program was formulated at American Greetings Corporation in 1969, with the help of Dr. Erwin K. Taylor, Personnel Research and Development Corporation, Cleveland, Ohio.

The seven factors measured in the questionnaire were (1) Relations with others; (2) Planning and Controlling; (3) Work approach; (4) Decision making; (5) Development of subordinates; (6) Initiative; and (7) Advancement potential and motivation. The layout of each of the scales was:

lowest
behavior
description

highest
behavior
description

With each of these scales an attempt was made to evaluate the person on his behavior rather than on some pre-selected list of traits which might or might not fit that individual. Thus, the rater had some leeway within each of the five scale categories to interpret the behavior descriptions.

The second project was to accurately evaluate the information collected and draw valid inferences and conclusions based on statistically acceptable procedures.

Adjustments to Raw Data

After the rating information was put on punch cards, it was necessary to convert the data into a form which could be processed by the computer programs which were developed for this project. In particular, alphabetic information had to be converted into its numeric equivalent. For example, a person with a Bachelors degree was given a number 4. By this procedure the number of years of education that each person completed was recorded. The range of assigned numbers was from 0 to 5, with 0 indicating a high school graduate and 5 being assigned to a person who had a Masters degree.

Some of the raters omitted certain information. "Subordinate Development" question number 5 was not rated in almost half of the cases. This was due to the fact that many people rated were in "staff specialist" positions and did not have subordinates. Because some of the computer programs could not be utilized with missing data elements, it was necessary to delete any case in which there was any missing information.

Types of Reports

Several reports were generated and used in analyzing the data. The first, "Cumulative Frequency," calculated a frequency distribution of rater responses for each of the seven attributes examined.

A frequency distribution tabulates the number of people who received a certain score. The absolute number of scores was then converted to a percentage so that it became possible to determine the percentage of all the people that received a certain score. By cumulating these percentages, a person's relative standing can be easily determined. For example, if a person who was being rated on his "Relations With Others" received a score of 12, this would indicate that he was in the 86th percentile or that that percentage of everyone who was rated received that score or less.

The mean score and the standard deviation of those scores were also calculated as part of the first report which covered about 760 people. (See Exhibit 1)

There was a suspicion that people in different pay levels (or different levels of management responsibility) might have significantly different average ratings. The hypothesis was that those people in higher management groups would have received, on the average, higher ratings. The expected difference between the management levels can probably be best explained by the fact that those individuals who are at higher management levels have already been somewhat successful and, therefore, are more likely to possess some of the desirable attributes being measured. A second possibility is that the raters themselves gave these people

Exhibit 1: Frequency Breakdown Program

RELATIONS WITH OTHERS

NUMBER OF DATA 761
MEAN OF DATA EQUALS 9.20
STANDARD DEVIATION IS 2.90

SCORE	ABSOLUTE FREQUENCY	CUMULATIVE FREQUENCY	RELATIVE FREQUENCY	CUMULATIVE RELATIVE
15	9	761	1.18%	100.00%
14	28	752	3.68%	98.82%
13	66	724	8.67%	95.14%
12	81	658	10.64%	86.47%
11	92	577	12.09%	75.82%
10	96	485	12.61%	63.73%
9	93	389	12.22%	51.12%
8	78	296	10.25%	38.90%
7	74	218	9.72%	28.65%
6	58	144	7.62%	18.92%
5	45	86	5.91%	11.30%
4	15	41	1.97%	5.39%
3	15	26	1.97%	3.42%
2	6	11	0.79%	1.45%
1	5	5	0.66%	0.66%

Exhibit 2: Ratings by Percentile: Levels 0–5

SCALE	RATING VALUE															N=	MEAN	STD. DEV.
	1	2	3	4	5	6	7	8	9	10	11	12	13	14	15			
RELATIONS WITH OTHERS	1	2	4	6	13	22	23	43	56	68	80	91	96	99	100	549	8.86	2.86
PLANNING AND CONTROL	0	1	1	5	11	18	25	37	48	59	73	85	95	99	100	543	9.42	2.83
WORK APPROACH	0	1	3	6	10	17	27	39	53	66	80	89	97	99	100	545	9.14	2.74
DECISION MAKING	0	2	4	7	11	17	28	42	56	66	78	88	95	99	100	540	9.05	2.88
DEVELOPMENT OF SUBORDINATES	0	1	2	4	8	13	21	34	43	60	76	86	92	98	100	289	9.61	2.74
INITIATIVE	0	1	1	2	7	11	18	29	39	55	70	82	92	98	100	548	9.96	2.65
ADVANCEMENT POTENTIAL AND MOTIVATION	2	14	22	32	46	57	62	68	71	83	97	99	100	100	100	544	6.45	3.28

RATINGS BY PERCENTILE: LEVELS 6–9

138

Use of Statistical Analysis for Performance Review

SCALE	1	2	3	4	5	6	7	8	9	10	11	12	13	14	15	N=	MEAN	STD. DEV.
RELATIONS WITH OTHERS	0	1	3	4	6	10	17	29	40	53	65	74	92	99	100	212	10.08	2.81
PLANNING AND CONTROL	0	0	0	0	3	8	14	22	32	43	58	70	87	98	100	213	10.63	2.59
WORK APPROACH	0	0	1	2	7	8	11	17	26	39	55	76	89	99	100	212	10.68	2.58
DECISION MAKING	0	0	1	2	4	7	9	18	27	40	56	74	91	100	100	213	10.70	2.46
DEVELOPMENT OF SUBORDINATES	0	1	2	3	8	10	17	27	36	46	64	75	90	99	100	157	10.24	2.77
INITIATIVE	0	0	0	0	1	4	8	15	23	33	45	62	80	96	100	213	11.31	2.40
ADVANCEMENT POTENTIAL AND MOTIVATION	1	9	20	21	24	27	30	38	44	55	78	89	95	99	100	213	8.69	3.74

RATINGS BY PERCENTILE: TOTAL

SCALE	1	2	3	4	5	6	7	8	9	10	11	12	13	14	15	N=	MEAN	STD. DEV.
RELATIONS WITH OTHERS	1	1	3	5	11	19	29	39	51	64	76	86	95	99	100	761	9.20	2.90
PLANNING AND CONTROL	0	0	1	4	9	15	22	33	44	55	69	81	92	99	100	756	9.76	2.82
WORK APPROACH	0	1	3	5	9	15	23	33	45	57	73	86	94	99	100	757	9.57	2.79
DECISION MAKING	0	2	4	6	9	14	22	35	48	59	72	84	94	99	100	753	9.52	2.87
DEVELOPMENT OF SUBORDINATES	0	1	2	4	8	12	20	31	41	55	72	82	91	98	100	446	9.83	2.77
INITIATIVE	0	1	1	2	5	9	15	25	35	48	63	76	89	98	100	761	10.34	2.65
ADVANCEMENT POTENTIAL AND MOTIVATION	2	13	22	29	40	49	53	60	63	75	91	96	99	100	100	757	7.08	3.56

higher ratings because their level in the organization presupposes that they already possess the managerial skills being rated. Third, there is a possibility that people in the lower pay levels may not yet have had an opportunity to prove themselves. The first reason seems to be the most plausible explanation of the differences.

In order to test this hypothesis, the total sample was broken into sub-samples to see if there were actual differences in average ratings. Two groups were created. The first consisted of the first six levels of responsibility, which corresponds to the Wage and Salary Administration Program of "pay level" ranges 0 through 5 (Lower Management). The second group consisted of pay levels 6 through 9 (Higher Management). Finally, as an additional test, means for each pay level (1–3 were grouped together) were computed.

The results confirmed the earlier suspicion; as a person progresses higher within the organization he tends to receive better scores. The lower management group (0–5) scored approximately 2 out of 15 points less on the average than the higher management group. The only exception to this relationship was found in the "0" pay level group. These people, first line supervisors, received higher average scores than the entrance level exempt jobs, levels 1–4. This is, of course, to be expected, based upon the difference in age and seniority between the two groups. Further research into these differences appears to be justified.

The second report was an overall summary of the individual attributes, as shown in Exhibit 2. The report merely summarizes in one table the cumulative percentiles for each attribute. This report is, in essence, a master by which a person's score on any one item can be converted into its percentile equivalent. A summary report was prepared for each sample (all employees, pay 0–5, pay 6–9).

It is important to get information back to the supervisors who initially made the original ratings. This gives them an opportunity to review the results and also gives them an idea of how their employees rated relative to everyone else. To facilitate this review, a computerized report was prepared for each rater (Exhibit 3). It lists each of the subordinates evaluated by the rater and the scores he assigned to each of that rater's subordinates.

To the right of each raw score is printed the percentile to which that score

Exhibit 3

		Headings	Rater	
1.	Names	Biographical	Scores and	Data
2.	of	Data	Percentile	About
3.	Subordinates	for each	of the	the
4.	Who	Subordinate	Evaluation	Rater
5.	Were		by	
n.	Rated		Each Scale	

is equivalent. Each rater can then see where his subordinates' scores fell. Because there were significant differences in the means of the different pay levels, it was decided to use the percentiles calculated by each of the pay levels rather than from the entire sample. It was felt that a clearer picture emerges of a person's relative standing if he is compared to those in a similar status or peer group. For example, a person who was in pay level 5 who scored a 10 on Advancement Potential would fall in the 83rd percentile, a very respectable rating, when compared with his peers. A person in the 6–9 pay level with the same rating would only be in the 55th percentile, at best an average rating.

A report comparing each individual to the average percentile generated from the total sample of everyone rated was also prepared in case that information were to be requested.

There was a natural concern about the possibility that the raters were somehow biased in their assessment of their subordinates. Because of the subjective nature of all performance appraisals, there was the possibility that rater's bias might influence the objective ratings and the results being sought. For this reason, a "Rater Bias Report Analysis" was constructed to try and identify any rater whose scores were significantly out of line with other raters' scores. (Statistically, because of the large number of raters involved and because only one person rated each subordinate, it would be very difficult to apply standard statistical difference tests to the data.)

Variations in average ratings between individuals could be due to three things: (1) that people of a particular rater are, in fact, better or worse than the average of all other ratees and that talent in the organization is not evenly distributed; (2) that there has been a misinterpretation of the questionnaire or any of the individual attributes rated, thus leading to an inaccurate rating of the subordinate; or (3) that there has been bias on the part of the rater.

In Exhibit 4, you will note that the total number of people rated was ac-

Exhibit 4: Rater Bias Report Analysis (a)

RATER NUMBER	NUMBER OF PEOPLE RATED	TOTAL ITEMS RATED	TOTAL RATINGS	AVERAGE RATING	STANDARD DEV. FROM MEAN
102	2	13	161	12.38	1.62
105	5	34	362	10.65	0.25
106	4	28	289	10.32	−0.01
107	2	14	163	11.64	1.03
108	4	28	272	9.71	−0.49
113	3	21	185	8.81	−1.20
116	2	14	126	9.00	−1.05
123	1	7	76	10.86	0.41
130	3	20	203	10.15	−0.14

(a) The total number of raters was equal to 182.

cumulated for each rater and the means of all the people rated by each rater were calculated. Then an overall average of all the people rated was calculated. From this, a standard deviation for the population was developed. Finally, each rater's average was compared to the population average to determine how far above or below the averages his ratings were. This difference was then divided by population standard deviation so that standard deviation from the mean was established for each rater. The formula used for this computation was:

$$\frac{\text{Standard Deviation}}{\text{from the Mean}} + \frac{\text{Rater Mean} - \text{Population Mean}}{\text{Standard Deviation Population}}$$

One would expect that about 68 percent of all the raters would have averages that would fall within one standard deviation from the mean, and approximately 95 percent of the population would fall within two standard deviations from the mean. Therefore, if an individual rater's standard deviation from the mean were greater than 1 standard deviation it would alert us to the possibility of rater bias. Whether or not there is rater bias, of course, would have to be established. As already pointed out, other factors might justify this deviation from the norm. It should also be noted that this bias test could fail to pick up any bias when it may have existed. For example, if a rater rated more than one person (the average number rated by a rater was 1.5 people) and if one ratee were rated very high and another very low, the rater's average could easily come out right on the population average as any bias would be simply cancelled out and would not show up using this test. However, it was believed that if there were any bias or misinterpretation of the questionnaire, a rater's entire group would have been affected rather than any one individual within the group.

Additional Quantitative Analysis

All of the ratings were subjected to two additional types of statistical analysis: Stepwise Regression and Factor Analysis. Regression Analysis is a statistical technique that can be used: (a) to quantify the correlation between variables; (b) to create an equation indicating the relative importance and statistical reliability of each of the attributes scored: and (c) to use the equation to forecast one of the attributes designated as the dependent variable, in this case, Advancement Potential and Motivation. Unfortunately, there was one major problem encountered. Since it is not possible to run a regression when you have missing data, the first regression was run with 447 employee observations, eliminating nearly half of the sample (this is still a large enough sample to get meaningful results).

The significance or importance of each of the variables was determined by the computer utilizing a technique called stepwise regression. Essentially, this means that the computer selects that variable which singly explains the greatest part of the variance or change in the dependent variable which in this case is

Exhibit 5: Regression Recap and Incremental Contribution of Each Variable (a)

Initiative	Alone	explained	.377	of	the	total	variation
Education	"	"	.09	"	"	"	"
Birthdate	"	"	.05	"	"	"	"
Decision Making	"	"	.05	"	"	"	"
Pay Level	"	"	.03	"	"	"	"
Relations w/others	"	"	.02	"	"	"	"
Work Approach	"	"	.004	"	"	"	"
Total Variance Explained (R²)			+.62				

(a) The variables are listed by the order which they entered the equation.

potential. Then the computer searches through the remaining variables and selects the next most important variable which explains the greatest amount of variance still remaining. This process continues until a point is reached where additional variables do not significantly reduce or explain any of the variance that still remains.

In Exhibit 5, it can be seen that three variables were statistically insignificant: Seniority; Planning and Control; and Subordinate Development. Because they are insignificant, they were deleted from the regression. The remaining seven variables explained approximately 60% of the total variation in potential, which represents a correlation of .78. After noticing that "development of subordinates" was statistically insignificant and since this one factor accounted for most of the missing data, the subordinate development category was entirely deleted. This made it possible to expand the sample to 742.[3]

In terms of the order in which these variables entered the regression, Exhibit 5 seems to indicate that those people who have (1) the most initiative, (2) the greatest amount of education, (3) are younger and (4) are able decision-makers, would have the greatest prospect for future potential advancement. These four variables and the other three significant variables together explained 62% of the variation in the potential ratings. The 62% of explained variation (coefficient of determination $= R^2$) also represents a multiple correlation coefficient of .79 between these seven variables and the potential rating. Statistically the results are satisfactory. However, it should be kept in mind that there is still 38% of the variation that these variables failed to explain; that is, there are still other factors which are unidentified and which could increase the predictive capability of the regression equation. In reality, it is virtually impossible to get a 100% explanation and results of better than 90% are often suspect. This is because there are certain random variations which could never be taken into account. Additional ex-

[3]Many people are in staff positions and thus do not have any subordinates to develop. They are considered management people, nevertheless, based upon their level of responsibilities, authority to influence corporate profits, etc.

Exhibit 6: Table of Residuals (a)

OBSERVATION	Y VALUE	Y ESTIMATE	RESIDUAL
1	14.0000	11.1761	2.82389
2	14.0000	12.6569	1.34307
3	3.00000	7.98721	−4.98721
4	11.0000	11.2357	−0.235683
5	8.00000	6.47370	1.52630
6	13.0000	8.57317	4.42683
7	8.00000	6.19785	1.80215
8	5.00000	5.17687	−0.176872
9	5.00000	6.30262	−1.30262
10	4.00000	7.23032	−3.23032
11	2.00000	2.36247	−0.362466
12	3.00000	7.59149	−4.59149
13	6.00000	7.96169	−1.96169
14	7.00000	5.53453	1.46547
15	15.0000	9.34431	5.65569
16	5.00000	4.18136	0.818643
17	2.00000	1.20944	0.790564
18	6.00000	3.94059	2.05941
19	2.00000	1.43458	0.565415
20	2.00000	1.84371	0.156292
21	4.00000	5.23077	−1.23077

(a) The total number of observations was equal to 742.

perimentation with the questionnaire might make it possible to increase the explanatory power of the equation.

As stated earlier, one of the desirable properties of regression is that it can be used for forecasting. In this case, given that the values of the seven variables in the final regression equation are known, one can predict the expected potential rating for each individual. By comparing his rating on potential and his estimated rating and by calculating any residual difference between the two, it is possible to spot any seemingly inconsistent rating of any one individual.

Exhibit 6 shows a portion of this table of residuals. Column one indicates how the individuals were actually rated by their supervisors on potential. Column two is an estimate of potential. This estimate is derived from the regression equation and is based upon the values (or coefficients) for each of the variables contained in Exhibit 5. If an individual had a set of ratings for the seven variables, the rating for expected potential could be predicted.

The last column is the residual difference between the individual's actual rating and his expected rating. If there is a significant difference between the two (residual is large) and if that residual is over one standard deviation (2.2 ratings

Exhibit 7

CORRELATION MATRIX

	Birth Date 1	Seniority 2	Pay Level 3	Education 4	Relations w/others 5	Planning Control 6	Work Approach 7	Decision Making 8	Development of Subord. 9	Initiative 10	Potential & Motivation 11
1	0.45114										
2	0.61283	0.40570									
3	-0.14115	-0.16089	0.46100								
4	0.12232	0.13412	0.56524	0.41580							
5	0.16052	0.04785	0.11694	0.10793	0.51194						
6	0.01658	-0.04717	0.24787	0.15900	0.50545	0.47620					
7	0.20249	0.09241	0.28453	0.26541	0.57836	0.50987	0.55090				
8	0.10565	-0.03204	0.29023	0.19174	0.57438	0.60195	0.63226	0.58532			
9	0.11532	0.02102	0.12835	0.11909	0.58006	0.55387	0.52198	0.56286	0.48293		
10	0.13862	0.02844	0.21133	0.12606	0.58224	0.55496	0.60615	0.59187	0.56896	0.54949	
11	0.29871	0.14945	0.40718	0.41789	0.53083	0.48279	0.58894	0.60231	0.46889	0.58331	0.60654

Exhibit 8: Rotated Factor Matrix (a)

Variable	Factor 1	2	
1	0.12946	{0.85710}	Birthdate
2	−0.00515	{0.73097}	Seniority
3	0.37554	−0.17143	Pay Level
4	0.30650	0.08982	Education
5	0.71151	0.08651	Relations with others
6	0.71267	−0.08246	Planning & Control
7	0.77033	0.12366	Work Approach
8	0.80455	−0.01809	Decision Making
9	0.69372	0.03263	Subordinate Development
10	0.76037	0.05024	Initiative
11	0.75782	0.21119	Potential & Motivation

(a) These factor loadings represent the correlation coefficient between each variable (1–11) and each of the two factors.

as derived from the regression equation), it would be sufficient reason to examine this individual's ratings in order to investigate this inconsistency. It should be pointed out that this residual could be the result of (1) bias on the part of the rater, (2) poor judgment on the part of the rater, or (3) that some other factor accounted for the difference, a factor which was not included in the questionnaire.

The final statistical test employed was the technique of factor analysis.[4] Factor analysis was carried out for two reasons: (1) To take into account any statistical bias that may have been present in the regression due to intercorrelation of some of the explanatory variables; (2) to test the dimensionality of the original questionnaire.

Factor analysis is also useful whenever the variables being considered are intercorrelated with one another. Since the seven items rated on this sample are all of the qualitative type, it is sometimes difficult for a rater to differentiate and determine the degree of independence of one attribute from another. For example, when work approach is correlated with decision-making ability, we find from the correlation matrix that the two are highly correlated. That is to say, if one of these were to change, the other one would also change in the same direction and degree which would be determined by the strength of the correlation between them. Whenever this problem exists to a critical degree, the ability to delineate an individual variable's contribution to explaining advancement potential (as is the aim in regression) is diminished by the degree of the correlation. Factor analysis, on the other hand, which takes advantage of the intercorrelation can be used very

[4]An orthogonally rotated matrix with squared multiple correlations of the data on the principal diagonal of the correlation matrix was utilized here.

effectively if this is the situation. Exhibit 7 is the result of the factor analysis.

The data did exhibit intercorrelation, but it was not felt to be strong enough to invalidate the results of the regression. Nevertheless, factor analysis was used as an additional check on the other statistical techniques employed. As the reader may recall, planning and control was not statistically significant. This may have been due to intercorrelation as the other variables that entered into the equation first (since they explained a greater amount of potential singly) left very little for planning and control to explain.

Factor analysis allows the investigator to determine how many different characteristics his questionnaire actually examines. In this case there were seven different attributes rated and other data collected, such as a person's age, education, etc. The question is: were seven different variables or characteristics of individuals actually measured or were there seven different questions about one characteristic?

The results of the factor analysis in this case revealed that the questionnaire was actually identifying two different factors or characteristics of the individuals rated. See Exhibit 8.

These factors were revealed by the clustering of the 11 variables (7 rated items and 4 personal items). Of the 11, the seven rated items, the pay level and the educational level all grouped together as one factor and can be labeled "management skills." The seven rated items were much more importantly related to this factor than were pay level and education. The second distinct factor was made up of a clustering of the two remaining variables which are the person's age and his seniority. This factor might be called a personal status characteristic. Of the two factors the first was quantitatively twice as important as the second as indicated by the percentage of variance that each factor explained.

Factor analysis also confirmed that seven questions were being asked about one attribute—management skills. That is what the questionnaire was designed to do.[5] The questionnaire can be considered unidimensional.

The analysis of the performance review data showed:

1. That there were significant differences in the average ratings with higher pay levels receiving higher scores.
2. That a person's initiative, education, age, and decision-making ability (in that order) were the most important factors affecting that person's advancement potential.
3. That the questionnaire was unidimensional, measuring primarily the individual's management skills.
4. That the coaching process was an effective way of minimizing the effects of rater bias.

---

[5]If, on the other hand, seven different characteristics were being sought, then additional questions would have to be added to the questionnaire.

In most organizations, the collection of performance review data is not the most difficult part of the task. The real payoff comes in the objective evaluation of the data collected and in putting the information gained to effective use. It is probably safe to say that in many companies, performance review information is collected and then merely filed away, with little or no effort made to use the findings to develop those involved in the evaluations and to strengthen the company's manpower resources.

The *Potential Evaluation Program* as it now stands has been in operation in its present form for four years. At the end of the fifth year, it is felt that a synopsis of organization trends and individual subordinates' growth can be accurately charted. Some comparison can then be made between the goal of the program— measuring an individual's potential to advance—and the general overall ability of the organization to foster its own growth through the development of its individual managerial personnel.

14.
Computer Simulation: A Training Tool for Manpower Managers

Thomas A. Mahoney and George T. Milkovich

Manpower planning appears to be one of the newest and most rapidly growing topics in personnel management. The number of articles, books and seminars concerned with the analysis and planning of manpower during the past few years seems to indicate a significant interest in the subject. This interest might suggest that manpower planning has developed from a concept to a set of accepted principles and practices. Any such conclusion would be wrong. While manpower planning is a much used term, it is not well understood or appropriately applied.

Managers universally attest to the important influence of sound manpower decisions concerning organizational effectiveness. However, these managers have typically been trained to view personnel management in terms of recruiting, employment, compensation, labor-relations and training. College programs and personnel management handbooks are similarly organized into separate functional areas. Subsequently, most managers tend to develop personnel policies and make personnel decisions related to separate functional areas, thus overlooking the essential interrelatedness of these personnel decisions to the firm's profits and other goals. In summary, many managers have been trained to view manpower management decisions in separate, neat categories and have not been trained to develop a more integrated approach to analyzing and planning manpower resource utilization.

Similarly, researchers have approached manpower issues in a piecemeal manner, studying a bit of motivation, a little training and development, a little selection and a bit of collective bargaining. They have not tried to study and understand either the interrelatedness and interactions of personnel decisions or their implications to cost and efficiency goals.

Concepts of system models and system analysis suggest a way of developing an integrated framework for the analysis of manpower management decisions. A system is conceived as a set of interrelated and interacting components. A model (an abstraction of the system) specifies the essential components and interrelationships important in solving a problem or gaining understanding. The power of such systems models comes not from their perfect replication of reality but from the models' representation of those details pertinent to the issues at hand.

Systems models specifying the essential components and interrelationships permit one to analyze key elements of the system and to analyze the interaction among these elements and the decision-making objectives. Such models also permit simulation by allowing one to vary single components of the system, observing the resultant changes in other variables.

A systems model or simulation model of manpower management would provide a means for enabling manpower management decision makers to consider the full range of manpower variables in their planning and decision making. No such systems model has been developed; rather, most work has been directed toward analyzing two-variable relationships. For example, the relationship between relative wages and turnover, incentive wages and performance, or training programs and changing skill levels have been studied. But the interactions among training programs, wage programs and changing skill levels, motivation and performance have been ignored. However, it is precisely these interactions and their relationships to organizational goals that manpower managers face. Each manpower manager, trying to solve and anticipate problems and make decisions, must develop his own such model, whether he does it implicitly or makes it explicit.

The authors developed a systems model incorporating the best evidence available concerning the two-variable relationships of manpower decision variables, manpower characteristics and their relationships to organizational objectives. The model is general and does not relate to any specific company.

Although this model was developed for research purposes, it was discovered that it has immediate application in the training and development of manpower

150

managers. In the remainder of this article we shall describe the simulation model and discuss our experience with the simulation and the advantages and shortcomings of using a computer simulation as a training tool for manpower managers.

The training objectives were to use the model in a manner which allowed managers and students to:

Gain insight into the interrelationships among personnel decisions and the relationship of these decisions to organizational costs and profit.

Sharpen their decision making skills and gain experience in the use of various manpower forecasting, analysis, planning and modelling techniques.

While there are many approaches to using simulation for developing skills of manpower managers, ours was to develop a computer simulation called the Minnesota Manpower Management Simulation, MMMS. It is based upon a model which represents as realistically as possible the most important personnel decisions, the consequences for manpower performance measures and achievement of corporate results. The model is based on a hypothetical casualty insurance firm called Minnesota Home Group (MHG). Each player or team takes the role of the manpower manager of MHG and makes quarterly manpower decisions. The manpower decisions required of each player are listed in Table I. Minnesota Home Group's performance depends upon the manpower decisions made by the player and is not affected by actions taken by other players. In order to produce profits, a player must develop and maintain an organization capable

Table I: Decisions Required of Each Player

Quarterly

Manpower forecasts and staffing
    Optimal staff levels and distributions
    Actual staff levels and distributions
    Recruiting levels
    Promotion, demotion, layoff levels

Manpower Programs
    Training: skills, supervisory and induction
    Job design
    Performance appraisal
    Selection research
    Recruiting

Wage Level and Structure

Information Purchases (Wage Surveys and Market Data)

Annually

Manpower Program Budget Request

---

of meeting the policy demand facing MHG at a minimum cost. Each player allocates a manpower budget on a quarterly basis among alternative manpower programs in order to maximize the performance of MHG's manpower. Each player's decisions are processed by the computer for a quarter. Decisions for succeeding quarters are implemented on the base of the previous quarters' results. Thus, each quarter's decisions, to be effective, ought to reflect long-term plans as well as single quarter plans.

The basic concept of the game is that MHG's profits are determined by deducting claims costs and manpower programs and labor costs from total revenue. Competition in the industry is such that all firms charge a comparable price per policy and uniformly change price as warranted by demand and inflation. Claims settlements also are the same proportion of revenues in all firms. All firms initially face the same basic demand for policy; whether or not this demand is realized depends on the firm's being adequately staffed with effective manpower. The variable elements influencing profits are the number of policies sold, the wage bill and the manpower program costs. The number of policies sold is a function of the productivity and effectiveness of the work force. The player is responsible for manpower program costs and the wage bill. It is through the effective management of the manpower programs and wage bill along with efficient levels and allocation of staff, that profits can be maximized.

A manpower program budget has been determined by the company president for the first year of play (4 quarterly decisions); the player is required to plan and submit a budget for subsequent years. The budgets granted to the players for the following year's play are determined by company performance, which, in turn is determined by the soundness of the player's manpower decisions. The manpower budget has fixed and variable expense items. Fixed items include supplies, overhead, etc., and are not under the player's control. The variable expense portion of the budget, with some exceptions, is used to finance the various manpower programs the player decides to institute. Each player allocates the variable portion of the manpower budget according to his manpower policies and plans.

The player goes through a process in which major manpower decisions are faced sequentially. Each player must determine the optimal number of employees for each job category in MHG. MHG has four occupational families, each with four job categories, resulting in sixteen different yet related jobs. Once a desired manpower level and distribution is determined and compared to the current internal work force, then the appropriate staffing strategies must be determined to achieve the desired manpower position. The desired number and distribution of employees is generated by players analyzing overtime hours, anticipated turnover, measures of productivity and labor costs and product demand data. Since recruiting and/or training employees takes time, players learn to plan beyond a single quarter in determining actions for each quarter. The player can recruit, promote, demote, hire and lay off employees. Manpower shortages and inefficient staffing are reflected in overtime and labor cost data and eventually in profits.

Each player also must set up and maintain a wage structure to attract, retain

152

Table II: Minnesota Home Group Insurance Company Quarter 1 Performance Report

	This Quarter	Year to Date
Policies Demanded	241503	241503
Policies Issued	241503	241503
Average Policy Price	50.00	
Total Revenue	12075144	12075144
Claims cost	6283821	6283821
Total wage bill	4859991	4859991
Personnel exp.	105464	105464
Total Costs	11249276	11249276
Net Profit	825869	825869
Return on Premium	6.8394	6.8394
Personnel Budget		
This year total		374388
After fixed costs		215273
Actual Expenditure		
Variable	65685	65685
Total	105464	105464
Remaining Budget		
Total		268924
Variable		149588
Forecast Policy Demand		
Next quarter	246591	
2nd quarter	249235	
Next year	260329	
2nd year	270369	
U.S. Unemployment		
Last quarter	.052	

and motivate employees. Wages are a major element affecting the success of MHG actions to build and maintain an effective staff; wages also relate to labor costs and profits. Any number of wage policy options are available to the players, such as across the board adjustments to meet inflation, linking wages to changes in market wages and revisions of the wage structure through selective wage increases. Players may purchase wage survey data, and other market information during the simulation.

Table III: Expense Report—Quarter 1

Expense Report	This Quarter	Year to Date
Total Fixed Costs	39779	39779
Variable Costs		
Selection Research		
Agency	0	0
Clerical	0	0
Claims	0	0
Admin.	0	0
Job Design		
Agency	1000	1000
Clerical	1000	1000
Claims	1000	1000
Admin.	1000	1000
Performance Appraisal		
Agency	1500	1500
Clerical	1500	1500
Claims	1500	1500
Admin.	1500	1500
Recruiting		
Agency	1100	1100
Clerical	900	900
Claims	1600	1600
Admin.	1100	1100
Supervisor Training		
Agency	1500	1500
Clerical	1500	1500
Claims	1500	1500
Admin.	1500	1500
Total Skills Training	30075	30075
Total Induc Training	9900	9900
Transaction Costs	2010	2010
Unemployment Data	500	500
Wage Survey Data	2500	2500
Total Variable	65685	65685
Total Expenditures	105464	105464

Finally, various manpower programs are available to the player. These programs have an impact on employee effectiveness and manpower costs. The effort devoted to each program, indicated by the player's allocation of his manpower program budget, can be varied at will each quarter, or maintained at some level throughout the year. The player can decide to implement three types of training programs: skill, induction and/or supervisory training. Each of these programs relates differently to manpower effectiveness and their effects diminish over time. Recruiting activities include agency fees, advertising and interviewing. Players must decide the degree of recruiting expenditure required based upon the number and quality of new employees required plus the length of time the job vacancies can be tolerated. Selection research involves developing and applying improved predictors of performance of recruits and enhances MHG's ability to identify competent recruits from the labor pool which in turn enhances the quality of MHG's labor force.

Table IV: Personnel Report—Quarter 1

	Policies Per Man Per Qtr	Labor Cost Per Policy*	Wage Rate Per Hour	* * * *	Training Breakdown	
					Skills	Induction
Agency						
Ag. Mgrs.	7318.3	.98	11.50	*	500	50
Sp. Acct.	4391.0	1.12	7.90	*	1000	250
Sr. Agnt.	2744.4	1.44	6.32	*	1500	500
Agents	2278.3	1.14	4.21	*	2000	1000
Clerical						
Secret.	5031.3	.39	3.16	*	3000	100
Clerks	2713.5	.62	2.70	*	3000	500
Typists	2046.6	.72	2.35	*	3000	1000
File Clerk	1610.0	.80	2.10	*	3000	2000
Claims						
Cl. Super.	4644.3	1.19	8.85	*	1500	100
Sr. Cl. Rep.	2367.7	1.85	7.01	*	2000	400
Fld. Cl. R.	1599.4	2.07	5.30	*	2000	800
Off. Cl. R.	1195.6	2.31	4.48	*	2000	1600
Admin.						
Div. Mgrs.	6708.4	.97	10.40	*	1000	100
Supertnd.	3450.0	1.52	8.43	*	1000	500
Supervisor	2515.7	1.42	5.71	*	1575	500
Prof. Tech.	1750.0	1.59	4.52	*	2000	500

*Includes fringe benefits at 30 per cent of straight time wage bill

Job design and performance appraisal programs also are available to the player. These programs affect the motivation and effectiveness of the work force. In order to be effective, most of the manpower programs require the player to make some minimum initial expenditure and to maintain continued expenditure.

After the quarterly decisions are made, they are processed by the computer, which simulates the company's operations based upon the player's manpower decisions and prints out three reports for each team. Examples of these reports, Performance, Expense, and Personnel, are shown in Tables II, III, IV and V. The reports provide players with a summary of their decisions, the resulting performance of MHG, and various indices that the players can use to analyze and monitor the impact of their decisions. Key indices included in the reports include labor cost per unit, profits, percent of potential demand realized, productivity, etc. Players also use this feedback to develop and subsequently revise their manpower plans and policies as well as to guide their next quarter's decisions. Players find

Table V: Personnel Report—Quarter 1

	Total Number Begin Quarter	Prom Out	Demo Out	Recr	Volun- tary Leaves	Invol. Leaves	Number at End Quarter	Weeks to Fill Reqis	Over- time Hours
Agency									
Ag. Mgrs.	33	0	0	0	1	0	33	0	0.0
Sp. Acct.	55	1	0	0	2	0	55	0	0.0
Sr. Agnt.	88	3	0	0	4	0	88	0	0.0
Agents	111	7	0	10	8	0	106	1	0.0
Clerical									
Secret.	48	0	0	0	2	0	48	0	0.0
Clerks	94	2	0	0	7	0	89	0	0.0
Typists	127	4	0	0	13	0	118	0	1.9
File Clerk	158	8	0	20	20	0	150	2	0.0
Claims									
Cl. Super.	52	0	0	0	1	0	52	0	0.0
Sr. Cl. Rep.	102	1	0	0	3	0	102	0	0.0
Fld. Cl. R.	155	4	0	0	8	0	151	0	0.0
Off. Cl. R.	208	8	0	15	13	0	202	2	0.0
Admin.									
Div. Mgrs.	36	0	0	0	1	0	36	0	0.0
Supertnd.	71	1	0	0	3	0	70	0	0.0
Supervisor	98	3	0	0	4	0	96	0	0.0
Prof. Tech.	142	5	0	10	9	0	138	2	0.0

they must deal with excessive overtime, production bottlenecks, high turnover, inability to attract sufficient manpower, high labor costs and an assortment of problems that face any manpower manager.

A simulation exercise (game) provides experience in the same way that a case study does. But learning solely through experience is difficult. There are a number of analytic techniques for use in manpower planning which can be tested and applied with the simulation. Forecasting models, manpower cost analysis and operations research decision models have been available for application in manpower decisions for some time but not applied. Introduction of these techniques in conjunction with the simulation exercise constitutes more meaningful learning. Participants learn the technique and then test it in their analysis and decision making. Illustrations of the techniques and topics that the participants learn and then practice in the simulation are listed in Table VI.

Experience with the Game

Since 1972, the game has been used as a training device in manpower analysis, planning and control seminars. Seminars have been conducted for managers, both for mixed groups of participants and within individual firms as a part of management development efforts. It has also been used as part of a required manpower analysis course in the University of Minnesota Industrial Relation Graduate Program.

Reactions to the simulation exercise and the related seminar materials have been positive from both students and professional managers. Students find that techniques for analysis can have relevance for "practical" manpower management; staff managers find that manpower decisions can be related to profit and productivity and develop an appreciation for the relevance of manpower modeling. Both students and managers develop skills in the generation and development of models for decision making.

As Mason Haire pointed out six years ago, "Personnel techniques in the past seem generally to have been used on a one shot of this and one shot of the other

Table VI: Topics and Issues Discussed During Seminar

Modeling Skills
Manpower Planning Approaches
Techniques of Manpower Analysis
Techniques of Manpower Forecasting Demand and Supply
Analysis of Internal Work Force
Techniques for Choosing Among Alternative Programs
Techniques for Monitoring and Evaluating Program Effects
Manpower Information Systems

basis, without any explicit analysis either of the effect of one shot or of its implications for the other shot."[2] Manpower management education, research and decisions seem to follow the "one shot" approach.

An integrated-analytical approach is at the heart of sound manpower management. Manpower educators, decision makers and researchers, often backgrounded in social and behavioral sciences, have generally lacked an appreciation for the development and application of modeling skills and systems analysis or the application of more quantitative and analytical approaches to decision making.

The authors have found the Minnesota Manpower Management Simulation a useful tool for students and managers to develop skills in modeling and to increase their understanding and experience with the various analytical approaches to manpower decisions.

REFERENCES

1. The authors wish to thank David Dimick and Frank Krzystafiak for their invaluable assistance in the development of the simulation.
2. Mason Haire, "Approaches to an Integrated Personnel Policy," *Industrial Relations,* 1968, pp. 107–117.

15.
An Interactive Multiple Objective Wage and Salary Administration Procedure

Ralph E. Steuer and Marc J. Wallace, Jr.

1. Introduction

The field of wage and salary administration has long been faced with the difficulty of balancing conflicting demands in the design and administration of internal wage and salary structures [1]. On one hand are internal demands for equity in the distribution of wages and salaries across positions within the structure. Evidence suggests that norms develop and are shared in organizations regarding relative rates of pay for positions that will be accepted as fair [4].

In contrast to norms of equity, there are often conflicting forces impinging upon the internal structure from external market forces. Although there are a number of strategies management might use to buffer these forces (such as limit-

Editors' Note: This article was written especially for this book.

ing entry to the organization to a few critical "portal" jobs), the internal structure can never be completely insulated from the market. Such forces include short-run market conditions that tend to place upward pressure on wage rates for occupations whose members are temporarily in short supply, upward pressure on wage rates for positions represented by organized labor unions in collective bargaining, and a variety of laws placing minimum wage floors under various positions. In some cases, market conditions may further stress the internal structure by placing downward pressure on wages or salaries for occupations that are temporarily oversupplied.

Up until this time attempts to resolve such conflicting forces have been very haphazard and unsystematic. Typically, a compensation planner approaches the problem of design in a two phase fashion. Phase 1 consists of establishing a relative rate of compensation for every position to be included in the pay plan. In complex organizations, similar jobs are clustered into "families" or homogeneous job classes for the sake of comparisons. Once this step is complete, some form of job evaluation is employed to estimate the relative worth of the job on a number of pay related (or wage-making) characteristics.

As a technical matter the results of job evaluation depend upon the specific technique employed. In its simplest form (the ranking method) job evaluation results in a simple ordering of jobs in a linear fashion, with very little detail about the proportionate economic value of jobs to the organization. In its most sophisticated form (the point system) several scales are developed assessing each of the compensable factors (aspects of the job creating worth for the organization, e.g., job responsibility, working conditions, credentials necessary, and degree of responsibility). These scales are used to assess each job's estimated worth. These points are then translated into percentages indexing each job's relative worth. In most cases point ranges are defined and all jobs falling into a given range are judged to be in the same job class or salary grade for pay purposes.

No matter which technique of job evaluation is used, the process itself is one that facilitates the pooling and blending of judgments within organizations regarding the relative worth to be assigned to jobs for the sake of setting wages and salaries. It is important to note that the process of job evaluation is based on judgment and perception, not on any market realities. For the purposes of job evaluation, there is no single "true" value for jobs in an objective sense. The technique, rather, is one for reaching consensus regarding perceptions of value.

Quite distinct from the internal process of job evaluation is the second phase of establishing the wage structure. It involves pricing each of the jobs in the structure. Usually a firm does not go directly to the market in order to price all jobs in its organization. A planner will typically choose a small subset of "key" jobs in each job family for pricing purposes. There are a number of important reasons for this strategy. First, jobs vary greatly in their comparability across organizations. Job titles are very deceiving. In many cases positions in one organization are not comparable to positions in others for which market information is available. The planner must then select only those jobs that are the most similar across organizations for making market comparisons. Second, in an attempt to insulate critical jobs from market forces, planners often try to staff these positions from within rather than going out onto the market each time a vacancy arises. A strategy of staffing from within calls for the establishment of "portal" or entry positions that will serve two purposes. First, they will link the firm to external supplies of labor in markets that are favorable, and second, will serve as training grounds from which to staff insulated positions. It is important to treat such portal positions as key jobs and obtain accurate price information for them. A third and final criterion for a key job is that the job be comparable on wage-making characteristics to other jobs within the organization. Thus once a price is determined for the key job, the results of the job evaluation can be used to accurately establish prices for other jobs in the family.

Very often the results of the wage survey in the second phase do not agree with the outcomes of the job evaluation in Phase 1. In addition there exists no systematic method for resolving these differences. Usually the results of the job evaluations are re-rationalized to come into line with external market information, and jobs may actually be redesigned and reclassified. Unfortunately, operations research and management science (OR/MS) techniques have been conspicuously absent as aids to the compensation planner. The purpose of the paper is to present a method using OR/MS techniques that will bring systematization to the compensation planning process. Specifically, the method allows the planner to resolve conflicts between job evaluation and market price results by sequentially testing a number of different strategies for bringing the two into line. The OR/MS tools to be applied are the following:

1. Linear programming
2. A criterion cone contraction process
3. A vector-maximum algorithm
4. Filtering methods

Although the reader is probably familiar with linear programming, the last three items on the list are relatively new (only having become available recently). As will be seen, most of the haphazardness in the wage and salary administration process can be eliminated using these techniques. Rather than employing them on a "one shot" individual basis, they are deployed in combination with one another in an interactive environment.

The solution procedure is based upon the interactive approach developed in [6] and applied in [7]. However, it has been modified to accommodate interactive adjustments to the feasible region that become necessary.

The paper is divided into six sections. In Section 2, the wage and salary administration problem to be solved is described. In Section 3 the multiple objective linear programming formulation is presented. Operation of the interactive procedure is discussed in Section 4, and a numerical example is solved in Section 5. Section 6 is the last section of the paper and it consists of concluding remarks.

2. Description of the Salary Midpoint Determination Problem

The job evaluation process described in Section 1 yields an internal structure of jobs ordered in terms of perceived importance or value. A typical structure is illustrated in Figure 1.

In this case the structure consists of six job classes each representing ten points of a 0–60 point evaluation method. In wage and salary administration there are two types of problems when dealing with the structure of Figure 1. First, the compensation planner must establish salary midpoints for each of the job classes (or pay grades). They are to be related proportionately across the pay grades as closely as possible to job evaluation judgments. For example, if a class 1 job is judged as 100% and class 2 is judged 90% in job evaluation, then the salary midpoint for class 2 should be 90% of that for class 1. Often outside market prices do not correspond to the job evaluation percentages and create conflict. This is the dilemma whose resolution constitutes one of the arts involved in solving wage and salary administration problems. Resolving the dilemma of the salary midpoint determination problem is the topic to be addressed in this paper.

The second type of wage and salary administration problem facing the compensation planner is to create salary ranges around midpoints within the classes

Figure 1: Internal wage structure

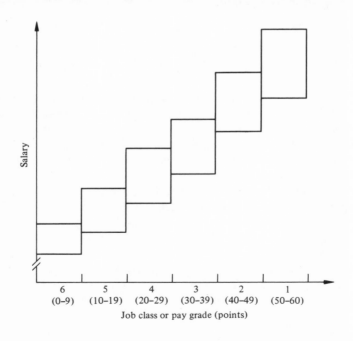

Job class or pay grade (points)

that (a) will provide sufficient breadth for individual treatment and (b) minimize overlap between pay grades. This problem will not be included in the subject matter of this paper.

Historically, when solving the salary midpoint determination problem, compensation planners have developed several remedial strategies for resolving discrepancies between job evaluation results and market prices:

1. Redesign troublesome jobs to allow additional job applicants to qualify for them.
2. Re-evaluate jobs to determine if any have been misclassified upward or downward. In most cases the re-evaluation is a post hoc rationalization in order to align job evaluation judgments with market realities.
3. Insulate certain jobs from direct market forces by limiting entry to "portal" jobs.
4. Re-examine the original job descriptions. It may be possible to make changes in order to minimize conflict with the forces stressing the wage structure.
5. "Red circle" positions that present insurmountable problems. Recognize them as being influenced by unique market circumstances. Do not allow them to affect the rest of the salary structure for wage comparison purposes.

In practice, the unstructured way compensation planners resolve differences between job evaluation judgments and external market constraints is as follows. After an initial wage plan is developed, it is "brought to market" for pricing. If it is within budget and does not conflict markedly with the constraints, the process stops. An acceptable internal wage plan has been obtained. However, this does not usually happen on the first iteration. Numerous adjustments (or iterations) typically characterize the process.

In cases where disparities exist, the five remedial strategies are variously applied to bring the pay plan more into compliance with requirements. An updated wage plan will result. Then it is priced against the market. The process of producing updated internal wage plans continues as long as avoidable differences are thought to exist between the pay plan and external forces. Obviously the process has to be brought to a conclusion. In practice, this usually takes place when the compensation planner reaches the limits of his patience trying to draft improved pay schedules. Due to the frustrations inherent in the compensation planning process, OR/MS techniques would be welcomed by the profession if they could be of any help. The remainder of this paper discusses how the salary midpoint determination problem can be addressed using interactive multiple objective linear programming.

3. Formulation of the Problem

The ultimate objectives of the midpoint determination problem are to establish an internal structure of wages that:

1. Fits within budget constraints
2. Is perceived and accepted as equitable by employees
3. Provides sufficient incentives for promotion from one job class to the next
4. Attracts and retains sufficient numbers of qualified employees

Unfortunately, these objectives are not actually obtainable with any given wage policy in the short run. Rather, they are long-run objectives toward which an individual wage plan can only contribute. Another difficulty with the four ultimate objectives is that they are not directly measurable. Consequently, planners must concentrate on more immediate and tangible "surrogate" objectives that are operational. In this paper five of them will be employed and they will be referred to as *proxy* objectives.[1]

In order to illustrate the five proxy objectives used in this paper, one of the candidate wage plans (Wage Plan 1–5) from the numerical example in Section 5 will be used. Six job classes or pay grades have been elaborated and wage information has been obtained for key jobs in each class. Let:

$n_i \sim$ number of employees in job class i

$p_i \sim$ inside relative worth of job class i with respect to job class 1 as estimated by job evaluation (3.1)

$x_i \sim$ proposed salary midpoint for job class i

$m_i \sim$ external market price for job class i as determined from wage survey information

In comparison to the inside relative worth percentages and outside market prices, Wage Plan 1–5 is given in Table 1.

With reference to Wage Plan 1–5, the five proxy objectives can be described as follows (assume that the budgeted amount is $200,000):

1. *Maximize a pool for individual job adjustments and/or incentive payments.* It is often desirable to allocate a small portion of the salary budget to create a discretionary reserve for making individual salary adjustments. Since the bill for Wage Plan 1–5 is $200,000, the pool for adjustments is zero. Thus, Wage Plan 1–5 would measure 0 according to this proxy criterion.
2. *Minimize average inside percentage deviation.* One way to measure a proposed wage plan's compliance with the salary profile determined by job evaluation is to minimize the average deviation from the value indicated by job evaluation judgments. Thus, averaging the absolute values of the Inside % Deviation column in Table 1, Wage Plan 1–5 would measure 11.3 according to this criterion.

[1]As defined in Keeney and Raiffa [2], *proxy* objectives reflect the degrees to which the higher level objectives are achieved but do not actually measure the higher level ultimate objectives themselves.

Table 1: Wage Plan 1–5

Job Class	n_i	p_i	x_i	Inside % Deviation	m_i	Outside % Deviation
1	1	1.00	26883	0.0	30000	−10.3
2	1	.90	24402	0.7	20000	22.0
3	1	.70	22402	17.0	25000	−10.3
4	5	.50	8961	−29.8	10000	−10.3
5	3	.30	7168	−9.9	8000	−10.3
6	10	.20	6000	10.3	6000	0.0

3. *Minimize maximum inside percentage deviation.* Another way to measure compliance with the job evaluation judgments is to minimize the maximum inside percentage deviation. Thus, Wage Plan 1–5 would measure 29.8 according to this criterion.
4. *Minimize average outside percentage deviation.* One way to measure a proposed wage plan's ability to attract and retain employees, without unnecessary overspending, is to minimize the average deviation from outside market prices. Thus, averaging the absolute value of the negative quantities in the Outside % Deviation column of Table 1, Wage Plan 1–5 would measure 10.5 according to this criterion.
5. *Minimize maximum outside percentage underdeviation.* Another way to measure a wage plan's attraction and retention ability is to minimize the maximum outside negative deviation. Thus, only considering the negative values in the Outside % Deviation column in Table 1, Wage Plan 1–5 would measure 10.3 according to the criterion.

Therefore, associated with each different wage plan would be values of the five proxy descriptors. This information will be sufficient for enabling the compensation planner to evaluate candidate wage plans.

The OR/MS tool that is central to the interactive procedure for generating candidate wage plans and proxy criterion information is multiple objective linear programming (MOLP). The particular MOLP formulation to be employed is organized as follows:

max	Pool for individual salary adjustments
min	Average inside percentage deviation
min	Maximum inside percentage deviation
min	Average outside percentage deviation
min	Maximum outside percentage underdeviation

s.t.

Budgetary Constraints
Inside Job Evaluation Percentage Constraints
Wage Floor Constraints
External Market Price Constraints
Minimax Constraints

As observed, there are five categories of constraints. Deviational variables, similar to those used in goal programming (see Lee [3]), will be utilized to implement the five proxy objectives. In addition to the symbols of (3.1), let

$B \sim$ total salary budget

$s_i \sim$ minimum allowable dollar salary spread between job class i and job class $i + 1$

$h \sim$ number of job classes in salary structure

The five categories of constraints are described as follows:

1. *Budgetary constraints.* In this category, an underachievement deviational variable (d_1-) is used to take up the slack between the cost of the wage plan and budget. The deviational variable is used to form the first proxy objective. For practical purposes, a limit of 5% of total budget is placed upon the size of the discretionary adjustment pool. The budgetary constraints are expressed as

$$\sum_{i=1}^{h} n_i x_i + d_1{}^- = B$$

$$d_1{}^- \leq B/20$$

2. *Inside job evaluation percentage constraints.* This category consists of two types of constraints. The first type attempts to enforce the relative worth percentage structure as determined by job evaluation. Underachievement and overachievement deviational variables $(d_{2i}-$ and $d_{2i}+)$ are employed to account for the percentage difference between proposed and ideal salaries. Constraints of this type are expressed as

$$-p_i x_1 + x_i + \frac{(p_i m_1)}{100} (d_{2i}{}^- - d_{2i}{}^+) = 0 \quad \text{for all } i \in \{2, \dots, h\}$$

The coefficient $(p_i m_1/100)$ is used to convert dollar deviations to percentage deviations. The value m_1 appears in the coefficient as a base since job class 1 is used as the benchmark. The sum of the $(d_{2i}-$ and $d_{2i}+)$ deviational variables multiplied by $1/h$ constitutes the second proxy objective. The second type of constraints provides for a minimum dollar spread between midpoints for adjacent job classes. They are written as

$$-x_{i+1} + x_i \geq s_i \quad \text{for all } i \in \{1, \ldots, h-1\}$$

3. *Wage floor constraints.* In addition to minimum wage legislation, there may be collective bargaining agreements and other stipulations placing floors under certain salaries. In the illustrative problem of this paper it will be assumed that the only constraint in this catagory is one specifying that all employees will be paid at least $6000/year.

4. *External market price constraints.* These constraints attempt to enforce compliance with outside market prices. Underachievement and overachievement deviational variables ($d_{4i}-$ and $d_{4i}+$) are employed to account for the percentage deviation between proposed and external salaries. Constraints of this type are expressed asThe sum of the ($d_{4i}-$ and $d_{4i}+$) deviational varia-

$$x_i + \frac{(m_i)}{100} (d_{4i}^- - d_{4i}^+) = m_i \quad \text{for all } i \in \{1, \ldots, h\}$$

bles multiplied by $(1/h)$ constitutes the fourth proxy objective.

5. *Minimax constraints.* There are two minimax objectives: the third and the fifth. A minimax literature reference is [9]. The purpose of the third objective is to minimize the maximum percentage deviation from the ideal relative worth schedule. This is accomplished by minimizing the scalar α_3 subject to the following constraints: The fifth objective endeavors to minimize the

$$d_{2i}^- \leq \alpha_3$$
$$\quad \quad \quad \text{for all } i \in \{2, \ldots, h\}$$
$$d_{2i} \leq \alpha_3$$

maximum percentage underdeviation from the outside market. This is accomplished similarly by minimizing the scalar α_5 subject to the following constraints:

$$d_{4i}^- \leq \alpha_5 \quad \text{for all } i \in \{1, \ldots, h\}$$

In addition to these constraints, there are the usual linear programming nonnegativity restrictions on all variables. That is, all x's, d's, and α's must be greater than or equal to zero. With the structure outlined in this section (along with one wage floor constraint), the salary midpoint determination problem will have $6h - 1$ constraints in $5h + 1$ variables. This is exclusive of all slack and surplus variables.

4. Interactive Procedure

The interactive MOLP procedure to be applied represents an improved version over the procedure used in [7]. Several modifications have been made. Some of them represent advances in the procedure's evolution. Others have been inserted in order to contend with the fact that the feasible region may undergo alterations each iteration. The modifications will be discussed at the end of this section.

Even though alterations may take place in the feasible region, the salary midpoint determination problem is tractable. This is because the *criterion cone* (i.e., the convex cone generated by the criterion function gradients) remains constant.

The main features of the iterative salary midpoint determination procedure are as follows:

1. The compensation planner does not have to specify any criterion weights, tradeoff ratios, or relaxation quantities.
2. No mathematical or computer sophistication is required on the part of the compensation planner.
3. A small number (determined by the compensation planner) of candidate wage plans is presented to the compensation planner at each iteration.
4. A generous (one week or longer) turnaround time between iterations is envisaged.
5. The procedure is organized to converge in a small number (determined by the compensation planner) of iterations.

The interactive OR/MS procedure of this paper provides a structured and straightforward decision environment for the compensation planner. The algorithm has been designed for the convenience of the compensation planner, not the management scientist. As a result of this philosophy, the chores of the analyst have become more complex. However, this is what he is trained and paid for.

The generous turnaround time allows for operational flexibilities. It enables both the compensation planner and analyst sufficient time to develop and reflect upon their iterative responses before performing another cycle of the interactive procedure. Also the long turnaround time does not require the compensation planner to possess a computer terminal or even be on-site with computer facilities. In fact, it would be possible to conduct communications at each iteration by telephone or even mail. Thus the analyst and his computational equipment could be hundreds of miles away. This would not harm the operation of the procedure.

Another advantage of the interactive procedure is that it is easy to explain to a client. Consider the following dialogue that might take place between a compensation planner and an analyst:

Compensation planner: Explain the details of your interactive procedure.
Analyst: Fortunately, the details are not very complicated. Basically, I will need to meet with you twice each week if that is all right with you. In

one of the meetings you will give me information. In the other I will give you information. We will go back and forth like this until the salary midpoint determination problem is solved.

Compensation planner: What kind of information do we exchange?

Analyst: I will provide you with a small group of candidate wage plans for each iteration. You will provide me with two things. One is periodic job evaluation information about how you are sculpturing the job class structure. The other is your choice as the most preferred from the groups of wage plans that I will give to you.

Compensation planner: I like the idea of groups of solutions. I don't think I will have any trouble telling you which one I like best. Also, I will be able to tell you intermittent information about how I might wish to reshape the job structure. By the way, how many wage plans do you plan to bring me each time?

Analyst: I can bring you as many or as few as you would like. Would eight be OK?

Compensation planner: Let me see. Eight might be too confusing. Can you make it six?

Analyst: Six would be fine.

Compensation planner: When during the week should we have these meetings?

Analyst: Let me suggest a Thursday for the meeting in which you provide me information and a Monday for me to bring you the six candidate wage plans. Would the three-day Monday/Thursday interval be enough time for you to tell me which plan is the best from the group?

Compensation planner: Oh, yes. Three days should be enough.

Analyst: Good. Then the four-day Thursday/Monday interval should be enough time for me to make my computer runs and get the next batch of six ready for you.

Compensation planner: How many Thursday/Monday pairs is this whole procedure going to involve?

Analyst: Once again, as many or as few as you would like. How about four?

Compensation planner: Can it really be done in as few as four?

Analyst: Research by other investigators [see (10)] tends to corroborate the observation that interactive algorithms of this sort converge in about three or four iterations. Four iterations will suffice. However, should you wish to extend the number of iterations by one or two while in the midst of the solution procedure, just let me know. It can easily be accommodated. However, for now, we will schedule four iterations.

Compensation planner: When can we get started?

Analyst: On the first Thursday that you have your initial job evaluation results ready for me. Then we will follow a Thursday/Monday/Thursday schedule. I will only need a little bit of your time for the Monday meetings

—perhaps 15 minutes or so for me to go over with you the six candidate wage plans. But for the Thursday meetings I will probably need about an hour. The one hour will be required for you to explain to me how you want to update your classification of the job structure.

Compensation planner: Sounds reasonable. It does not seem that difficult.

Analyst: Well, we've deliberately tried to make interfacing with the interactive procedure uncomplicated. Unfortunately, my part of the interactive procedure gets pretty hairy. But don't worry about me. That's just part of my job. I'm ready to get started as soon as you are.

Compensation planner: Wait a minute! This is interesting. I've got an idea. Let's not solve the real problem yet. Let's make a pilot run first for me to get familiar with the procedure. Then we can go back to the real problem later. In order to keep from getting carried away with the pilot run, can we do it in three iterations?

Analyst: That's a great idea. The idea of a "dry run" is excellent. Sure, three iterations would be fine for demonstration purposes. How about the following schedule that I have jotted down on this piece of paper? [Shows sheet of paper.] Please note how we would still be following the Thursday/Monday/Thursday format.

1st iteration	Thursday (7/6/78)	Communicate results of initial job evaluation to analyst.
	Monday (7/10/78)	Receive first group of six wage plans.
2nd iteration	Thursday (7/13/78)	Indicate most preferred from first group of six and communicate results of second job evaluation.
	Monday (7/17/78)	Receive second group of six wage plans.
3rd iteration	Thursday (7/20/78)	Indicate most preferred from second group of six.
	Monday (7/24/78)	Receive third group of six and make final selection.

Compensation planner: That schedule looks fine. I will mark the dates down on my calendar. I will expect you, then, here in my office on July 6th to get started.

Figure 2 flowcharts the interactive procedure. As seen it is composed of 16 blocks. Blocks 2, 5, 7, 11, 13, and 16 are performed by the compensation planner. The rest are supervised and performed by the analyst. Variable N is the intended number of iterations pre-specified by the compensation planner. The compensation planner, however, can extend the value of N in block 12 and request further

Figure 2: Flowchart of interactive procedure

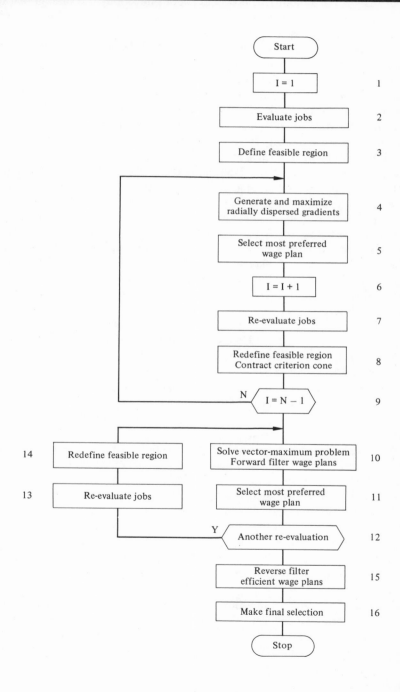

iterations if so desired. The item of note here is that the compensation planner, not the analyst, is extending the procedure. The philosophy throughout the whole iterative process is to put the compensation planner in control. The role of the management scientist is to be that of a facilitator.

The flowchart may look complicated but this is because it is portrayed from the management scientist's point of view. Admittedly, it is complex for the analyst. However, it is simple for the compensation planner. It is as simple for him as the one hour Thursday meeting and the 15 minute Monday meeting.

Before discussing the modifications that have been installed, the theoretical justification for the interactive procedure will be outlined.

In the absence of a utility function (which is the case in this paper), a solution to a MOLP problem is an efficient point. A point is said to be *efficient* (i.e., nondominated, Pareto optimal) if and only if it is not possible to improve one of the criterion values without worsening at least one of the others. In other words, "to pay Peter you will have to take from Paul." Efficient points are of interest because under nonsatiety the decision-maker's optimal point is always efficient.

The size of the set of all efficient points is related to the size of the criterion cone. In the case of single-objective linear programming (which is a special case of MOLP), the number of efficient (optimal) points is usually one. This is due to the fact that the criterion cone is simply a one-dimensional half-ray. However, in cases where there are several objectives, the one-dimensional half-ray expands in size to a multi-dimensional cone.

The resulting efficient set is normally not a single extreme point but usually consists of a portion of the surface of the feasible region. Since it is typically a nondiscrete set, its extreme points are often used to characterize it in a finite fashion. Procedures that are able to solve for all efficient extreme points are called vector-maximum algorithms. The vector-maximum algorithm that will be used in this paper is [5]. The main difficulty, however, of the vector-maximum approach is that MOLP problems have notoriously large numbers of efficient extreme points.

When using vector-maximum algorithms, two things can be done. The first involves contracting the criterion cone to limit the number of generated efficient extreme points. In many cases, however, the reduced number of extreme points may still be too large. In such situations filtering techniques can be applied.

There are two types of filtering processes. The first will be referred to as filtering in the "forward" direction. By comparing criterion distances among the generated efficient extreme points, the most redundant versions of other points can be indentified and eliminated. In this way the number of points presented to a decision-maker can be reduced while still preserving the full range of choice available.

Assume that the decision-maker selects his most preferred from the forwardly produced reduced list. Then instead of discarding blurred versions of other points, the closest neighbors to the point selected should be re-introduced. This is accomplished by filtering in the "reverse" direction. Thus moderately

Table 2: Parameters of the First Iteration

i	n_i	p_i	s_i	m_i
1	1	1.00	2000	30000
2	1	.90	2000	20000
3	1	.70	1000	25000
4	5	.50	1000	10000
5	3	.30	1000	8000
6	10	.20	—	6000

Table 3: Candidate Wage Plans of the First Iteration

	Wage Plan					
	1-1	*1-2*	*1-3*	*1-4*	*1-5*	*1-6*
z_1: pool	10000	0	0	0	0	0
z_2: average inside	9.6	3.7	9.8	14.5	11.3	7.9
z_3: minimax inside	20.9	22.2	12.3	36.0	29.8	16.8
z_4: average outside	12.4	15.1	12.7	5.3	10.5	9.0
z_5: minimax outside	21.1	34.6	36.6	28.0	10.3	18.2
x_1	23707	23333	26304	30000	26883	24942
x_2	21707	21000	20347	20000	24402	22448
x_3	19707	16333	15826	18000	22402	20448
x_4	8707	11666	11304	9600	8961	9942
x_5	7112	7000	7000	8000	7168	7482
x_6	6000	6000	6000	6000	6000	6000

large numbers of efficient extreme points can be analyzed without having to present the decision-maker with more than a small number of candidates at any one time.

The main modification of the interactive salary midpoint determination procedure is that the criterion cone is reduced at a slower rate than in [7]. As recommended in [6], each successively reduced criterion cone should have a cross sectional volume of only 20% (when $k = 5$) of that of its predecessor. In this paper, a slower rate of reduction is recommended since the feasible region undergoes alterations. A figure of 33% was used instead of 20%. Which 33% of the predecessor criterion cone is used to comprise the newly contracted cone is determined by which radially dispersed gradient (in block 4) produced the most preferred point in block 5. The newly reduced criterion cone is contracted about this gradient. Another modification that has been made is to enable the decision-maker to extend the number of iterations (in block 12) beyond the pre-specified number if such is his inclination.

The method works because of the following. It is to be noted that some small subset (perhaps even a singleton) of gradients in the criterion cone will produce (in the sense of the objective function gradient in linear programming) the decision-maker's optimal point. As long as each contracted criterion cone intersects this small subset, the interactive procedure should produce the decision-maker's optimal point or a point close enough to it to suffice in its stead.

5. Numerical Example

Using the MOLP structure of Section 2, the pilot run alluded to in the dialogue of Section 4 will be used to illustrate the interactive salary midpoint determination procedure. Since the number of pre-specified iterations is three, N is set to 3 for use in the flowchart in Figure 2. It will be assumed that the total salary budget is $200,000. Also, let it be assumed that at the first Thursday (7/6/78) meeting the initial job evaluation (block 2) was parameterized (in block 3) as in Table 2.

After solving for the maximal points (in block 4) produced by six radially dispersed gradients, the list of candidate wage plans in Table 3 is delivered to the compensation planner on Monday (7/10/78).

At the Thursday (7/13/78) meeting the compensation planner identifies (in block 5) Wage Plan 1–5 as his most preferred. He also indicates (in block 7) that he wishes to modify his original job class structure. By redesigning job class 3, it is possible to change p_3 in Table 2 to .65 and m_3 from 25000 to 19000.

Since I = 2 in block 9, all extreme points of the altered feasible region that are efficient with respect to the reduced criterion cone are solved for in block 10. Upon forward filtering, the six most dispersed extreme point wage plans are obtained. They are presented in the form of Table 4 to the compensation planner on Monday (7/17/78).

At the Thursday (7/20/78) meeting the compensation planner selects (in block 11) Wage Plan 2–5 as his most preferred of the six. Deciding not to iterate further, the vector-maximum produced efficient extreme points are reverse filtered about Wage Plan 2–5. The results are presented to the compensation planner in the form of Table 5 on Monday (7/24/77). Selecting (in block 16) Wage Plan 3–2 as the best compromise, the pilot run terminates. Perhaps with some rounding off of the dollar figure amounts for $x_1 \rightarrow x_6$, the salary midpoints for the different job classes have been established.

6. Concluding Remarks

In this paper OR/MS techniques have been used to solve a difficult problem in wage and salary administration upon which OR/MS tools have not ever been applied previously. This has been because OR/MS tools have never shown that they can be of assistance here. The achievement of OR/MS techniques on the multiple criteria salary midpoint determination problem has come about because

Table 4: Candidate Wage Plans of the Second Iteration

	Wage Plan					
	2-1	*2-2*	*2-3*	*2-4*	*2-5*	*2-6*
z_1	10000	9613	3673	5763	2153	0
z_2	94	9.0	9.3	10.2	10.3	6.6
z_3	16.6	15.9	16.8	18.5	25.6	30.4
z_4	9.1	8.7	7.6	7.9	3.4	8.0
z_5	16.6	15.9	12.5	12.5	7.6	8.6
x_1	25000	25217	26249	26249	27692	27412
x_2	18000	18391	19062	18625	20000	24670
x_3	16000	16394	17062	16625	18000	17817
x_4	10000	10217	10590	10347	10000	9137
x_5	7000	7000	7000	7000	7384	8137
x_6	6000	6000	6000	6000	6000	6000

Table 5: Candidate Wage Plans of the Third Iteration

	Wage Plan					
	3-1	*3-2*	*3-3*	*3-4*	*3-5*	*3-6*
z_1	2153	2210	2846	3000	3461	3673
z_2	10.3	10.9	9.3	6.6	9.5	9.3
z_3	25.6	31.5	30.2	28.8	30.7	16.8
z_4	3.4	2.6	3.9	8.3	3.9	7.6
z_5	7.6	5.2	7.6	11.1	7.6	12.5
x_1	27692	28421	27692	26666	27692	26249
x_2	20000	20000	20000	24000	20000	19062
x_3	18000	18000	18000	17333	18000	17062
x_4	10000	9473	9307	9000	9230	10590
x_5	7384	8000	8307	8000	8230	7000
x_6	6000	6000	6000	6000	6000	6000

of the recent availability of multiple objective methods, particularly those used in this paper.

Another interesting aspect of this application is that two different types of iterative processes are superimposed upon one another. Not only is the decision-maker conducting an exploration for his optimal point, but interwoven with it the decision-maker is refining the shape of his feasible region. Thus, beyond obtaining the most preferred solution with respect to a given feasible region, the decision-maker is able to obtain his most preferred solution over the wide variety of feasible regions at his disposal.

REFERENCES

1. Belcher, D. W. *Compensation Administration.* Englewood Cliffs, N.J.: Prentice-Hall, 1975.
2. Keeney, R. L. and H. Raiffa. *Decisions with Multiple Objectives: References and Value Tradeoffs.* New York: Wiley, 1976.
3. Lee, S. M. *Goal Programming for Decision Analysis* Philadelphia: Auerbach, 1972.
4. Nash, A. N. and S. J. Carroll. *The Management of Compensation.* Belmont, Ca.: Wadsworth, 1975.
5. Steuer, R. E. "Operating Manual for the ADBASE/FILTER Computer Package for Solving Multiple Objective Linear Programming Problems," (Release: 5/78), No. BA 7, College of Business and Economics, University of Kentucky, 1977.
6. Steuer, R. E. "An Interactive Multiple Objective Linear Programming Procedure," *TIMS Studies in the Management Sciences,* Vol. 6, 1977, pp. 225–239.
7. Steuer, R. E. and A. T. Schuler. "An Interactive Multiple Objective Linear Programming Approach to a Problem in Forest Management," *Operations Research,* Vol. 26, No. 2, 1978, pp. 254–269.
8. Steuer, R. E. "Vector-Maximum Gradient Cone Contraction Techniques," *Multiple Criteria Problem Solving,* Heidelberg: Springer-Verlag, 1978, pp. 462–481.
9. Soyster, A. L., B. Lev and D. I. Toof. "Conservative Linear Programming with Mixed Multiple Objectives," *OMEGA,* Vol. 5, No. 2, 1977, pp. 193–205.
10. Wallenius, J. "Interactive Multiple Criterion Decision Methods: An Investigation and an Approach," Helsinki: Helsinki School of Economics, 1975.

16.
Computerization of Absentee Control Programs

John Scherba and Lyle Smith

An aspect of absenteeism that is currently growing in volume and importance is absence *with* permission. An analysis of attendance records of chronic absentees will frequently reveal large numbers of absences that are excused by supervisors. This factor which is almost always present in attendance records of alcoholics is now becoming more prominent in those of the nonalcoholic absentee. We might speculate that this is being caused by a general growth of permissiveness coupled with employee job boredom, high wages, and liberal benefits.

The chronic absentee, like the alcoholic, learns to become a very talented teller of tales when he requests permission for a day off work. It is an unfortunate fact that the supervisor will often "go along" and grant the request. This usually happens because the supervisor doesn't have current and concise information of the extent or pattern of absences for his employees. Supervisors also tend to be more tolerant of employees in jobs that do not need to be filled by other employees on overtime. If the job "runs dry," the inefficiency is there, but the pressure of a direct overtime cost isn't present.

Need For Detailed Individual Attendance Records

Many companies keep statistical records of attendance by plants or departments, but fail to maintain current records on individual employees because of the sheer volume, expense and drudgery of such recordkeeping.

Departmental summaries are valuable in detecting trends or identifying departments with special problems. However, they can also hide the single chronic absentee in a large department and distort records in a small one. In some instances it is difficult to identify a chronic absentee if he spreads his absences and is not involved in problems of poor workmanship or discipline.

A broad attack on the program requires that chronic absentees be identified and dealt with on an individual basis. Individual employee trends in absenteeism should be monitored to make possible counseling of problem employees before they become chronic.

Individual absence records can also reveal patterns in absences such as days after payday, Mondays and Fridays, or weekend absences for rotating shift employees. Analyses of absence records can also provide clues to cases of alcoholism, drug abuse, poor adjustment to the job, and mental illness.

Absenteeism has actually raged out of control on occasion in individual plants that embody large work forces and heavy automation. An article in Fortune Magazine described an incident in a major automobile manufacturing plant where over 200 absences occurred on one shift employing 2,000 men. In most companies, absenteeism isn't that dramatic, but it exists virtually everywhere as a major problem.

Computerization as a Tool

The mechanics of an absentee control program are often cumbersome and involve lengthy and tedious clerical operations, with accompanying errors, especially in programs covering large numbers of employees. Computerization of absence records is a logical solution to the problem of identifying employees with absenteeism problems and providing accurate records of attendance. A concise and accurate report that is current can be a tool of great value to supervisors in carrying out attendance control at the first-line level.

The following is a description of a computerized program in a plant of approximately 2,000 employees that evolved over a ten year period from a manual clerical operation.

178

Objectives of the Program

The program has two main objectives:

1. To accurately and efficiently record absence information through data processing with print out sheets using language that is in readable form rather than codes. This permits thorough and easy understanding of the information by persons not accustomed to computer information.
2. To establish a method of identifying problem absentees so that individual counseling or necessary disciplinary action can be taken as steps to reduce absenteeism and its accompanying costs.

General Description of the Program

Information regarding absences is provided daily on record sheets by the supervisor who is responsible for timekeeping in his department. In an effort to reduce clerical work and accompanying costs, absence information is handled in conjunction with a report for pay purposes dealing with daily job assignments (Exhibit 1). Absence information is later extracted by the Data Processing section.

This method of getting information to the computer is arbitrary. In smaller plants, it may be more practical to place central responsibility for reporting absences in the Personnel Department and information may be put into the computer weekly rather than daily.

The output from the computer consists of two major sections. The first section covers basic reporting and permits a fast and efficient method of recording and reviewing an employee's attendance record. The second section involves a special chronic report which identifies employees with poor attendance records and provides detailed information about their attendance. Below, the output is briefly outlined.

BASIC REPORTING / *Weekly*—This is an alphabetical listing of all absences for the week. There are no totals (Exhibit 2).

Monthly and Quarterly—These are alphabetical listings of each employee's absences for the month and quarter. There is a section below his name which summarizes his monthly or quarterly record and his year-to-date record. This report also contains a separate section which summarizes the total absentee record for the quarter by departments (Exhibit 3).

Annual—This is an alphabetical listing of each employee's absences for the year. There is a section below his name which summarizes his yearly record (Exhibit 4). This report also contains a separate section which summarizes the total absence record for the year by departments (Exhibit 4).

Because of the requirements that exist at the plant in question, this division in reporting was considered necessary in order to have at least a weekly updating

Exhibit 1

ABSENTEE/FORCE REPORT

DEPT. ___45___   DATE ___8-11-72___

REASON FOR ABSENCE CODES

NON-CHARGEABLE	CHARGEABLE
II – INDUSTRIAL INJURY LA – LEAVE OF ABSENCE SW – SHARE THE WORK NA – NO WORK AVAILABLE U – UNION J – JURY DUTY F – OFF - ELIG. FOR FUNERAL PAY USE ABOVE REASONS WITH "EXCUSED" TYPE OF ABSENCE.	OS – SICK AW – AUTO WRECK SF – SICKNESS IN FAMILY OT – OUT OF TOWN DR – DOCTOR EH – EMER. AT HOME PB – PERSONAL BUSINESS DL – DISCIP. LAYOFF SL – OVERSLEPT C – COURT CT – CAR TROUBLE W – WEATHER DO NOT USE ABOVE REASONS WITH "EXCUSED" TYPE OF ABSENCE.

NOTE: OFF FOR "VACATION" OR "SCHEDULED OFF" SHOULD BE "√" OR "X" IN THE APPLICABLE COLUMN. DO NOT SHOW "VACANCY FILLED" FOR THE ABOVE.

VACANCY FILLED — SHOW HOURS OF ABSENCE IN THESE COLUMNS FOR COLUMNS 3-9 AND HOW FILLED

COLUMN	1	2	3	4	5	6	7	8	9	ST	OT	DT	NF
NAME / I.D. No.	VACATION	SCHEDULED OFF	EXCUSED (E)	DID NOT REPORT (DN)	REPORTED OFF (RO)	LATE REPORTED OFF (LR)	LATE TO WORK (L)	HOME EARLY (HE)	DISCIPLINE LAYOFF (DL)				
John Doe — 35	X												
Frank Smith — 1012			J								8		
William Williams — 1927								PB					2
Fred Thompson — 2012					OS								8
Sam Doe — 123					CT						8		
Joe Blue — 463							SL						1

APPROVAL _____

Exhibit 2: Weekly Absentee Report

Week Ending: 8-30-72

NAME	INIT.	CLOCK NO.	DEPT.	SHIFT	DAY	DATE	TYPE OF ABSENCE	REASON FOR ABSENCE	NO. HRS. OFF	HOW FILLED	CHRONIC
BLACK	R.	1	2	1	MON	08-24-72	REPORTED OFF	SICK	8.00	NF	PROD – CHRONIC
BLACK	R.	1	2	1	TUE	08-25-72	REPORTED OFF	SICK	8.00	NF	PROD – CHRONIC
BLACK	R.	1	2	1	WED	08-26-72	REPORTED OFF	SICK	8.00	NF	PROD – CHRONIC
BLACK	R.	1	2	1	THU	08-27-72	REPORTED OFF	SICK	8.00	NF	PROD – CHRONIC
BLACK	R.	1	2	1	FRI	08-28-72	REPORTED OFF	SICK	8.00	NF	PROD – CHRONIC
BROWN	S.	7	13	1	THU	08-27-72	EXCUSED	JURY DUTY	N/C 8.00		
DOE	J.	10	50	1	MON	08-24-72	REPORTED OFF	SICK	8.00	NF	MAINT – CHRONIC
DOE	J.	10	50	1	TUE	08-25-72	REPORTED OFF	SICK	8.00	NF	MAINT – CHRONIC
DOE	J.	10	50	1	WED	08-26-72	REPORTED OFF	SICK	8.00	NF	MAINT – CHRONIC
DOE	J.	10	50	1	THU	08-27-72	REPORTED OFF	SICK	8.00	NF	MAINT – CHRONIC
DOE	J.	10	50	1	FRI	08-28-72	REPORTED OFF	AUTO WRECK	8.00	NF	
GREEN	J.	21	36	1	WED	08-26-72	EXCUSED	UNION N/C	8.00	NF	
GREY	F.	29	27	1	FRI	08-28-72	EXCUSED	LV. OF ABS. N/C	2.50	NF	
JONES	A.	35	16	1	MON	08-24-72	REPORTED OFF	SICKNESS-FAMILY	8.00	NF	PROD – CHRONIC

Exhibit 3: Monthly Absentee Report

Month Ending 07-31-72

NAME	INIT.	CLOCK NO.	DEPT.	SHIFT	DAY	DATE	TYPE OF ABSENCE	REASON FOR ABSENCE	NO. HRS. OFF	HOW FILLED	CHRONIC
JONES	R.	301	51	1	WED	07-05-72	REPORTED OFF	PERSONAL BUS.	.50	NF	
		(YTD* TOTALS)	NO. OCCURRENCES	OCCURRENCES		11	(MONTHLY TOTALS)	NO. OCCURRENCES	1		
			HRS.	CHG.		80.00		HRS. CHG.	.50		
			HRS.	N/C		2.00		HRS. N/C	.00		
			HRS.	EXCUSED		.00		HRS. EXCUSED	.00		
SMITH	D.	4199	53	1	WED	07-05-72	REPORTED OFF	CAR TROUBLE	2.50	NF	
		(YTD TOTALS)	NO. OCCURRENCES	OCCURRENCES		12	(MONTHLY TOTALS)	NO. OCCURRENCES	1		
			HRS.	CHG.		144.00		HRS. CHG.	2.50		
			HRS.	N/C		6.50		HRS. N/C	.00		
			HRS.	EXCUSED		.00		HRS. EXCUSED	.00		
DOE	J.	9208	02	1	SUN	07-16-72	HOME EARLY	SICK	2.00	NF	
		(YTD TOTALS)	NO. OCCURRENCES	OCCURRENCES		1	(MONTHLY TOTALS)	NO. OCCURRENCES	1		
			HRS.	CHG.		2.00		HRS. CHG.	2.00		
			HRS.	N/C		.00		HRS. N/C	.00		
			HRS.	EXCUSED		.00		HRS. EXCUSED	.00		

* YEAR TO DATE

Exhibit 4: Annual Absentee Report

DATE: 12-31-71

NAME	INIT.	CLOCK NO.	DEPT.	SHIFT	DAY	DATE	TYPE OF ABSENCE	REASON FOR ABSENCE	NO. HRS. OFF	HOW FILLED	CHRONIC
SMITH	D.	2348	24	1	MON	02-13-71	REPORTED OFF	OVERSLEPT	8.00	OT	PROD - CHRONIC
SMITH	D.	2348	24	1	THU	02-18-71	REPORTED OFF	CAR TROUBLE	8.00	OT	PROD - CHRONIC
SMITH	D.	2348	24	1	FRI	02-19-71	OFF CONTINUED	SICK	8.00	OT	PROD - CHRONIC
SMITH	D.	2348	24	1	SAT	05-27-71	REPORTED OFF	DISC. LAYOFF	8.00	OT	PROD - CHRONIC
SMITH	D.	2348	24	1	MON	06-28-71	REPORTED OFF	SICKNESS-FAMILY	1.00	NF	PROD - CHRONIC
SMITH	D.	2348	24	1	FRI	07-02-71	REPORTED OFF	SICKNESS-FAMILY	6.00	NF	PROD - CHRONIC
SMITH	D.	2348	24	1	THU	07-08-71	REPORTED OFF	SICKNESS-FAMILY	8.00	OT	PROD - CHRONIC
SMITH	D.	2348	24	1	SAT	12-06-71	REPORTED OFF	SICKNESS-FAMILY	8.00	OT	PROD - CHRONIC

(YTD TOTALS) NO. CHG. OCC 20

HRS. CHG. 155.00

HRS. N/C .00

HRS. EXCUSED .00

of information. When the quarterly report is published, the weekly reports are discarded. This occurs on a continuing basis. The annual report is the only report maintained as a permanent record.

CHRONIC REPORTING / Each quarter a special Chronic Absentee Report is compiled. This section of the program is designed to produce a list of the top 100 absentee offenders. These 100 or so employees have met special requirements which identify a chronic absentee based on that employee's previous 12 month record. It consists of a combination of the number of days missed and the number of separate absences (approximately 14 days and 7 occurrences). Once the record identifies the employees as chronic, a list of their individual records is prepared. This list is arranged by departments, and has a section below each employee's name which summarizes his quarterly record and his year-to-date record.

From the 100 absentee offenders identified by this list, the computer then selects the top 25 people in Production and the top 25 in Maintenance departments. These 50 people are then followed for the entire next quarter. A list, by department order, is prepared weekly for the Production Department and a separate list is prepared for Maintenance Department, covering the weekly record of these 50 people. This list is sent directly to the designated supervisor in the respective areas who is charged with the responsibility for implementing corrective action in his department.

The Chronic Report output is designed to allow line personnel to follow a limited number of people in an effort to correct their records. Operating on a management by exception basis, it has been shown that by concentrating on a few people, there is a greater chance for more effective, immediate results. The overall program has also served as a deterrent to those absentees not identified as top offenders.

Special Individual Reports

The computer program has also been designed so that on special request, a record of a particular department or a particular man for a specific time period can be run anytime during the year. This phase of the program can be used for a specific employee or employees and is especially valuable if discipline is being considered.

When the employee is identified as a chronic absentee, his supervisor is in a position to be alert to subsequent absences. The employee can then be counseled concerning his attendance. If unauthorized absence persists, absentee investigations at the employee's home are conducted by members of the Personnel Department and progressive discipline is administered, if warranted.

If medical problems are present, the case is referred to the plant physician for review. When identified, alcoholics are counseled by the Personnel Department and are also referred to the local Alcoholics Anonymous Chapter.

Absentee investigation at the employee's home has proven important in securing information relative to the cause of the absences. It has also served as a deterrent in controlling some cases. Considerable success has been experienced in departments where supervisors use individual attendance records in employee counseling on a continuing basis. Detailed records also serve as effective documentation for administering progressive discipline where all other attempts have failed.

The control of absenteeism is a mandatory program in any business or industrial operation that seeks effective management of its workers. Where large numbers of employees are involved, a move to computerization from manual posting or from no individual records at all may be an effective and economical move.

17.
The Computer's Uses and Potential in Bargaining: A Management View

William G. Caples

Introduction

The technological response to demands of physical systems and scientific-engineering applications in both the public and the private sector has been phenomenal in the past decade. A concomitant of this development has been the growth and refinement of information technology essential to the manipulation and communication of factual data. The precision of treatment and predictability of data in the physical sciences provided logical fields for computer applications in the past two decades.

Editors' Note: Reprinted from *The Impact of Computers on Collective Bargaining* by Abraham J. Siegel, ed., by permission of The M.I.T. Press, Cambridge, Massachusetts. Copyright © 1969 by The Massachusetts Institute of Technology.

The quantification, manipulation, and communication of data reflecting human action and interaction present a somewhat more difficult problem. Perhaps this accounts for the lag in computer utilization in the industrial relations field.

There can be no question of the fact that the computer has increasingly come to play a significant role in the management of American business. At the same time, it should be noted that its use has been uneven when viewed against the wide variety of possible applications. Only limited use has been made of EDP in industrial relations; and, as Charles Myers observed at the winter meeting of the Industrial Relations Research Association in 1966, ". . . the use of computers in preparing for collective bargaining is even newer. Possibly some firms have used computerized employee records to calculate costs of alternative management proposals or union demands, but I am not aware that any have access to data banks containing information on what other firms have done in collective bargaining."[1]

Since we are at the threshold of possible expansion of information technology into the field of collective bargaining, it seemed to me that it would be most helpful to explore two principal areas: one, the current practice or state of the art in management's use of EDP in collective bargaining; and two, suggestions regarding current limitations and the prospects for future applications.

A search of the literature and a variety of personal contacts revealed that considerable attention has been given to the application of EDP to the general field of personnel administration.[2] There is no need on this occasion to review this material in depth, but I would like to call attention to two surveys in which reference was made—or significantly omitted—to applications to collective bargaining.

Bueschel,[3] for example, surveyed eighty-nine industrial firms, government agencies, and nonprofit institutions to determine actual and potential applications of data processing in the personnel department (broadly defined). Bueschel's primary interest was in the impact of real-time systems on the personnel function, but some of his findings are pertinent to our discussion.

Of the eighty-nine companies surveyed, about two-thirds had been using data

[1]C. A. Myers, "Some Implications of Computers for Management," *Proceedings of the Nineteenth Annual Winter Meeting, Industrial Relations Research Association,* San Francisco, December 28–29, 1966, Madison, Wisconsin: The Association, 1967, p. 200.

[2]Barrie Austin, "The Role of EDP in Personnel," *Management of Personnel Quarterly,* Vol. 3, No. 4, Winter 1965, pp. 24–30; R. T. Bueschel, "How EDP Is Improving the Personnel Function," *Personnel,* September/October 1964, pp. 59–64; R. T. Bueschel, *Management Bulletin 86: EDP and Personnel,* American Management Association, 1966; R. T. Bueschel, "Real-time Data Processing for Industrial Relations," *Management of Personnel Quarterly,* Spring 1966, pp. 24–30; E. Lanham, "EDP in the Personnel Department," *Personnel,* March/April 1967, pp. 16–22; Julius Rezler, "Automation and the Personnel Manager," *Advanced Management Journal,* Vol. 32, No. 1, January 1967, pp. 76–81; University of California, Institute of Industrial Relations, *Electronic Data Processing and Personnel Management,* Los Angeles, California: The Institute, 1967.

[3]Bueschel, *supra.*

processing for an average of three years. This fact may be somewhat misleading in terms of computer applications since about a third of this number were still using electric accounting machines (EAM). Data processing was being used extensively in the personnel function by about 25 percent of the companies surveyed. Of those not using data processing, fully two-thirds had plans to implement a program within a year. On the other hand, one in ten companies had no intention of using data processing.

Pertinent to the present inquiry is the frequency of use in these eighty-nine companies of EDP for labor relations. Seventeen companies, or 27 percent of the sample, reported using computers for "labor relations and seniority." This is substantially below the 82 percent who reported EDP applications for employee records and the 78 percent reporting uses for compensation purposes. In terms of other functional applications, 36 percent of the companies surveyed used EDP for skills inventory, 26 percent for employment, 18 percent for testing, 8 percent for attendance, 6 percent for personnel research, 4 percent for medical, and 3 percent for safety.

Elizabeth Lanham[4] surveyed 333 companies in a wide variety of industries to determine the impact of EDP on the personnel function. Of these firms, 254 utilized EDP in one or more phases of their operation. When it came to EDP applications in the personnel field, however, applications were much less frequent. Only 142 of the 254 EDP users were using it for personnel records and reports; 97 companies were planning to extend EDP to include personnel uses; and 94 of the 333 companies reported no EDP planning for personnel records and reports. Lanham's report referred to bargaining-related usage (e.g., grievance records, payroll analysis) but it did not reveal any specific applications to collective bargaining.

The Survey

In the absence of any systematic collection of data dealing with the applications of EDP to collective bargaining, we decided to conduct a questionnaire survey in an attempt to identify the state of the art in this specific field. The questionnaire was designed to obtain information regarding:

1. The availability of data for EDP processing.
2. Computer usage in preparation for bargaining.
3. Computer usage during bargaining.
4. Problems and limitations in the use of computers for bargaining and preparation for bargaining.
5. The use being made of computers by unions with which respondents were negotiating.

[4]Lanham, "EDP in the Personnel Department."

6. Their viewpoints regarding limitations and the prospects for use of computers in collective bargaining.

The survey sample was drawn from the firms listed in the 1967 *Fortune* Directory; and it included the one hundred largest manufacturing corporations, twenty-five transportation companies, twenty-five life insurance companies, twenty-five commercial banks, twenty-five merchandising organizations, and twenty-five utilities.

THE RESPONDENTS / Replies were received from 96 of the 225 organizations included in the survey. As might be expected, the heaviest response came from industrial and manufacturing organizations. A detailed analysis of respondents by industry group in relation to company size measured by number of bargaining unit employees can be found in Table 1.

You will also note that ten of the ninety-six reporting companies indicated that they had no collective bargaining agreements. An additional eighteen companies replied by letter stating that although labor agreements were negotiated, they made no use or only very limited use of computers in their bargaining. Three of these eighteen companies reported that they were exploring the use of computers for bargaining. Four others replied that bargaining was done locally at many different locations involving small numbers of employees. It was their feeling that the circumstances did not seem conducive to computer usage. It was not possible to include these companies in the cross-tabulations, but they will be considered later in the analysis.

Completed questionnaires were received from sixty-eight organizations including fifty-five manufacturing corporations, six transportation companies, six utilities, and one merchandising organization. The number of bargaining unit employees in these companies ranged from 2,500 to just over 400,000 employees. The median bargaining unit employment was approximately 22,000 employees.

NUMBER OF UNIONS / Presumably one of the important variables in determining computer usage in collective bargaining would be the number of unions involved in negotiations with a particular company. A simple tabulation (Table 2) indicates that responding companies negotiate with as few as one union in a single location to as many as eighty-five independent unions at as many locations.

Between these two extremes, however, the data are not as clear-cut. Some respondents reported only the names of international unions with whom they negotiated. Others reported in terms of local unions, and some companies reported both the internationals and the number of locals in each with which bargaining agreements were made.

An examination of the data shows no clearly discernible pattern of relationship between the number of bargaining unit employees and the number of unions involved in negotiations. One company dealing with 85 independent unions had 7,700 employees in bargaining units ranging from 6 to 2,150 employees. Another

Table 1: Distribution of Respondents by Company Size and Major Industrial Classification

Industry Group	Number of Companies Solicited	Respondents by Letter: Do Not Use Computers in Bargaining	Respondents with No Bargaining Unit Employees	Respondents by Questionnaire: Number of Bargaining Unit Employees (in thousands)						Total Respondents
				Under 10	10–24	25–49	50–99	100–Over	Subtotal	
Manufacturing	100	16	3	15	17	12	8	3	55	74
Transportation	25	1		0	2	3	1	0	6	7
Finance	25		5	0	0	0	0	0	0	5
Utilities	25			2	3	1	0	0	6	6
Merchandising	25			0	0	0	0	1	1	1
Insurance	25	1	2	0	0	0	0	0	0	3
Totals	225	18	10	17	22	16	9	4	68	96

Table 2: Number of Unions Dealt With, by Company Size (Number of Bargaining Unit Employees)

Number of Unions	Number of Bargaining Unit Employees (in thousands)					
	Under 10	10–24	25–49	50–99	100– Over	Total
1	3	2	2	0	0	7
2–5	6	12	8	4	4	34
6–10	4	3	2	2	0	11
11–20	2	0	1	0	0	3
21–50	0	4	3	3	0	10
Over 50	1	1	0	0	0	2
Unreported	1	0	0	0	0	1
Total Number of Companies	17	22	16	9	4	68

company reported 150 individual plant agreements with 27 international unions covering a total work force of 22,000 people. At the other extreme, a steel company reported one union agreement covering a 25,000 employee bargaining unit.

However, for the sample of responding companies, multiple unions are the rule. The median number of independents or international unions bargained with is probably about four per company, while the median number of locals is on the order of eight per company. Because of reporting variations, there is a distinct possibility that these estimates are understated. A complete enumeration of the number of separate agreements per company would, I suspect, double these median figures.

A further examination of the data reveals that where multiple union representation is found, there is no simple pattern of distribution of employees among bargaining units. There is a range from a concentration of employees in one union with only small numbers in all others to a fairly even distribution among all unions represented. For example, one manufacturer reported as follows: International Association of Machinists and Aerospace Workers (IAMAW)—22,341 members; International Brotherhood of Electrical Workers (IBEW)—309; International Brotherhood of Firemen and Oilers (IBFO)—39; International Brotherhood of Teamsters, Chauffeurs, Warehousemen, and Helpers of America (TCWH)—76; UPGWA—211. This pattern was more or less typical in steel, auto manufacture, aircraft manufacture, and the farm equipment industries. In chemical, oil, and other industries the number of workers per union tended to be more equally distributed. For example, in one such company, the distribution was: International Chemical Workers Union (ICWU)—2,480 members; Oil, Chemical, and Atomic Workers International Union (OCAWIU)—2,320; International Union of Operating Engineers (IUOE)—930; United Steelworkers of America

(USWA)—830; United Mine Workers of America (UMW)—240; International Brotherhood of Electrical Workers (IBEW)—240; and 17 other unions with less than 200 members each.

The existence of multiple unions in a company is important, I believe, with regard to the use of computers in bargaining for two reasons: first, the presence of multiple unions and many agreements suggests the desirability of a system of contract comparison which might be computer based; and second, one pattern of distribution may be more conducive to the adoption of EDP for bargaining purposes than other patterns of distribution.

FREQUENCY OF CONTRACT NEGOTIATIONS / Another factor to consider in terms of preparation for bargaining is the frequency with which contracts are renegotiated. At one extreme is the possibility of continuous bargaining such as exists under the railroad agreements. Although such conditions may involve only a limited number of issues, preparation for bargaining may be pursued on a continuing basis. At the other end of the continuum, a contract reopened as infrequently as every five years tends to result in a burst of preparatory activity beginning a few months before the reopening date. In companies with multiple agreements, it is characteristic to find that contract termination dates are spread out in time so that collective bargaining at some location is almost a constant occurrence (Table 3).

In the sample of companies for which data were available, the modal frequency of contract negotiations was every three years. Almost half (thirty-one) of the companies reported that their agreements covered this span of time. Only two companies reported longer term agreements.

Table 3: Average Frequency of Contract Negotiations, by Company Size (Number of Bargaining Unit Employees)

Negotiation Frequency	Number of Bargaining Unit Employees (in thousands)					
	Under 10	10–24	25–49	50–99	100– Over	Total
Every 1–3 Years	2	1	0	0	0	3
1–4 Years	0	1	1	0	0	2
Every 2 Years	3	7	2	0	0	12
2–3 Years	6	2	4	1	0	13
Every 3 Years	5	10	8	6	2	31
3–5 Years	0	0	0	1	0	1
Continuously	0	0	0	0	1	1
Unreported	1	1	1	1	1	5
Total Number of Companies	17	22	16	9	4	68

THE DATA BASE / In terms of current practice, the spread of union agreements and the frequency of contract negotiations are only two of many significant variables to consider in evaluating computer usage for contract negotiations. A highly significant factor is the data base available for use in this regard.

In an attempt to assess this important variable, thirteen items were listed in the questionnaire for respondents to check if they were maintaining data on machine records and had them available for electronic data processing. The items selected included a sample of those which seem most relevant to preparation for collective bargaining. For any one company, the median number of items reported in this sample was six. There were no significant differences found in the availability of data on the basis of comparisons by company size (Table 4).

On the basis of this information it must be concluded that only limited data are currently available on machine records. Most companies—at least seven out of ten—have a basic employee record, a machine records current payroll system, a record of premiums paid for the employee benefits package, and a machine records pension system. However, less than half of the companies maintain historical wage and salary data. Of those that do retain historical data in this area, the most frequent retention time is five years. A number of reporting companies maintained records for one or two years while a few have data for ten or more years. It was interesting to note that companies with the longest historical payroll records were not necessarily those companies with extensive data bases in other areas. Just over a third of the respondents maintain machine records on time not worked where significant costs might be incurred (i.e., absenteeism, vacation time off, sick leave, and so forth).

Looking at the employee benefit area, we find that two-thirds of our reporting companies have machine records showing data on plan participation and premiums paid. Almost half of them have information available on charges and benefits paid out. On the other hand, only eighteen percent had case data available to analyze such factors as length of hospital stay, surgical procedures, nature of illness, and so forth. This type of information is of real significance in terms of negotiations for benefit packages. Most companies find it necessary to go to the jacket files, pull a large sample of cases, and tabulate case history data in order to tailor coverages to areas of greatest need. Studies of this type are required prior to most negotiations. In our own case (i.e., Inland Steel), we have not maintained this type of information on machine records largely because of the cost. Apparently other companies have also concluded that the need does not warrant the cost.

Finally, the data base of reporting companies is almost nonexistent in areas of crucial interest. Five companies indicated that they have information about grievances and arbitrations in their data base and only two have used computers for recording and analyzing company labor contract clauses. No companies reported computer usage in connection with contract clauses in other company contracts.

Overall, one is forced to the conclusion that the data base on which bargain-

Table 4: Frequency of Inclusion of Items in the Data Base, by Company Size (Number of Bargaining Unit Employees)

Data Base Items	Number of Bargaining Unit Employees (in thousands)					Total	
	Under 10	10–24	25–49	50–99	100–Over	Number	Percentage
Basic Personnel Data[a]	17	17	15	8	3	60	88
Wage and Salary Data							
Current	17	15	16	9	3	60	88
Historical	7	6	9	5	2	29	43
Absenteeism	7	9	4	2	3	25	37
Sick Leave	10	10	3	5	2	30	44
Vacation Time Off	10	8	5	3	2	28	41
Grievances and Arbitrations	0	2	1	1	1	5	7
Employee Benefits							
Part. & prem. paid	13	15	11	7	3	49	72
Charges & ben. paid out	7	11	6	5	4	33	49
Case data[b]	1	5	2	3	1	12	18
Pensions	11	14	13	9	3	50	74
Contract Clauses							
For company contracts	0	1	0	0	1	2	3
For other-company cont.	0	0	0	0	0	0	0
Total Number of Companies	17	22	16	9	4	68	100

[a] Age, sex, length of service, marital status, etc.
[b] History of each hospital claim.

ing judgments must be made is limited. For most companies, available data involve a few standard items which are in the personnel records for other purposes including employee identification, payroll administration, and work force reporting.

USE OF COMPUTERS IN PREPARATION FOR BARGAINING / With this as background information, let us take a look at the way in which computers are currently being used to prepare for bargaining (Table 5).

The most common usage is to have routine reports produced by EDP and then have them reviewed and analyzed by hand methods with regard to bargaining issues. Another frequent application is to have special runs made to obtain computations and estimations through machine methods.

Only seven companies reported that anticipated demands are coded and entered into the computer with specially designed programs to obtain cost estimates directly from the computer. One company reported the development of mathematical models to project such factors as work force composition and enable them to use such projections in estimating the impact of probable or known bargaining demands.

Little or no use of computers in preparation for bargaining was reported by seventeen of the sixty-eight companies replying to the questionnaire. To get a

Table 5: Uses Made of the Computer in Preparation for Bargaining, by Company Size (Number of Bargaining Unit Employees)

Use Made	Number of Bargaining Unit Employees (in thousands)					
	Under 10	10–24	25–49	50–99	100– Over	Total
Little or None	7	6	3	1	0	17
Routine EDP Reports Reviewed and Hand Analyzed	12	14	14	5	2	47
Special Runs Obtained for Hand Analysis	10	15	9	6	3	43
Anticipated Demands Run on Speically Devised Programs	0	3	0	3	0	6
Mathematical Models Developed	0	1a	0	0	0	1
Total Number of Companies	17	22	16	9	4	68

aSuch models are being developed, and have not yet been used.

more realistic picture in this area, we should include in this analysis the fact that eighteen companies replied by letter to the effect that they did not use computers in their bargaining. This results in a finding that just over forty percent of our respondents are not using computers for this purpose. Again, we must conclude that the use of computers to prepare for bargaining is in its infancy—or possibly it is still in the foetal stage.

Anticipating this result, we asked these same companies to help us identify the problems which they encountered in attempting to develop computer applications. We have already noted the fact that the data base is quite inadequate at most companies. As you can see in Table 6, this is confirmed through the report of thirty-eight of the sixty-eight companies that necessary basic data are not available in a usable form for computer applications.

Another very common problem relates to programming. Almost half of the companies indicated that programming for special reports takes too long or they are faced with the fact that programmer time is not available. In reviewing this with our programmers, they felt this could have other causes, such as requests for special report programming failing to be clearly and simply stated or failure to ask for reservation of programmer time sufficiently in advance of need. Difficulty in obtaining time on the computer was cited as a problem by twenty of the sixty-eight companies. In the opinion of twenty-seven companies, the type of analysis they required could be done just as quickly by hand methods.

The basic problems in using computers in preparation for bargaining can be summarized under the headings of utility, programming, and the high cost of both computers and programming time.

Table 6: Problems Encountered in Using Computer, by Company Size (Number of Bargaining Unit Employees)

| Problem | Number of Bargaining Unit Employees (in thousands) | | | | | |
	Under 10	10–24	25–49	50–99	100– Over	Total
Data Not Available	9	9	13	5	2	38
Difficult to Get Computer Time	5	6	5	3	1	20
Programming Takes Too Long	7	9	10	3	2	31
Hand Methods as Fast	10	7	6	2	2	27
Other	2	4	1	2	1	10
Total Number of Companies	17	22	16	9	4	68

USE DURING BARGAINING / Another dimension of the topic under discussion involves the use of computers during bargaining (Table 7), as opposed to their use in preparing for negotiations. As might be expected, companies reported even less usage of computers during bargaining than in their preparatory work.

We received no indication of any company having developed mathematical models or simulations in order to test and keep current an analysis of the effects of alternate demand packages and company offers. Three companies reported that bargaining demands are fed into the computer for cost estimates and similar analyses on a real-time basis.

The most common usage was in the preparation of routine or special reports that required further analysis by hand methods in order to obtain meaningful information. Over one-half of the companies reported that they made little or no use of computers during bargaining, if we include our letter responses along with those obtained from the questionnaire.

The same kinds of problems were noted with regard to using computers during bargaining as those identified in the area of preparing for negotiations. In addition, there were a number of comments which might best be summarized in the words of one respondent who wrote: "The use of computers presupposes considerable advance understanding of the problem scope, availability of accurate input, reliable factor weighting, and logical resolution of problems; somehow those elements still are rarities in the bargaining process."

Table 7: Use Made of Computers During the Bargaining, by Company Size (Number of Bargaining Unit Employees)

Uses	Number of Bargaining Unit Employees (in thousands)					
	Under 10	10–24	25–49	50–99	100– Over	Total
Practically None	12	9	6	1	0	28
Routine Reports Analyzed by Hand	6	5	5	2	2	20
Special Reports Analyzed by Hand	7	11	11	7	3	39
Demands Analyzed on Real-Time Bases	0	1	1	1	0	3
Simulations and Math Models Used	0	0	0	0	0	0
Describe	0	4	3	2	2	11
Total Number of Companies	17	22	16	9	4	68

UNION RELATIONSHIPS / With this rather dismal view of current management practice with regard to computer usage for bargaining purposes, we can turn briefly to an examination of the subject in relation to unions. We asked for a response to two general questions:

1. How does your use of computers enter into your relationship with the union(s) with which you negotiate?
2. To what extent do you judge the *principal* union with which you negotiate makes use of computers in preparing for your negotiations?

Table 8: Use of Computers and Relationship with Union, by Company Size (Number of Bargaining Unit Employees)

Use	Number of Bargaining Unit Employees (in thousands)					
	Under 10	10–24	25–49	50–99	100– Over	Total
Make Little Use	14	12	8	2	0	36
Use Results Insofar as Necessary	3	6	7	6	4	26
Share Data and Analyses	0	0	3	1	0	4
Cooperate with Union in Planning Special Analyses	1	3	1	1	0	6
Other	0	4	1	2	1	8
Total Number of Companies	17	22	16	9	4	68

Table 9: Estimated Union Use of Computer, by Company Size (Number of Bargaining Unit Employees)

Estimated Uses of Computer	Number of Bargaining Unit Employees (in thousands)					
	Under 10	10–24	25–49	50–99	100– Over	Total
Little or None	14	12	9	2	1	38
May Use, but Lack Data for Effective Job	4	7	7	5	2	25
Makes Sophisticated Use of Computers	0	0	1	1	1	3
Describe	2	2	2	2	1	9
Total Number of Companies	17	22	16	9	4	68

The pattern of replies is very similar to both of these inquiries (see Tables 8 and 9). Over fifty percent of the companies indicate that there is little or no use of computers in their union-management relationships. In the opinion of fifty-six percent of our respondents, the principal union with which they negotiate is not making use of computers in preparing for bargaining.

A number of companies indicate that they use the results of their analyses in discussions with the union if relevant issues arise. Only four companies indicated that they share their data and analyses with union representatives. There were six companies who stated that they do cooperate with the union in planning special analyses of data pertaining to bargaining issues. A few comments were received indicating that, in some instances, reports in tabular form are given to the union in such matters as seniority listings, work force additions, dues deductions, and the like.

In terms of union usage of computer applications, over one-third of the respondents indicated that while unions may use computers to analyze some data, they lack the data sources to do a very effective job. Three companies reported that the principal union with which they negotiated was making sophisticated use of the computer in developing, analyzing, and defending contract demands.

Since Mr. Ginsburg has prepared a paper on the unions' use of computers in bargaining, there is no need for me to devote any further time to this matter except to note that the state of the art appears to be about the same for both parties.

PLANS AND LIMITATIONS / I think it is fair to state further that we are probably at the same stage of the game in terms of future applications (Table 10). Two-thirds of our reporting companies stated that they did not have any plans formulated for computer applications in this area, but that they intended to develop applications at some future point in time. Thirteen of our companies stated that they had definite plans for such applications, while ten acknowledged that they had no plans for future applications at this time.

The kind of planning which is being done suggests that most attention is being given to the refinement of basic personnel data along with more sophisticated treatment of wage and benefit data. The other significant area of attention involves plans to develop internal catalogues of grievances, arbitrations, and contract clause references for use by the company.

We have already referred to some of the limitations expressed by our respondents. Cost factors, along with time considerations, were frequently mentioned. The function of the computer is viewed as being limited primarily to economic matters. In the view of many managers, contract issues do not lend themselves to mathematical treatment. Whether, or how, good models of complex gaming or strategy situations can be developed will be discussed elsewhere in this symposium.

It was pointed out by some companies that frequent bargaining in decentralized situations poses some difficult problems in special applications of computer

Table 10: Future Plans for Use of EDP in Bargaining, by Company Size (Number of Bargaining Unit Employees)

Plans	Number of Bargaining Unit Employees (in thousands)					
	Under 10	10–24	25–49	50–99	100– Over	Total
None	5	4	1	0	0	10
None Formulated, but Intend to Develop Uses	9	14	9	7	3	42
Plans Made	3	4	4	1	1	13
Total Number of Companies	17	22	16	9	4	68

technology. Others feel that computer hardware and software simply have not yet reached the level of sophistication required for use in collective bargaining. One of my colleagues in reading this disagreed, saying, "Not so; it is the human ability to make the logic explicit that is lacking." This issue, I am sure, will also be debated.

This does not mean, however, that the outlook for future usage is dim or discouraging. The utilization of coalition bargaining is seen as a force in the direction of greater application of information technology. Several companies indicated that while costs might be prohibitive to develop a computer application for their company, there is a real possibility of such a development if groups of employers can pool their resources or share a computer at a central location. Another force in the direction of computer applications is the acknowledged increase in the complexity of wage items, benefit packages, and other economic factors.

All in all, there is good evidence that most management people believe that there will be an increased use of computers in collective bargaining; but they aren't quite sure how or when this will come about.

The Problems and Potential for Computers in Collective Bargaining

In concluding this paper, I thought you might be interested in my own views on the matter. In order to present an informed viewpoint, I think we must examine the needs of collective bargaining, the problems which arise, and then ask ourselves how computer capabilities can serve these needs. We need to examine these relationships within the context of time, cost, and trends.

THE INFORMATION NEEDS / As I see it, there are three phases of bargaining activities that need to be examined with regard to potential computer applications.

Phase I encompasses all of those activities which relate to preparation for actual negotiations. The range of activities moves from statistical studies through problem areas under the existing agreement to an analysis of the social, economic, and political climate within which negotiations will be carried out.

Phase II might be defined to include activities carried out during the period of actual negotiations. Such activities involve face-to-face discussions across the bargaining table and the exchange of information, demands, and positions leading to discussions which culminate in a final agreement.

Phase III involves activities associated with the interpretation and administration of the contract provisions agreed upon at the bargaining table. Such activities would range from the processing of grievances and arbitration cases to recording and analyzing the impact of an economic package.

Information for effective decision making is vital during all three phases of the bargaining process. However, there are meaningful differences with regard to the type of information which may be required, the time factors involved, and the significance of the data in resolving issues.

As one of our respondents pointed out, "Contract issues are not of a mathematical nature." Furthermore, I am occasionally reminded of a printed admonition that reads, "My mind is made up—don't confuse me with facts." For a number of reasons such as these, I would predict that the development of computer applications in connection with Phase II activities will be the last to come on the scene.

We have already observed that applications in the human relations field have lagged behind computer usage for the manipulation and control of physical processes and interactions. Within the industrial relations area, we find the greatest use being made of computers in the field of personnel administration for purposes of counting and identifying people, recording and analyzing personnel actions, and the collection or payment of money. For these purposes, definitions can be precise and the process can be easily translated into symbolic language.

The same cannot be said with regard to most activities in the field of labor relations and collective bargaining. In this field, initial efforts have been associated with the manipulation of financial data reflecting cost per manhour, cost of insurance claims, and the cost of other benefit programs. Activities of this nature are primarily associated with Phase I, Preparation for Bargaining, or Phase III, Administration of the Agreement. This is not to say that information of this nature is not pertinent to the ongoing collective bargaining activities in Phase II. It is to say that computer applications with regard to manipulation of quantifiable data for use during negotiations have encountered some real problems. The treatment of data in Phase I and Phase III is based upon existing and known conditions. Basically, it is a recording of what has happened, not a projection of what will happen.

Projection of future events, even in the realm of economic data, rests on a set of assumptions. In many respects, such assumptions with regard to human behavior are founded on belief rather than experience. The importance of assumptions with regard to problem resolution in the mathematical and physical science fields is well known. They are equally important in dealing with problems of human behavior, but all too often assumptions relative to anticipated human behavior have proved to be erroneous when tested against actual experience. Rapid calculations, speedy transmission of data, and impressive printouts are of little value if the data rest on a set of assumptions that are open to question. It is true that you can set up a variety of hypotheses and assumptions to reflect various alternatives. When this is done, however, you run into some real problems in terms of time and cost pressures.

The critical factor is the problem of gaining acceptance of the assumptions upon which the data are based. The use of computers for the generation of data utilized at the bargaining table offers no greater assurance that the results of the analysis will be any more acceptable to the opposing party than data laboriously developed by hand methods. It is reasonable to assume that data which do not support a bargaining position or objective of one of the parties will be rejected by that party regardless of how it was developed.

For these and other reasons, I find it difficult to believe that computer applications will be a positive force in resolving bargaining issues at the bargaining table. Their greatest value will be in helping to arrive at positions prior to bargaining and identifying the results of agreed-upon contract provisions reflected in experience after the agreement has been reached.

The second application in the labor relations field involves attempts to compare contract clauses, provisions, and language in agreements with different unions or agreements with the same union in different geographical locations. The possibility of such action has already been demonstrated, and it would appear knowledge gained from the use of computers to retrieve case law, locate patents, and similar types of library activities would be helpful here. In many instances, such comparisons are already being made by hand methods. Machine methods would certainly be helpful as the number of contracts to be compared increases and the provisions of the agreements become more complex. Again, the value of such analysis relates to Phase I and Phase III of the negotiations. Results may lend support or weaken positions at the bargaining table, but they are not likely to be significant in resolving the issues.

As I see it at the present time, then, the growth area for computer applications relative to collective bargaining will be in preparing for negotiations and analyzing the impact of collective bargaining agreements in company operations. The use of computers during actual negotiations is apt to lag behind both of these areas.

PROBLEMS IN USING EDP / Within this conceptual framework, it might be well to note that there are some very real problems to be overcome in expanding the use of EDP for collective bargaining purposes. As indicated earlier, we need to examine the informational requirements of collective bargaining which might be served by machine methods within the context of time, cost, and trends in collective bargaining.

Computer applications in terms of machine capabilities can be divided into two general categories: one, applications involving the solution of programmed or well-structured problems; and two, those calling for the solution of nonspecifically programmed or poorly structured problems.

Examples of the former can be drawn from clerical and other routine jobs such as pricing orders by catalogue and working out payroll deductions, plus a long list of somewhat less repetitive jobs such as planning production and employment schedules or determining the product mix for an oil refinery. Examples of poorly structured problems are generally drawn from areas of decision making for which there is no exact precedent; i.e., a general's decision to attack or a company's decision to launch a particular sales campaign.

While it is true that the machine is developing many more capabilities than we dreamed of a few years ago, most of the "profitable" applications are still confined to such routine jobs as payroll functions, processing insurance data, making out accounts payable and receivable, and other ordinary business tasks.

Few people have speculated more boldly about the role of the computer in management than Herbert Simon. In his view, heuristically programmed computers (discovery of solutions to loosely structured problems) will be a long time surpassing men on jobs where they exercise their senses and muscles as well as their brains; i.e., examining a piece of tissue in medical diagnosis or the performance of work in face-to-face service jobs. Relative costs, Simon goes on, will decide who does the job.

Collective bargaining applications, by and large, fall into the area of poorly or loosely structured problem solving. As yet, computers put to heuristic problem solving do not have anything remotely like the advantage they have over man in arithmetic and scientific computing. There is still a substantial area of research and development required in this area. Hardware and software costs are, and will be, substantial. Yet, these are only a portion of the total cost considerations. For the moment, let us confine our discussion to applications involving existing equipment and techniques.

In many instances, the information required for collective bargaining is not collected in a routine fashion. In other cases, data available from routine reports designed for other purposes must be differentially treated. This means that something unusual or different has to be performed in order to obtain the desired results. Lacking the data base, time and money must be expended to secure the necessary information.

Furthermore, establishing data collection procedures to be carried out on a continuous basis where the use is limited to collective bargaining purposes is a costly matter. As we have seen, negotiating a contract is a sporadic and infrequent occurrence for any one company. Continuous bargaining is the exception rather than the rule. Issues change and information requirements vary in relation to the issues. The alternative to providing for continuous data collection is to develop specific programs and procedures for the collection of data to be used in each negotiation. Adopting this alternative poses time and cost problems that are equally serious although of a different type.

The problems of special programming and batch operations are not unique to computer applications in the field of collective bargaining. Frequent reference was made in our survey to difficulties in getting time on the computer. Others indicated that programmer time was not available. Computer personnel and equipment must be fully utilized in the day-to-day operation of the business if the cost of such an operation is to be supported. Intermittent demands for special applications are difficult to accommodate. Similarly, special programming skills required to service collective bargaining requirements may not be available within the company.

I feel sure that in many instances a cost-benefit analysis would reveal that hand methods of analyzing and interpreting data for collective bargaining purposes would be less costly from the standpoint of both time and money than machine methods. It is highly unlikely that small, single plant operations would either need or could afford the use of computers for their negotiations. As a company increases in size and scope of operation, communication requirements become more voluminous and complex. More machine applications become possible. Under some forms of coalition bargaining, computer applications may become almost mandatory. Clearly, the potential for EDP application is greater under conditions of industrywide bargaining than it is for negotiations involving one company and one bargaining unit.

To put it another way, the greatest impetus to the use of EDP for collective bargaining will come from trends toward increasing centralization of negotiations and the growing complexity of economic issues. In terms of present requirements and the state of the art, it seems to me that we would have to view the future of EDP applications in collective bargaining with cautious optimism.

THE FUTURE FOR COMPUTERS / We need to be alert to the progress and expanding technical capabilities of both hardware and software in the computer field. Advances in time-sharing and on-line capabilities should increase the feasibility of utilizing electronic data processing for collective bargaining purposes. We need to explore the possibility of computer applications in a number of areas. Some of the areas which might lend themselves to such applications are:

1. The analysis of actual costs of past contracts and their relation to the costs estimated at the time of the agreement.
2. Determination of relative costs of various package proposals.

3. Computation of costs to individual companies involved in industry or area-wide bargaining.
4. Analysis of the impact of compensation changes upon rate structures or price and profit levels.
5. The possibility of using the computer as a retrieval device for ascertaining comparable contract clauses during negotiations.
6. Analyzing the impact of contract clauses on workers and groups of workers depending upon different profiles, geographic areas, and production methods.

Such a listing is limited only by the imagination of people and a knowledge of machine capabilities. Perhaps we should examine the implications of computers for mediation and arbitration with programs and data available for analysis of prior agreements. It is certainly within the realm of possibility to consider the computer as a retrieval device for prior decisions and settlements. The day may even come when it is possible to resolve disputes through an essentially unbiased evaluation of facts. This, however, is easier to speculate upon than to achieve.

Taking a cold, hard look at the future of computer applications for collective bargaining from a management standpoint, it seems to me that much will depend upon four considerations:

1. A determining factor will be the extent to which we can develop a data base for collective bargaining so that it fits into other current and continuous uses.
2. The expansion of industrywide or coalition bargaining would be a strong positive force in the development of future applications.
3. The degree of attention, time, and money devoted to the development of software for use in bargaining will be a factor.
4. The progress which can be made in the development of computer utility service will influence the possibility of future applications.

Man-computer communication is increasing rapidly. Computers can provide management with an extension of time, personnel, and knowledge. Early computer applications were made possible by fitting a problem to a solution which could be programmed. Today, the types of problems which can be solved are restricted to those which fit certain closely defined rules. Eventually we can anticipate that computers will be available to people for use in problem solving and information processing, and the users will find that they have increasing power to structure and carry out solutions tailored to their problems.

Regardless of these developments, we will still be faced with the question, "To what extent can union-management negotiating issues be resolved on the basis of fact?" And, we are still faced with economic realities. The economics of the situation is well summarized in the remark of an airline pilot who, when asked if he worried over being replaced by an electronic guidance system, replied, "No. Where can you get a nonlinear servomechanism control device which can be produced by unskilled labor for $2,000 a month?"

An examination of current uses of the computer in business suggests that its key role might well be described as "artificial intelligence" *within well-defined business systems.* Research on computer methodology may lead to increases in the "artificial intelligence" aspects of the computer, but it is highly speculative to predict new computer capabilities which will be sufficiently basic and powerful to cause the development of a new outlook on business problems or a restructuring of the collective bargaining process.

Negotiating a labor agreement can scarcely be identified as a well-defined business system. On the other hand, the bargaining process is certainly a part of a highly complex informational system. Before we answer the question regarding computer applications in this field, it is important that we do some basic research with regard to the total informational system. Only then can we decide whether the technique and methodology are pertinent and effective.

I believe this is what our survey respondents implied when they indicated a posture of exploration and investigation. All would probably agree that the rate of progress of information technology in collective bargaining will be partially a matter of technological feasibility and partially a matter of economics. There is a third barrier—and an important one—which must be handled. This is the barrier of human acceptance and interpersonal relationships.

ADDITIONAL REFERENCES

"Computer Sits in on the Bargaining," *Business Week,* September 10, 1966, p. 154.

Norbert J. Esser, "The Computer—A Challenge to the Personnel Profession," *Personnel Journal,* Vol. 44, No. 6, June 1965, pp. 292–294.

Woodrow L. Ginsburg, "Labor Turns to the Computer," *IUD* Agenda, Vol. 3, No. 9, September 1967, pp. 26–30.

John F. Griffin, "Management Information Systems—A Challenge to Personnel," *Personnel Journal,* Vol. 46, No. 6, June 1967, pp. 371–373.

Daniel E. Knowles, "The Personnel Man as Business Systems Engineer," *Personnel,* Vol. 41, No. 2, March/April 1964, pp. 41–44.

John R. McNulty, "Computers May Have To Be Used To Keep Up With The Unions," *Canadian Personnel and Industrial Relations Journal,* Vol. 14, No. 1, January/February 1967, pp. 4–6.

Charles A. Myers, "New Frontiers for Personnel Management," *Personnel,* Vol. 41, No. 3, May/June 1964, pp. 31–38.

Part V
Issues

The basic issue raised in considering the application of computers in personnel administration can be simply stated: Do the benefits derived from such applications exceed the costs of developing and utilizing these methods? Several of the articles in this text have emphasized the importance of evaluating the cost effectiveness of computerized personnel information systems and problem-solving techniques. In addition to this issue, several others confront the personnel administrator in turning to electronic data processing for assistance. Three of these issues are explored in this section: the possible conflict between managers and computer specialists, the use of time-sharing consulting services, and the legal restraints and requirements upon personnel administration.

The communications gap between the users of computer systems and the technicians who design and maintain them has too often been a limiting factor in the application of computer technology to organizational problems. Elliot and Haynes discuss the nature of the problem and point out the key role held by top management in narrowing this communication gap. They offer six specific steps that can be taken to reduce the conflict and bring about more effective use of the computer.

It is often difficult for an organization to know when to rely on its own services and when it would be more feasible to engage the services of an outside consultant. Dukes, in his article on "The Role of Time-Sharing Consulting Services for Personnel," attempts to provide some guidelines for making use of outside services with respect to the organization's personnel resource system. The article also provides information concerning those functions related to the initial and continuing development of a personnel resource information system and to the ways in which the best combination of the organization's and the consultant's resources and services can be used.

The proliferation of labor laws and regulations has put extra demands upon personnel administrators to insure that all personnel programs are in compliance with legal requirements and that sufficient information is available to supply required reports and records. Miller examines selected laws and regulations that affect information management and information-handling activities of organizations in both the public and private sectors. Of particular interest to the personnel administrator is the section on employee protection laws: the Equal Employment Opportunity Act, the Occupational Safety and Health Act, and the Employee Retirement Income Security Act. The author suggests that managers and information specialists take a more active role in gaining knowledge about present and future laws and regulations and applying such knowledge when developing and operating organizational information systems.

18.
Resolving a Growing Conflict: Management and Computer Specialists

Clifford Elliott and Joel Haynes

A growing problem in today's business world is that the technical capabilities of computer systems often outpace management's ability to utilize them effectively.

As a consequence of rapid technological advances, the quality and quantity of technical skills must be increased as part of the basic business knowledge of managers, analysts and programmers. In particular, operating management needs special assistance in comprehending more complex computer systems, which many non-computer personnel fear or dismiss as esoteric. It is the operating line or general staff manager, however, who is the major user and potential beneficiary of management systems which utilize computers.

The roles played by the operating manager as user, and the computer special-

Editors' Note: Reprinted by permission of the publisher from *University of Michigan Business Review*, March 1977.

ist as initiator and implementer of systems, are vital to the better employment of computer systems. While an understanding between data processing management and general management is a necessary prerequisite to effective utilization of systems, both groups have a different frame of reference and tend to see problems in a different perspective.

Frames of Reference

Clear understanding and rapport between operating management and data processing managers are hindered by differing characteristics prevalent within each group.

An *operating manager* must be a generalist who has developed beyond the confines of any one specialization, such as accounting, personnel or engineering. He needs skill in interpersonal relations, sensitivity to organizational politics and the ability to persuade others in the organization to accept or reject certain programs or policies. He plans, coordinates and controls by interaction and communication with other people. The operating manager is generally more senior in age, less concerned with narrow professional interests, and owes his advancement to successful performance within the company. The background and the training of line managers in most companies is focused on traditional activities such as sales, finance or engineering. Practitioners in these fields communicate with one another in concise but usually non-technical language, unless there is special reason for not doing so (e.g., a special report on a subject in their own field).

A *computer specialist* develops in a markedly different environment from that of the operating manager. His formal education is more likely to have emphasized the physical sciences, statistics and engineering, with little attention paid to the social sciences. The college and business training of a computer technologist requires logical analysis and accuracy in results. He is responsible for developing and maintaining systems which are fast, consistent and accurate. Data processing specialists communicate in scientific languages which use a large vocabulary of new technical words and, given the infancy of computer technology, the present vocabulary can be expected to increase greatly.

The non-computer, generalist manager may feel isolated from the scientific jargon of the technician. The technician may be limited in his ability to explain, persuade or understand his operating counterpart.

The Contrast Between Roles

When the typical frames of reference of functional managers and computer specialists are juxtaposed, they present a striking contrast. Members of the two groups perform according to different criteria. The systems expert achieves his position by virtue of technical ability, with increasing emphasis placed upon professional qualifications, such as the well-regarded Certificate in Data Processing. Due to the recent growth of the computer industry, specialists skills are in short supply. Scarcity of computer personnel diminishes the likelihood that professionally qualified individuals are specifically committed to their current employer. The functional manager is apt to be more company-oriented, owing his position to knowledge of the operating situation of the organization.

Expectations concerning their inter-managerial relationships are likely to be frustrated due to divergent backgrounds and training, on-the-job experience, and the range of qualities necessary to maintain their respective positions. Members of each group may bring to organizational problems ingrained attitudes which produce friction or disharmony. As a result, there may be a number of misunderstandings which adversely affect communication and interaction between technicians and non-computer personnel.

The fact that computer specialists are often deficient in interpersonal relationships, due to their strong task-orientation, has been explored in a number of journal articles.[1] Writers on this subject explain there is a need for systems managers to understand and respect the frailties and dignities of people. Arnold Keller suggests the systems man is in large measure responsible for the gap between himself and operational management:

> Systems power will eventually decide many of the competitive battles in the business community. Assuming that the systems professional understands this power better than anyone else—and he should—his task is to communicate this understanding to management. If properly approached, management will listen.[2]

Bridging the Gap

The number of computer applications is being increased as organizations learn how to use computers, not only for basic administrative purposes, such as payroll and inventory, but as an extension of management capability permitting better control over events. Information provided by the systems unit is, in effect, an extension of the manager's own intellect.

The extent to which the data processing group is able to assist general management in the control and direction of the organization depends greatly on the ability of the EDP professionals to create a receptive climate for change. If the systems managers lack administrative ability and are insensitive to the organizational problems faced by operating managers, it will be difficult for new applications to be implemented successfully. John Diebold provides a three-stage evolution of computer use: First, computers are applied to routine administration (accounting, payroll, general ledger, orders, etc.); second, to supervision (inventory control, sales analysis, cost accounting) and third, computers provide management information.[3]

In the third stage, the systems specialist is called upon to design and implement systems which give information for management control, simulate future conditions, aid management strategy, analyze investments, provide market research, etc.

This stage of computer use tests the interactive skills of the systems specialists to a much greater degree than the first or second. The systems professional designs management information systems which cross the boundaries of several departments. There is likely to be friction between the systems unit and the managers of the affected departments if the new application is perceived as a threat to departmental autonomy. Without the collaboration of operating managers, the development of new computer applications is jeopardized. Indifference, intransigence or covert resistance can hamper the introduction of systems which subordinate the division or department to the wider interests of the organization. Operational managers tend to be "sub-optimizers," that is to say, they may maximize the performance of their own department to the detriment of the larger group.

As the third stage of computer utilization dominates business usage, the "gap" in managerial communication increases. These gaps or separations can be described as functional, informational and spatial.

Functional separation is inevitable because of the special skills required in each role; it is increased by lack of knowledge of what is required of a person in the other role. Clearly, the role played by computer specialists has an important influence on the effective operation of computer systems. But there are good reasons why the role of EDP staff in many companies is not clearly defined:

a. Recent growth of the industry.
b. The newness of the specialization.
c. The fact that EDP is a cross-functional activity which involves the cooperation of various other departmental groups.
d. Absence of a positive direction supplied by top management.

A corporation is an amalgam of groups competing for more control over processes, each seeking to influence the corporate policy in order to enhance its own position. The EDP specialist, in dealing with the various rival groups, becomes aware of the importance of data processing for the organization as a whole. The computer staff pioneers new systems, and in so doing they cut across established departments, adopting a more innovative approach to business operations. Any manager in this position can be expected to suffer stresses and uncertainty. He tends to look to senior management for support and assistance in clarifying his role within the organization.

The line or operating manager is functionally separated from the data processing specialist as a result of background, aptitudes and particular working environment. Whereas a high degree of disciplined thought and procedure is required by computer specialists, operating managers can be more flexible in their solutions to problems. They can avoid difficulties by choosing new techniques, policies and forms of organization whenever necessary. Computer systems, however innovational, are not capable of such day-to-day flexibility. The rules of a system must be clearly defined and, once established, the operating manager is faced with constraints which did not formerly apply. The requirement to adhere to strict procedural rules may give the operating manager the feeling he is hindered, rather than assisted, by data processing. The necessary precision with which the objectives and operating criteria of a computer system are stated is unfamiliar to the line manager. He is inclined to think mainly in terms of final results, taking short-cuts when they seem necessary and issuing instructions which do not always conform to the limitations of the computer system.

Informational separation is a consequence of the semantic barrier between general management and computer specialists. The informational gap results from the generalists' failure to appreciate the technical language of the systems specialist, or it may be a problem of confused language between the groups. In the latter case, both parties may think they are talking about the same thing but, because of their differing frames of reference, they may differ considerably.

For example, when a system specialist initiates a system in consultation with the relevant departmental managers, he will explain that tasks need to be performed according to certain rules. The department managers may agree, but without appreciating the full implication of those rules. The operating manager will expect to make exceptions when he feels it is necessary to bypass the established procedures. His own background has been pragmatic and heuristic, rather than programmed and consistent. When the operating manager wants to make changes or modifications, he will feel frustrated by a system which rigidly defines operating procedures. For computer systems, "small" changes may be major changes which the systems staff cannot accommodate. From the systems viewpoint, all the details of an operating situation have to be considered at the time the system is designed. The non-computer manager is unlikely to set forth all the factors which should be introduced ideally even though he is aware of them.

Thus, the implementation of a computer system may become an exercise in mutual frustration. The manager feels the computer professional is too rigid and rule-bound and has restricted his flexibility unnecessarily. The systems specialist wonders why the manager cannot explain in detailed fashion exactly what it is that he wants, since the department manager should know his own operation better than anybody else. Management may come to feel that computers, far from being sophisticated tools for analysis and strategy, are a form of straight-jacket, which unduly limits maneuverability. The specialist, for his part, is surprised the organization has gone on so long, managed by people who are imprecise and non-systematic. This scenario reaches a gloomy impasse brought about by confusion of language.

To overcome this form of informational separation, both sides need to understand the expectations of the other. As a first step, the systems users should be more realistic relative to what computers can do in terms of both the negative and the positive aspects of introducing computer systems. The benefits must be weighed against the constraints in operating procedures. The computer specialist should become more versed in the operational problems of the organization. Where there is a gap in communication between computer staff and general management, the former may tend to "take refuge in refining the internal operating efficiency of the computer department."[4]

Spatial separation is the physical separation of EDP facilities from plant or administrative offices. This poses a barrier to interaction between computer and non-computer personnel. Where special "systems units" are formed with premises remote from other parts of the organization, the normal day-to-day patterns of interaction, both formal and informal, will be limited. This situation often occurs as a consequence of centralization of data processing activity. Costs can be reduced by centralizing the EDP activity of such common services as accounting, inventory and personnel information. As the capacity of large computers is increased, it becomes feasible for one computer to take over the work of several divisional or departmental computers. There is also a trend toward use of a common data base for a number of different systems. Development of ancillary equipment, such as remote terminals and use of time-sharing schemes, has also encouraged centralization of data processing services. While there may be substantial economic advantages to be derived from central systems, the spatial separation of systems specialists and non-computer personnel can have adverse effects. EDP personnel may be regarded as "outsiders," rather than integral members of the organization.

Top Management Involvement

Leadership by top management can be an important factor in reconciling computer staff and non-computer personnel. The objective should be to combine all personnel resources so they work together effectively to achieve common goals for the benefit of the organization as a whole. Top management has the final responsibility for the success of computer operations. Data processing staff have the task of designing, implementing and maintaining systems for the organization, subject to the planning approval of top management. Support by top management to achieve the goals of the organization is vital if computer systems are to operate effectively. This has been the conclusion of a number of major studies.[5] Researchers at Ohio State University found that, while top managers favor more involvement in the overall conduct of computer operations, they spend very little time in consultation with data processing management.[6] Two-thirds of a sample of 130 top managers spent less than two hours per week with senior computer staff. In view of the fact that in recent years EDP systems have absorbed 10 percent of new investment spending, this appears to be a disproportionately small amount of time to allocate to such an important function.

214

Many top managers relegate the task of forging links between general management and EDP management to functional middle-managers. Brady made a study of the impact of computers on the decision-making process of 100 top managers in a sample of manufacturing and industrial research firms.[7] He concluded that the use of computers has little direct impact on top management decision making. What impact there was resulted from the manner in which middle-managers contributed to the decision-making process. However, use of the computer did give top managers more time to make decisions, more alternatives to consider and other indirect advantages. Nevertheless, top managers generally have been insulated or shielded from personal involvement in data processing activity and have little first-hand awareness of the problems of computer systems operation.

What specific steps should top managers take to help bridge the communications gap between the groups?

1. Executives should acquire more knowledge of the operations of computer systems, starting with basic computer concepts, through the rudiments of the applications in use in their organizations. This would facilitate top-level interaction with computer professionals.

2. Programs to educate non-computer personnel in EDP concepts and systems should be initiated for those employees whose functions benefit from systems operations.

3. Top managers should play a more active role in directing the course of and defining objectives for systems development.

4. Operating managers, the "customers" of data processing services, should be brought into discussions at the design stage of a new system, so they will regard it as "their system," rather than something imposed upon them by computer and professionals.

5. Systems specialists should be exposed to the work of other departments in the organization so they do not retreat into the computer department through an inability to recognize the general problems of their particular organization. Remote, centralized data processing departments merely reinforce the isolation of EDP staff. Remoteness can also produce unhappy psychological effects when the EDP staff concentrates on improving its own operating efficiency instead of providing the services the functional departments need. Helping the users specify their needs is an important task for the computer professional.

6. Where possible, top managers should assign to operating managers the administrative and financial responsibility for computer systems within their domain. If functional managers are accountable, they will be involved more actively in the operations of data processing systems.

Conclusions

The communication gap between the users of computer systems and the technicians who design and maintain them can be bridged if unifying measures are instituted by top management. Top managers can initiate important steps to create better understanding between users and specialists. Both parties will be better prepared to reconcile differences if they are aware of the sources of conflict. Neither group can operate effectively without the other. It is, therefore, in their mutual interest to minimize the level of conflict.

1. Arnold E. Keller, "Putting Systems Into Management," *Business Automation*, (July, 1968); Rudolf Borchardt, "Computer Systems: How Now Their Effects on the Organization?" *Systems and Procedures Journal*, (May-June, 1967); George Glaser, "Computers in a World of Real People," *Datamation*, (December, 1968); Milton Reitzfeld, "Marketing the Systems Function," *Systems and Procedures Journal*, (November-December, 1971); Joseph A. Cook, "Association Management Challenges in Data Processing" *Association Management*, (August, 1967).
2. Keller, *op. cit.*, p. 45.
3. John Diebold, "Bad Decisions on Computer Use," *Harvard Business Review*, (January-February, 1969), p. 14.
4. McKinsey & Company, Inc., *Unlocking the Computer's Profit Potential.* (New York: McKinsey & Co., Inc., 1968). John Dearden, *Computer and Business Management*, (Dow Jones-Richard D. Irwin Inc., Homewood, Illinois 1966).
5. *Ibid.*, p. 22.
6. Clifford Elliott, *A Behavioral Study of Managers of Business Computer Systems: With Special Reference to the Role of Top Management*, Unpublished Ph.D. Dissertation, Ohio State University, Columbus, Ohio, 1970.
7. Rodney J. Brady, "Computers in Top-Level Decision-Making," *Harvard Business Review*, (July-August, 1967).

19.
The Role of Time-Sharing Consulting Services for Personnel

Carlton W. Dukes

"What can a consultant service do that our own internal systems and/or departments can't do for our own organization's needs?"

That's the first question asked of a Personnel System consultant, so let's consider that first. Obviously, the best judgments of an organization's capabilities and needs are necessarily going to come from within. But the extent to which an organization can solve the demands of a computerized Personnel Resource System can only be partially evaluated in terms of past successes implementing financial or material resource systems. However, people usually do not behave in the same way that money or things function. And in dealing with the only truly unique resource of a company, it may be well to consider using the experience and resources of those organizations who have specialized in "People Parame-

Editors' Note: Reprinted with permission from *Personnel Journal*, Copyright March 1975.

ters." There are some definite reasons for considering engaging outside consultant services, which should be discussed in some detail as to their desirability, particularly regarding Personnel Resource Systems. Broadly speaking, there are four major considerations which should be examined first:

1. The consultant has expertise not sufficiently available in the client organization.
2. Their organization can be dedicated to the task, not subject to the internal priority contests clients experience.
3. Certain services or equipment are unique to the consultant—or are not otherwise available to the client company.
4. Flexibility in options or approach are a necessary by-product of consultant-client relationships and are the most important consideration of all.

Looking at each of these considerations in detail will help not only to describe precisely what is meant by Personnel Resource Information Systems, but provide some explanation of the system architectures built around needs for personnel data.

Expertise—which is another way of indicating extensive experience—may be summarized by the saying, "Don't re-invent the wheel." Frankly, the implementation of system #10 is a great deal easier than implementing system #1. There are some things which can easily be put into the initial system design, but which might be troublesome trying to include at a later date. The number of weeks in a year can be calculated as 52.00, 52.14 or 52.18 (depending upon what formula you use) and relates directly to weekly or hourly pay equivalents. Good system design should include the possibility of modifying the payrate/week formula. Or, for another example, is there provision for automatic calculation of salary administration controls such as compa-ratio or percentage of salary range by group? Are deviations systematically identified? What about saving time and errors by having annual/monthly/weekly/hourly equivalents calculated automatically?

These are rather basic examples when compared to data convenience and system efficiencies gained when using tabular data to shorten record length and to effect mass changes for large numbers of employees. Nevertheless, they should illustrate that there are some system aspects requiring hard experience.

Dedication—more in terms of time availability than religious fervor—can make or break a system undertaking. Realistically speaking, personnel projects are not usually found at the top of most organization's priority lists. Inevitably, the internal project-assigned programmers and analysts are diverted one by one for "more important projects" (usually capital-related) and the Personnel Resource System will undergo several false starts. Then, when some organizational crisis occurs, a "crash" project is initiated.

Unless there is some guarantee that internal people will remain dedicated to the Personnel System, then the commitment to an external organization in terms of time and dollars is the only other way an organization is likely to continue with

218

the project, usually because "we've already made the commitment/investment—so let's continue with it."

Unique services or equipment—is different from expertise in that the consideration here is the relative unavailability of an essential service—in this particular instance time-sharing. Expertise in the development of Personnel systems is an outgrowth of implementing a series of such systems and learning from the experience. But some services or equipment such as time-sharing computers—particularly Personnel systems applications—are simply not available as in-house resources. In-house systems are usually concerned with batch-run systems involving a multitude of essentially similar transactions or analyses, and are not set up for the often unpredictable conditions generated by human beings doing unpredictable things.

Unless the client organization is unusually fortunate, there is no alternative to engaging an outside consulting service to obtain, for example, a truly interactive, immediately responsive, computer system to handle personnel data.

On the broadest level, the option exists of developing a Personnel Resource System on an in-house basis, versus utilizing outside consulting services. If both the consultant and the client organization have had no experience in implementing a Personnel Resource System, then the choice of options would be about equal in value. But when the consultant has had experience with prior systems, then the range of options becomes wider. The experience gained with other companies may in great part be applicable to a given client company, or that experience may be best utilized by clarifying the incorrect way to proceed.

In either event, it would seem that a consultant's experience can serve as an effective multiplier of knowledge in evaluating the best approach for a client company to follow in the implementation of a Personnel Resource System.

Flexibility—a compelling aspect of basic system design directly concerned with the level and type of services one should expect from a Personnel Resource Information System—an aspect directly related to time-sharing. It is important to note here that flexibility—particularly in computer services—is a one-way street. Basically, one cannot go from a rigid system of architecture to a flexible one, although one can proceed from the flexible to the less flexible. Let us examine flexibility.

In general, there are three basic modes of processing Personnel Data:

A. *Batch Processing Systems*—probably the most common method utilized by Personnel functions today. This is because most in-house systems utilize batch, and because most of the companies marketing Personnel Systems are graduates of the Batch school of processing.

   Batch systems are characterized by their adherence to a large, fixed data base (reprogramming is required to modify it), and by reliance on a "turnaround document," essentially a Personnel Data Profile with keypunch fields/codes preprinted on the form.

   But most important, companies are limited by the processing limits of batch operations. One consulting firm prides itself on the large number of error/audit messages produced by the system. (When you input only once or twice a month, you have to provide for a large number of accumulated errors, which were input sometimes weeks before processings.) But most of all, batch processing limits needed access to data, particularly in the increasingly tight time constraints faced by Personnel functions today.

Waiting weeks for report application programs to be written, long ago yielded to generalized retrieval systems, simplified to write limited data and using English-language commands. However, at least 24 hours is considered "realistic" for turnaround. But this writer knows from experience that if four sequential report runs are required to analyze data, the total time cycle can exceed one week! (Keypunch errors for the report request, improper field names, unexpected data and low priority on the computer can and do work against the user.)

An interesting sidelight is that in many such systems using a generalized report writer, specified output is transferred onto punch cards and the cards are themselves read in the next cycle as input (to effect "mass changes").

Even basic updates to records can be plagued by a series of problems so that a salary increase may take 6 weeks to get into the system. For example, a salary increase effective the 1st of the month is submitted on the 20th. But a keypunch error is encountered and the system rejects the transaction because of alpha data in a numeric field. Then, on the next run (by now it is the 15th) the transaction is rejected because the increase exceeds the salary maximum. On the next run (the 1st of the month) the transaction is finally accepted by the system.

Under batch runs, there is no way of finding an error until the whole run of inputs, etc., is made.

However, batch systems will be with us for some time, if for no other reason than the investments already made in existing hardware installations. Meanwhile, batch operations result in system-driven users, rather than putting users first.

B. *Remote Batch Processing Systems* range from mailing in a change notice or modified Profile form to remote terminal input. This mode of processing is in itself a compromise between batch run pre-structured programs and terminal input with special instructions for delayed processing.

Essentially, the best use for such processing is to take advantage of "off-hours" computer loads, when more time is available—and usually a lesser scale of charges.

For regular monthly reports or for large input/processing situations (survey processing is an example), remote batch can provide the service the user needs, provided the customer is not in a hurry for the data.

C. *Time-Sharing, Interactive Processing Systems*—relative newcomers to the scene for Personnel data users—their flexibility is their major advantage. Literally, users can get their data when it is needed—not at the month's end, or every Monday, or even overnight—but immediately, if the situation demands.

Able to perform virtually every operation the Batch Systems can perform, with the ability to effect remote batch input/output, Time-Sharing can function in whatever mode desired, with no degradation in quality.

There are, however, certain requirements which should be taken into account in the development of Time-Shared Personnel Resource Information Systems which are worth looking at in detail.

The basic system architecture of Time-Shared Personnel Resource Information Systems has two major constraints which must be built in if they are to operate efficiently and economically:

1. The *Data Base* should be flexible, preferably modular. Dictated by the nature of Time-Sharing, blanks or unnecessary data cost as much to store/process as does valid information. Therefore, data bases must be more tailored to client needs than batch systems. However, the ability to add or delete fields in a record, with simple commands, is also necessary to permit data base flexibility under *user control,* with no programmers required. This means unanticipated fields can be added, unused ones deleted, and usable fields made longer or shorter.

   (a) A segmented data base should be utilized, since employee groups require varying extents of data. Though all employees will have basic name, address, sex/race, etc., not all employees will have benefits plan data, performance review information, etc., or other data more appropriate to managerial than to production personnel.

   (b) The file structure of a Personnel Resource Information System should then be modular in design, allowing for a variable number of files (History, Skills Bank data) to be assigned to each record as appropriate, rather than having one large record in which to fit all employees (with many blanks for most employees) or setting up different files according to employee type. Simple commands should permit intersecting/merging separate files into one as needed.

2. *Processing,* and particularly input/output, can be made very simple for users. Data can be entered by helpful prompting by the system to preclude not only keyboarded errors, but validation against user-specified rules for data propriety.

   (a) The other facet of system architecture should allow for priorities in processing. Some information entering or coming out of a system should be processed on an interactive basis so that the user gets exactly what is needed when it is needed—immediately.

   (b) However, if it is not important to have the processing occur during prime business hours, then remote batch can be used. Periodic inputs or reports can be run at night, over the weekend, or at the month's end. Under remote batch, processing costs are lower because runs are made during off-hours, and to the user, the system behaves like the well-known batch mode systems. But for standardized inputs, reports or creation of sub-files, remote batch is efficient and economical and operates according to user priority.

However, users impressed with the quick and complete responses to their queries, enjoy demonstrating the system to associates. Unfortunately, any system costs money to operate, a fact easily forgotten when demonstrating how easily a telephone number is found or how interesting histograms, plots and statistical analyses can be.

Users, particularly new ones, cannot be expected to jump into a new system, so guidance is needed. This can take the form of providing some types of prestructured input/output routines. In that way, the individual can get data into and out of the machine without costly initial experimentation. But as he becomes more proficient, he can modify those routines or develop suitable new ones. For instance, entering "GENERATECOSTINCREASE" can ask the user what data base is to be used, the field (salary) to be used for calculations, and whether the user wishes to add dollars and cents or percent increases as alternatives or cumulatives.

When reasonable experience is gained, the user can fully interact with the system "HELP" commands, keying in "WHY" for detailed error messages, or "HELP" when a several-paragraph explanation of current transactions is needed.

And if that fails, "linking" to the office in the user's city—or to the central computer—will permit a two-way conversation between the user and an experienced programmer, so that proper, efficient use of the system provides the user with exactly what is needed.

Use of a Time-Sharing System

What most people seem to look for in a System are answers based on the information put into the System and kept up to date. But the author feels that this is not sufficient in today's world, in which no magical single answer will suffice.

Human Resource Management requires alternatives and analysis, not merely answers. For example, if a salary increase of 5% is contemplated for a particular group, why not see what 4¾% and 5¼% would cost and examine what that will do to the salary averages, ranges and key salary figures? By analyzing those figures, Personnel *planners* should be able to decide whether to increase or decrease the proposed alternatives; or to create/evaluate additional alternatives within the same problem solution period without waiting until tomorrow's computer run is ready.

The writer believes that since the methods of developing a Human Resource System are limited to:

Make (internal Edp group develops and runs on own system)
Buy (purchase software, run on own hardware)
Service (lease software capability and terminals)

Everything should be done to permit the Personnel user to "Try Before You Buy." To do this, provide the systems representative with 100–500 records and in *no more than 3 weeks* demonstrate capability.

Recognize the writer's prejudice here, in that Time-Sharing Systems permit effecting a demonstration within one week in the Personnel office, using actual company data provided, thereby allowing the Personnel department to use the full system capability "hands-on."

Though batch systems may take longer to set up and interactive "hands-on" is not possible, this does not mean such a test should be ignored. The management of Human Resource data is too critical to be promised or implied as a capability, but not delivered.

User-oriented commands, adequate decimal points, calculations on fields, descending sorts, mass increases in salary, are areas the writer knows are overlooked by Systems Representatives, and Personnel is left with inadequate capability if the questions are not asked.

In summary, it should be noted that the most important consideration in any system design is the requirement for flexibility. A Time-Sharing System goes from a fully interactive mode (wherein the user has direct interface with his data and programs) to a batch operation (with its rigid pre-structured constraints).

A user should have the ability to create/add/change/delete fields in a data base, modify the fields as they apply to individual employees, create/interface with other files, retrieve and analyze data with full statistical and graphic programs, and—most importantly—do these operations *when the user desires.*

A Human Resource System should provide this flexibility, and with segmented data bases and variable time options, could do so effectively. In this way, an organization can devote proper attention to the management of its only truly unique asset—its Human Resources.

20.
Law and
Information Systems

Lawrence R. Miller

A great deal of the information an organization gathers, processes, or distributes may be subject to—or triggered by—various Federal, state, and local laws and regulations. Some of these laws and regulations have been developed by legislative and administrative bodies. Others have evolved through the interpretations and decisions of judicial agencies.

Usually, two main components of a law or regulation can affect the content, form, frequency, and flow of information into, within or out of an organization. These could be termed the law's: (a) compliance component; and (b) its record-keeping and reporting component:

Editors' Note: Reprinted by permission of the Association for Systems Management from *Journal of Systems Management,* January 1977.

1. The *compliance* component of a law or regulation stipulates the standards, activities, and conditions an organization must follow in order to live up to the intent of that law or regulation. This component may focus primarily upon information itself (e.g., advertising, credit information, securities information, etc.) or it may focus upon activities that have information-based implications (e.g., on-the-job operations, employment and promotion practices, production processes affecting the environment, etc.).

2. The *record-keeping and reporting* component of a law or regulation usually defines: (a) what information an organization is supposed to develop, maintain, and make available *to the government* to prove compliance; as well as, (b) the form, content, frequency, volume, accuracy, and distribution of that information.

For some laws, the compliance and record-keeping/reporting components are so intertwined that no clear distinction between the two is possible. For others, record-keeping and reporting may be required but only *after* a violation has been identified or some legal action has been initiated.

This article examines some of the laws and regulations that most directly affect the information-handling, recording, retrieval, and/or dissemination activities of organizations in both the private and public sectors. Because of the number and complexity of such laws and regulations at *all* levels of government, only a few recently enacted or amended laws at the *Federal* level will be dealt with.

Each law or regulation has been assigned to one of three categories which reflects the target group it is designed to protect: (a) employees; (b) consumers; or, (c) citizens in general. Whenever possible, the record-keeping and reporting component of a law or regulation has received primary emphasis.

Employee Protection Laws

The three most controversial acts affecting employees in recent years appear to be the Equal Employment Opportunity Act of 1972, the Occupational Safety and Health Act of 1970, and the Employee Retirement Income Security Act of 1974.

EQUAL EMPLOYMENT OPPORTUNITY ACT (EEOA) / The Equal Employment Opportunity Act was developed to ensure that applicants or employees are treated without regard to race, color, religion, sex, or national origin in situations involving hiring or promotion. This act gave the Equal Employment Opportunity Commission judicially enforceable powers to carry out the Civil Rights Act of 1964.

The law affects management's rights (and the procedures management follows) in hiring or promoting people to certain positions to fulfill organizational objectives. In addition, it affects what information is to be displayed (through

225

advertisements, bulletin board notices, etc.) or elicited (through interviews and applications) in the hiring and promotion process.[1]

The record-keeping and reporting component of the EEOA requires private, governmental, educational, and labor organizations to follow strict record-keeping and reporting requirements. Fifty-five separate sections of Part 1602 of the *Code of Federal Regulations* define records to be made or kept, preservation methods, exemptions, filing requirements, penalties, and applicability of state or local laws to these records requirements.

Here is a sample of some of the more salient record-keeping and reporting provisions:

1. Any personnel or employment record made or kept by an employer (such as an application form or other records having to do with hiring, promotion, demotion, transfer, layoff, termination pay rates, other terms of compensation, selection for training or apprenticeship, etc.) must be preserved for two years from the date the record was made or from the date personnel action (such as firing, etc.) was taken.
2. Records on the ethnic identities of employees as well as those for race, religion, or sex must also be maintained and reported but kept separate from the file folder on the actual employee.
3. Once a charge of discrimination has been filed or an action by the Attorney General has been initiated against an employer, all personnel records relevant to the charge or action must be preserved until the charge or action is finally disposed of. "Relevant" records would include those relating to the charging party, to other employees holding similar jobs, to application and test forms completed by the charging party and other candidates for the same job, etc.
4. Employers of 100 or more employees are required to file Form EEO-1 annually; any employer who conducts apprenticeship programs must file Form EEO-2-E annually.[2]

OCCUPATIONAL SAFETY AND HEALTH ACT (OSHA) / The Occupational Safety and Health Act requires all employers to make sure their operations are free from accident and health hazards to workers. Through the Occupational Safety and Health Administration, OSHA affects on-the-job activities in all kinds of organizations from a health and safety standpoint. It also affects how, what, and where information is to be displayed and distributed to help employees benefit from the law.[3]

The record-keeping and reporting component of OSHA (Part 1904 of the *Code of Federal Regulations*) contains 19 separate sections on records creation, maintenance, access, reporting, applicability to state law, and other requirements. Records are supposed to assist compliance and safety officers in making inspections and investigations as well as aid the Bureau of Labor Statistics in developing reliable measures of injury and illness rates.[4]

Employers must:

1. Keep records at each separate work site.
2. Maintain a log of each recordable injury and occupational illness.
3. Maintain a supplementary record that elaborates on circumstances, people, medical assistance, and other activities related to injury or sickness.
4. Maintain an annual summary of log entries.
5. Post copies of the annual summary as well as explanations of employee protection and responsibilities under the act.
6. Report any accident which results in one or more deaths or in hospitalization of 5 or more employees to the Federal Occupational Safety and Health Administration (or to the state OSHA administration if such an approved agency exists).
7. Maintain all records for five years after the year to which they relate.

A penalty of not more than $1,000 can be assessed for a serious violation of the Act and a $10,000 civil penalty can be assessed for each willful or repeated violation of the Act.[5]

EMPLOYEE RETIREMENT INCOME SECURITY ACT (ERISA) / The Employee Retirement Income Security Act is designed to protect the pension and welfare rights of workers in the private sector. Although ERISA gets involved with fiduciary responsibilities and participation and vesting rights, the act heavily emphasizes disclosure methods, procedures, formats, timing, content, and modes of expression employers must use to inform employees about benefits, plan changes, etc.[6]

ERISA requires disclosure to two principal information consumers: (a) plan participants and beneficiaries; and, (b) the government. Most of the forms and reports listed below are to be distributed to employees and beneficiaries and must also be filed with, or made available to, the Labor Department:

1. A summary plan description for each benefit plan provided to employees.
2. Summaries of benefit amendments.
3. A summary annual report.
4. A statement of accrued and vested benefits on termination.
5. Plan documents such as texts, trust agreements and contracts, personal statements of pension benefits.
6. Written explanations of claims denials.

Highly specific timetables and schedules affect submission of reports and information to the Federal government. In addition to the forms and reports mentioned above, ERISA also requires an employer to file Form EBS-1, Form EBS-2, an annual registration report, and a special report on changes in plan status with the Federal government.

ERISA's vesting, participation and funding standards are administered by the Internal Revenue Service; ERISA guidelines primarily involved with reporting and disclosure to employees are administered by the Labor Department.[7]

Consumer Protection Laws

Two major types of consumer protection laws focus upon information that is disseminated *to* or *about* consumers. One type is primarily involved with advertising, labelling, and related promotional information; the other type is primarily involved with financial information (consumer loans, consumer credit, and consumer investment).

Advertising, labelling, credit information, and loan information are basically within the purview of the Federal Trade Commission; financial information affecting consumers as investors in securities is monitored and controlled by the Securities and Exchange Commission.

FTC-ENFORCED PROMOTIONAL INFORMATION RULES AND REGULATIONS / The FTC derives its power to monitor and prevent false and deceptive advertising, labelling, and other promotional information from: the FTC Act; the Consumer Products Safety Act; the Fair Labelling and Packaging Act; the Wool, Fur, and Textile Fiber Products Labelling Acts; the Magnuson Moss Warranty-FTC Trade Improvement Act; and others.[8]

In addition to the duties and procedures spelled out in these acts, the FTC generates its own guidelines and trade practice rules for specific industries (more than 200 at this time).[9]

Since so many industries are covered by FTC regulations, only one industry —the office machine marketing industry—will be dealt with here for example purposes.

According to Part 175 of the *Code of Federal Regulations* for the office machine marketing industry:

> It is an unfair trade practice to make or cause to be made, directly or indirectly, verbally or through advertising, pictorial representation, invoice, tag, label, mark, or writing upon the product itself, or otherwise, any false, misleading, or deceptive statement or representation concerning the construction, composition, utility, performance, condition, age, name, serial number, model, durability, life expectancy, speed, ease of operation, manufacture, distribution, price, or terms or condition of sale, lease, or rental, of any office machine; or concerning any service or training offered in connection with the sale, lease, or rental of any such machine; or concerning the repair and replacement of parts of any consumer's machine; or, which is false or misleading in any other respect.[10]

More specific requirements govern when, how and where industry members can use certain language about office machines. The following information-related actions are considered to be illegal by the FTC:

1. Deceptive concealment of the fact that a machine is not new, deception as to discontinued or obsolete models; deception as to price reductions or price quotations; and deceptive guarantees or warrantees.

2. Misuse of the terms "new," "demonstrator," "factory rebuilt," "rebuilt," "remanufactured," "reconditioned," "overhauled," "special," "bargain," "closeouts," "discontinued lines," etc.
3. Misrepresentation as to character of business operated, quality of a machine in terms of industry standards, installment sales contract terms and conditions.
4. Alteration or removal of serial numbers, false invoicing, inducing breach of contract.
5. Defamation of competitors or disparagement of their products.
6. Bribery of an employee or an agent of a competitor to obtain information about the business of that competitor; use of false or misleading statements or any unfair means to get such information; use of information thus gained to injure the competitor's business, to suppress competition, or to unreasonably restrain trade.[11]

In this and other industries under FTC jurisdiction, a complaint about a deceptive information practice can be lodged by a consumer or a competitor as well as by the FTC itself or some other government agency at the Federal, state, or local level.

Informal means of settlement are used first and if this does not work, formal procedures are instituted. These include a preliminary injunction or an order to cease and desist by an administrative law judge or U.S. District Court judge.

Violations of an order to cease and desist subject an offender to civil penalties of up to $10,000 for each violation and for each day a violation continues, For dissemination of false advertising of a food, drug, device, or cosmetic where use of the commodity may be injurious or where there is intent to defraud or mislead, there is a fine of up to $5,000 and up to six months in jail; succeeding convictions may result in a fine of up to $10,000 or up to one year of imprisonment or both.

All respondents against whom cease and desist orders have been issued *must* file reports with the FTC to substantiate their compliance.[12]

FTC-ENFORCED CONSUMER CREDIT AND LOAN INFORMATION LAWS AND REGULATIONS / The FTC's enforcement power in relation to consumer credit and loan information is derived from the Fair Credit Reporting Act of 1970 and the Truth-in-Lending Act of 1970. (Closely allied to these acts is the Equal Credit Opportunity Act of 1974 which prohibits discrimination in granting credit on the basis of sex or martial status.)[13]

The *Fair Credit Reporting Act*—was designed to protect consumers against circulation of inaccurate or obsolete credit reports and to insure that consumer reporting agencies exercise their responsibilities in a manner that is fair and equitable and in conformity with requirements of the Act.

The law applies to any person or organization that:

1. Provides written or oral information on consumers to third parties for fees, dues, or on a cooperative basis; and/or
2. Assembles or evaluates information on a consumer's creditworthiness, credit

standing, credit capacity, character, general reputation, or personal character.

The information reported, assembled, or evaluated must be used in whole or in part as a factor in establishing a person's eligibility for: (a) credit, (b) insurance, (c) employment or promotion; or, (d) license or other benefit provided by a government agency.

Certain types of information about consumers are *not* to be reported if a certain number of years have passed. For bankruptcies, reports are not to be made 14 or more years after the bankruptcy has occurred; for tax liens, suits, judgments, accounts placed for collection, arrests, or other adverse items, reports are not to be made 7 or more years after the action has occurred.

Consumers have the right to request identification of sources of information and recipients of information up to two years after an information request affected their employment and up to six months after a request that affected their credit, insurance, government licensing, or government benefits.

Updating and correction procedures are also included in this act. Civil liabilities on reporting agencies *or users* of this information include damages for willful or negligent noncompliance (plus court, attorney and related costs).[14]

The *Truth-in-Lending Act*—is designed to insure that credit terms are clearly disclosed to a consumer so that the consumer will more easily be able to compare the various credit terms available to him and avoid the uninformed use of credit. Various amendments to the Act cover issuance of credit cards and the procedures that credit card customers can follow in resolving billing disputes.

Willful violations of the Truth-in-Lending Act are punishable by a fine of up to $5,000 and up to one year imprisonment. Improper disclosures result in the creditor being liable up to twice the amount of the finance charge (up to a maximum of $1,000), court costs, and attorney fees.[15]

SEC-ENFORCED INVESTOR PROTECTION INFORMATION LAWS AND REGULATIONS / The SEC's powers to regulate investment-related information are derived from the Securities Act of 1933, the Securities and Exchange Act of 1934, and subsequent amendments and official interpretations.[16]

Whenever securities are offered to the public in interstate commerce through the mail, directly, or through some other party, the issuer of the securities must file a registration statement as well as annual and other reports with the SEC.[17] If the issuer has assets of $1-million or more and 500 or more shareholders of record, the registration statement and reports also must be filed with national securities exchanges.

Issuers of securities are expected to provide the SEC with information that keeps their registration statements reasonably current and to provide annual reports that are certified by independent public accountants. Appropriate disclosures must be made, whether or not an issuer's stock is listed on a particular stock exchange.

Anything which could be considered a materially important event must be reported to the SEC on Form 8-K within 10 days after the close of any month during which that event occurs. Typical examples of such events would be:

1. A change in control of the stock issuer.
2. Acquisition or disposition of a significant amount of assets by the issuer.
3. Material legal proceedings to which the issuer or any of its subsidiaries has become a party or to which any of its property is the subject.
4. Material modifications in the issuer's securities or material revaluation of assets.
5. Excess increase or decrease in the amount of securities outstanding of any particular class of stock.[18]

Much of the information that is reported to the SEC must also be reported to the investment public. For example, the annual report to stockholders is to contain certified financial statements for the past two years, a summary of operations for the last five years (plus an accompanying management analysis), identification of director's principal occupations, stock market and dividend information for the past two years, notice of Form 10-K availability (the required annual report that goes to the SEC and stock exchanges), and a brief description of business and line-of-business breakout similar to what is reported in Form 10-K.[19]

According to SEC Rule 10b-5, faulty disclosure of material information to the investment public can constitute a criminal violation of SEC rules whether this information is disseminated through standard company publicity channels or through annual, quarterly, or other periodic reports. In fact, liability may result ". . . if a public announcement that provides adequate disclosure of material *favorable* corporate developments does not also provide information on other material *adverse* corporate developments that have not been publicly disclosed."[20]

The SEC has also closed the loopholes in an earlier rule that deals with public knowledge of conditions that led to the termination of a company's independent auditors. Companies are now required to tell their stockholders when and why they fire their auditors. Letters from the company and the fired auditor explaining any serious disagreements in the preceding *18* months are to be attached to public reports normally filed with the SEC. Other new requirements concerning the management-auditor relationship are also in operation.[21]

Citizen Protection Laws

Several landmark pieces of legislation in recent years have clarified or reaffirmed citizens' rights in several areas, including rights to privacy, rights to information about their government, and rights to a clean and healthy environment. Most prominent among these are the Privacy Act of 1974, the Freedom of Information Act of 1974, and Executive Reorganization Order #3 of 1970 (which consolidated power to protect the environment within the Environmental Protection Agency).

PRIVACY ACT / The Privacy Act amends Title 5 of the *U.S. Code* by adding Section 552a to protect individual citizens from invasions of their privacy through the use or misuse of Federal records. The act also allows citizens to gain access to records about them that are maintained by the Federal government and to get inaccurate information corrected.

Although the Privacy Act currently applies to organizations at the Federal level only, similar legislation is being considered for application to business and industry as well as to professional, non-profit, and other governmental (state, local) organizations.

Some of the provisions of the Act which may also be duplicated in an act aimed at the private sector include:

1. Accounting for disclosures—agencies must keep an accurate accounting of the date, nature, and purpose of each disclosure of a person's record and the name and address of the person to whom the disclosure is made. This accounting is to be retained for at least five years or longer (depending upon the authorized life of the record) and should be made available to the person named in the record on request. Any corrections or notations of dispute must be disseminated to agencies or persons who previously used the record.
2. Procedures for persons to gain access to their records—agencies must allow a person to review the information they have on him or her and to have a copy made. If a person requests a correction and it is refused, he may ask for it to be reviewed at several different levels (including judicial review) within certain specified deadlines.
3. Procedures for maintaining records—agencies must tell people who are asked to supply information what authority lies behind the request, the purpose of the request, the routine uses to which the information will be put, and any penalties there are for not providing part or all of the information. Every year each agency is to publish categorized lists of records used by that agency and methods available to gain access to those records. Whenever possible, an agency must notify a person when any record is made available to some individual or organization for use in legal proceedings. In addition, an agency must continuously train people in procedures and penalties involved in the privacy protection process and safeguard the security and confidentiality of records.

For failure to live up to the provisions of the law, the agency responsible for records on an individual can be sued. Any officer or employee of an agency who knowingly gives information to someone not entitled to receive it or who fails to meet the notice requirements of the Privacy Act will be found guilty of a misdemeanor and fined up to $5,000. (Anyone guilty of obtaining information under false pretense would also be guilty of a misdemeanor and be fined up to $5,000 as well.)

Several state and local governments have already enacted privacy legislation similar to the new Federal law. Like the Federal Privacy Act, many of these laws require agencies to develop and make available to the public various types of indexes to categories and locations of personal information as well as to procedures citizens can follow to discover and correct this information.[22]

FREEDOM OF INFORMATION ACT / The Freedom of Information Act (as amended in 1974) affects any department, government-controlled corporation, or independent regulatory agency within the purview of the executive branch of government. Several state and local governments have already enacted similar legislation.

Essentially, the Federal FOI Act requires each agency to make available to requesting citizens (at a reasonable fee): final opinions and orders, statements of policy and interpretations, administrative staff manuals, and instructions to staff. Current indexes to information must be maintained and made available to the public at least quarterly. Regulations and procedures to be followed by the requesting citizen must also be published, including updates, charges, supplements, etc.

If an agency fails to provide information as stipulated under the act, disciplinary action may be taken against the executive or employee responsible for withholding it.[23]

REORGANIZATION ORDER #3 (EPA) / Through Reorganization Order #3, the Environmental Protection Agency was given power to help regulate business, industrial, and other operations (including governmental) that may contaminate air, water and other environmental elements that sustain the lives of citizens.[24]

In attempting to carry out provisions of this act, the Environmental Protection Agency requires a massive amount of information from organizations to analyze the possibility of contamination and pollution as well as to monitor the extent to which these organizations are complying with Agency standards.

For some types of pollution, the Environmental Protection Agency has wide authority to set standards and enforce them; for others, most authority rests with state or local governments. Some of the laws that come under the jurisdiction of the Environmental Protection Agency include: the Clean Air Act, the Federal Water Pollution Control Act, the Resource Recovery Act, the Federal Environmental Pesticide Control Act, and the Federal Noise Control and Abatement Act.[25]

Here is an example of the record-keeping requirements from one subchapter of one act under the EPA's jurisdiction—the Clean Air Act (Subchapter I, Section 1857c-9):

> The [EPA] Administrator may require the owner or operator of any emission source to establish and maintain such records, make such reports, install, use, and maintain such monitoring equipment or methods, sample such emissions (in accordance with such methods at such locations at such

intervals and in such manner as the Administrator shall prescribe) and provide such other information as he may reasonably require. . . . The Administrator or his authorized representative, upon presentation of his credentials shall have a right of entry to, upon or through any premises in which an emission source is located or in which any records required to be maintained are located and may at reasonable times have access to and copy any records, inspect any monitoring equipment or method required and sample any emissions which the owner or operator of such source is required to sample. . . . Each state may develop and submit to the Administrator a procedure for carrying out this section in such state. If the Administrator finds the state procedure is adequate, he may delegate to such state any authority he has to carry out this section (except with regard to new sources owned or operated by the United States). Nothing in this subsection shall prohibit the Administration from carrying out this section in a state.[26]

The act also sets forth provisions that protect trade secrets from public exposure if they are contained in any records, reports or other information the Administrator has access to.

Any person who knowingly makes false statements in any document required to be maintained or filed or who falsifies or tampers with monitoring equipment or methods can be punished by a fine of up to $10,000, imprisonment for up to six months, or both.[27]

Difficulties Involved with Compliance and Non-compliance

From this brief presentation, it should be apparent that managers and information specialists who fail to consistently monitor and evaluate the effects of Federal laws and regulations on their information-handling and distribution activities may be putting themselves and their organizations into serious jeopardy.

Personnel information systems, marketing information systems, etc., are often prime targets of the compliance and record-keeping/reporting provisions of Federal laws and regulations. Civil and/or criminal penalties may accrue for failure to adequately comply with various provisions of these laws. And, major dislocations in organizational operations, morale, and public image may be a by-product of any actual or potential litigation.

THE ROAD TO COMPLIANCE: OFTEN MURKY AND EXPENSIVE / In addition to penalties and other problems that may be involved with partial or total *non-*compliance, managers and information specialists may also have problems when *trying* to live up to the provisions of Federal laws and regulations.

Often, requirements are stated in ambiguous or vague terms which do not provide adequate direction for people and organizations that want to comply.

234

Some are selectively enforced, haphazardly enforced, over- or under-enforced, and possibly, unenforceable. Except for some short-cuts enforcers can use under OSHA and acts enforced by the EPA, many of the laws and regulations allow time-consuming due process and appeal procedures that may mitigate or blunt their very intent. Loopholes built into the laws (intentionally or otherwise) may also dilute or fragment their effectiveness.

Much of this confusion may be due to the failure of Congress and various regulatory agencies to adequately or consistently consider the administrative hardships and costs that result from the laws and regulations they generate.

One such result is the increasingly heavy burden of paperwork and other information-handling activities that Federal laws and regulations impose on organizations in both the private and public sectors. This burden usually forces an organization to *add* or *re*allocate human, machine, and other resources. Such *non*-productive additions may require *increases* in income to cover the increased costs to the organization. And these costs may then be passed on to consumers, taxpayers, and other income sources in the form of increased prices for goods and services, new or higher taxes, etc.

Another costly (and frustrating) result of regulatory agency and Congressional inconsistency is the situation in which several government agencies compete or conflict with each other over the same organization and its possible violation of government requirements. Quite often that organization ends up in the unenviable position of being both right and wrong for doing (or failing to do) the same thing.

Beyond these actualities and possibilities are the thousands of laws, codes, and regulations of an international, Federal, regional, state, and local nature which elaborate on, extend, supplant, or otherwise interact with the Federal laws and regulations that have been covered in this paper. Continuing changes in or additions to these laws and regulations as well as enactments of new laws and regulations can seriously strain an organization's information systems and procedures.

HOW TO KEEP UP WITH THE REQUIREMENTS EXPLOSION / In some organizations, legal counsel, lobbyists, and other advisors keep managers and information specialists regularly informed about relevant developments on the regulatory and legislative fronts. In other organizations, such a program of continuing legal updating either does not exist or exists in only sporadic or limited form.

Unless the information pipeline from legal and political advisors is unusually effective, an organization is not only inadequately equipped to live up to *current* legal requirements, it is also quite unprepared to accommodate to *future* requirements. Well-informed managers and information specialists can help an organization to build systems that more flexibly respond to change (thus avoiding the dramatic cost increases and operating inefficiencies that plague organizations with less-informed personnel).

WAITING FOR ADVICE IS NOT ENOUGH / Although legal and political advisors may be familiar with current and proposed laws and regulations that affect an organization's activities, they may not necessarily be *legally accountable* for that organization's failure to properly live up to those laws and regulations. Managers and information specialists responsible for an information system affected by a particular law or regulation *may* be so accountable.

It is incumbent upon managers and information specialists to *actively* seek information about: (a) the extent of their accountability (if any) under various laws and regulations; and, (b) the implied and actual effects of these laws and regulations on organizational information systems and related operations. Their strategy should be to *ask,* to ask *regularly,* and to ask to be *updated* regularly.

In addition to consulting in-house and contract legal/political advisors, managers and information specialists should actively pursue other avenues of information. Some of the following possibilities could prove helpful:

1. Subscribing to information services that keep track of relevant legal developments and their implications (e.g., association publications, government publications, private news services and hot-lines, etc.).
2. Interviewing professors and others who keep up with current proposed, and future possibilities.
3. Creating ongoing updates through seminars offered by or available through professional associations, industry groups, management consultants, college and university programs, etc.
4. Creating ongoing intra- and interdepartmental committees or task forces that focus on information-related procedures and systems that may be open to legal control or litigation.

Active information-seeking by managers and information specialists may not be enough, however. Newly gained knowledge must be *actively applied* in order to make organizational information systems more effective and efficient. The successful coupling of such knowledge and application should help an organization to: (a) meet its operational goals and objectives; and, (b) live up to compliance and record-keeping/reporting requirements of the government at the same time.

Summary

Selected laws and regulations at the Federal level have been presented as examples of laws, codes, regulations, etc., at all levels of government that affect information management and information-handling activities or organizations in both the public and private sectors.

For convenience, cited laws were divided into three categories (with primary emphasis on their record-keeping and reporting requirements, if any): (a) Employee Protection Laws; (b) Consumer Protection Laws; and, (c) Citizen Protection Laws.

Cited laws and regulations included: the Equal Employment Opportunity Act; the Occupational Safety and Health Act; the Employee Retirement Income Security Act; various FTC regulations on advertising, labelling, packaging, and trade practices; the Fair Credit Reporting Act; the Truth-in-Lending Act; various SEC regulations involving financial disclosure; the Privacy Act; the Freedom of Information Act; and the Clean Air Act (one of the many acts under the jurisdiction of the Environmental Protection Agency).

The changing nature of these and other laws and regulations as well as inconsistencies in their application, enforcement, and enforceability were mentioned as part of a total package of variables which adversely affect organizational efficiency and productivity.

Managers and information specialists were asked to take a more active role in: (a) gaining knowledge about present and future laws and regulations; and, (b) applying such knowledge when developing and operating organizational information systems.

The flexible response capability resulting from this coupling of knowledge and application was thought to be critical to organizational cost control, systems efficiency, and overall organizational effectiveness.

REFERENCES

1. Title 42, Chapter 21, Subchapter VI, *U. S. Code 1970: Supplement IV, 1974,* Volume III, January 1975.
2. Title 29, Parts 1602 and 1610, *Code of Federal Regulations,* 1975.
3. Title 29, Chapter 15, *U. S. Code 1970,* Volume 3, January 1971.
4. Title 29, Parts 1903 and 1904, *Code of Federal Regulations,* 1975.
5. *Record-keeping Requirements Under the Occupational Safety and Health Act,* U. S. Department of Labor, Occupational Safety and Health Administration, Revised 1975.
6. "Department of Labor," *United States Government Manual 1975/1976,* May 1975.
7. Title 29, Chapter 18, *U. S. Code 1970: Supplement IV, 1974,* Volume II, January 1975.
8. "Federal Trade Commission," *United States Government Manual 1975/1976,* May 1975.
9. Title 16, Subchapters B and D, Parts 18–254 and Parts 400–417, *Code of Federal Regulations,* 1975.
10. Title 16, Chapter I, Part 175, Section 175.1, *Code of Federal Regulations,* 1976, p. 102.
11. Title 16, Chapter I, Part 175, Section 175, *Code of Federal Regulations,* 1976.
12. Title 15, Chapters 2 and 39, *U. S. Code 1970: Supplement IV, 1974,* Volume I, January 1975.
13. Title 15, Chapter 41, Subchapter IV, Section 1691, *U. S. Code 1970: Supplement IV, 1974,* Volume I, January 1975.
14. Title 15, Chapter 41, Subchapter III, *U. S. Code: Supplement IV, 1974,* Volume I, January 1975.

15. Title 15, Chapter 41, Subchapter I, Part D, *U. S. Code: Supplement IV, 1974,* Volume I, January 1975.
16. "Securities and Exchange Commission," *U. S. Government Manual 1975/1976,* May 1975.
17. Title 15, Chapter 2A, Subchapter I, *U. S. Code 1970,* Volume 3, January 1971.
18. Title 17, Parts 210, 239, and 249, *Code of Federal Regulations,* 1975.
19. Taft, R. W. and Hamby, A. F., "Disclosure: Another Busy Year Ahead," *Public Relations Journal,* April 1975.
20. Flom, J. A. and Atkins, P. A., "The Expanding Scope of SEC Disclosure Laws," *Harvard Business Review,* July-August 1974, p. 112.
21. "The SEC Bears Down Harder on Disclosures," *Business Week,* October 19, 1974.
22. Title 5, Part I, Chapter 5, Subchapter II, Section 552a, *U. S. Code 1970: Supplement IV, 1974,* Volume I, January 1975.
23. Title 5, Part I, Chapter 5, Subchapter II, Section 552, *U. S. Code 1970: Supplement IV, 1974,* Volume I, January 1975.
24. "Reorganization Order #3 of 1970," [H401–32, H403–24, S403–7], *CIS Annual 1970,* Part I, Washington: Congressional Information Service, 1971.
25. *Your World, My World,* Washington: Environmental Protection Agency, 1973.
26. Title 42, Chapter 15B, Section 1857c-9, *U. S. Code 1970,* Volume 9, January 1970, p. 10192.
27. *Current Laws: Statutes and Executive Orders,* Volume I, Update 1973, Washington: U. S. Environmental Protection Agency, 1973.

Name Index

Subject Index